Maggie Moor is the author of *I Am: Your Guide to Mind and Body Union for Total Awareness*, and her psychoanalytic paper, *Coloring Outside the Lines: Sadomasochistic Defense and the Search for Identity,* was nominated for the NAAP Gradiva Award. She lives in New York City, where she is a licensed psychoanalyst and works with people recovering from trauma and addiction. Maggie is also a three-time national figure competitor and a jazz-rock singer/songwriter. She has recorded three albums with Grammy-award-winning musicians. *Skinless: The Story of a Female Survivor* is Maggie Moor's first fiction novel.

For my father.

Maggie Moor

SKINLESS

The Story of a Female Survivor

AUSTIN MACAULEY PUBLISHERS™

LONDON • CAMBRIDGE • NEW YORK • SHARJAH

Ordering Information
Quantity sales: Special discounts are available on quantity purchases by corporations, associations, and others. For details, contact the publisher at the address below.

Publisher's Cataloging-in-Publication data
Moor, Maggie
Skinless

ISBN 9781645361626 (Paperback)
ISBN 9781645361909 (Hardback)
ISBN 9781645366089 (ePub e-book)

Library of Congress Control Number: 2020909723

www.austinmacauley.com/us

First Published (2021)
Austin Macauley Publishers LLC
40 Wall Street, 33rd Floor, Suite 3302
New York, NY 10005
USA

mail-usa@austinmacauley.com
+1 (646) 5125767

I would like to thank Kate Larder, author of *Shut Up He Explained: The Memoir of a Blacklisted Kid*, for her mentorship and Stacey Donovan, author of *Forbidden Zone* and *Dive*, for her editorial contributions.

In each of us, there is another whom we do not know.

C. G. Jung

***

Prologue

This story has characters who some may not like or care about because they're considered low life on the barometer of what people are worth in society, but if you choose to judge them, you're probably not looking at something about you. A guy told me recently, "If you knew all the parts of someone, you would love them." If you could connect the dots. Sometimes I think about excavating all the shit I've done—I figure, what's the point, you'll think I'm self-involved. But despite what everyone and his mother is telling me about just forgetting it and moving on, I figured maybe if I actually let myself feel the love I had for Sam back then or anger or fear, I can clear stuff out; allow my true voice to lead me in heart-led action rather than fear-based reactions.

I recently read words Maya Angelou said, "If I decide something with an open heart, I usually make the right decision."

They say, killing a person is the most intimate you can be with them. That's how they brief the vets when they go into the field. A guy who fought Nam told me once.

Me and Sam were like two street cats, moving toward, bouncing off each other; each like we got a magnet stashed in our hearts. Who knew in life that people with similar type of emotional wounds often hook up as an opportunity to connect deeply and heal. Too bad we couldn't see that trigger before it got pulled, shown up with some tenderness for one another. It's a delicate balance: the bullet line or bedsheets.

I used to contemplate that shit. Could spend all day in my room staring out the window at the layers of leaves on the tree. *Drifting,* I called it. Sunlight behind makes them blend transparent, morph new shapes.

"Like Laura in *The Glass Menagerie,*" Sam used to pipe.

He saw me play that role at Stella Adler's during those six months before, taking acting class together. He played Brick and I played Maggie in *Cat on a Hot Tin Roof.* Sam said I was better at Laura the way I liked to space out, navigate visual things with my eyes. I never told him, felt to me like I'd been born with some cursed mongo antennae inside; soaks up all the nasty, pus-filled wounds of the world. I often had to hunker down, submerge, to re-up—sometimes get intuitions on how to go back out, handle people.

Wished I could have used it to fix things with Sam. But it had turned teeth, fingernails, and hair. He yelled at me in Spanish. I didn't speak Spanish. Anyway, this story is about transformation from manipulation and getting over to living from a true place of confidence.

They say if you've been through abuse as a kid, find some good memories. My favorite thing to do was sing next to my daddy. We'd sit together, front some big ol' fire, night outside a Quaker meeting house we went, or family went camping The Cape. Couple of times he laughed, make jokes. Other times I'd catch him gazing off, somewhere else. Thought his eyes looked real nice then; like the water. He just gazin' out, looked real quiet inside, almost mystical. I thought I understood it 'cause I felt that same way inside; never knew how to put it into words. Something about the music, the fire that helped.

Part I

Lower East Side, New York

Good Morning

A wind tapped lightly at heavily drawn aluminum shades, wishing to breathe newness amidst the howling chaos. Me and Sam had one thing to cling to on this banal rock, and that was each other. Well, each other and whatever else we could get our hands on.

Bare springs, mattress. Me. Cool air, tawny skin. Long dancer's limbs, lanky legs. Naked on my back. Gold chestnut waves; my hollow eyes blindly, wide open staring into hue, blue.

Cold chills from the cheap AC cranked up in the middle of September rattled my bones, a fixture insisted on by my hot-blooded Cuban choice of man, forever running everything in his life as a quick means to get by and a quick means to die. Sam set for sleep like he will the morgue, when he's done doing his time.

"That ass is mine," he said. My thighs pressed his tattoo-inked delts. Sam's silver sacred heart Jesus chain slid supple against my slender neck bone.

"Sam." Matted goosebumps crept slowly up my spine. I pulled him deeper, "Sam."

Shift, wrap, fetal style. Cranky radiator steam spit behind our slumbering heads. Early evening waking, actually. I pulled myself from Sam, tried stretching my overworked limbs. Though I appeared lithe and strong from several years of childhood dance class, and my teenage road-roughing homeless, natural living I couched it as, I still to that day (and maybe even today sometimes) found it impossible to gather strength to stand. That morning, not unlike many of the rest, the chill in the air got me up from bed. Perhaps, it was more the cold of my inner unrest, my screaming wish to enliven a life force within that I had quieted by my own mind, my daily endurance of cruel and jarring commands on my own innocence and self. Those internal mental lashings had been going on since I was a young child, before the junior high dance classes, before the Miss Teen New York pageant, and probably started right around the first time my mother's drunk boyfriend grabbed my clean-then pussy.

A salmon-colored rotary phone rang from its perch on our hardwood floor, just across the beige flimflam hanging. A sheet to separate the mattress from the living was all we had in this Lower East Side dive studio. The fifth of our sublet apartments since we'd begun dating a few years back.

"God, it's fucking cold," I sighed. I slipped my ankle from Sam's clutch, pulled the pink sham from our bed tight 'round my shaking ribcage.

"Don't answer the phone, babe." Sam grabbed at the air as I—Groan, I did, and crawled under that flimsy beige, across cool bare wood, in that New York, studio sublet.

"I'm serious, babe," Sam yelled. "If it's Jess, tell him I been under flu, few days past layin' low, watchin' like, *Mean Streets*, watchin' something…ah, You never remember." Sam loved his Scorsese flicks. I swear I think he thought or we thought we lived in one. Or any movie, really. This was our life. I didn't realize then that most people watch TV and flicks to vicariously live through, while keeping themselves safe at home. I, we, lived like there was no tomorrow. I swore by it.

"Live like you're gonna die tomorrow, 'cause you never know." There's some spiritual truth to that, ten years later and to this day even, twenty years later, I might hear myself say the same thing—but meaning, don't cow-tow to fears and social moorings. Back then I meant, I didn't care if I died, and secretly hoped I would, every single day.

"Remember what?" I mumbled absently, lost in my usual foggy and anxious. *Why get bogged in memories. I pride myself in not remembering,* I probably thought, and often said.

Venetian blind tapped, half-slid. My cover dropped; shoulders drooped. Breeze spilled pink sundown on that dusty wood flooring. I stretched, a cat in sun slip.

"Fuckin' symp softees…Life is fleeting." Softee was a word I always used then for people I thought were weak: hadn't survived the streets, had parent's money, had no grit, had no backbone, worried about what everyone else thought. Maybe add: went to college, worried about the future, didn't follow their gut, their heart. That was my basic definition for a softee. I hated weakness in a person. I wouldn't stand for it in myself. When you been touched funny as a kid, and especially you don't tell, you got a fortress built up.

Morning stream of conscious, "Girl, don't hide your face from nothin'…" my lips-flow, "Pull your hair back…Don't worry you're alone…" I found myself humming barely audible, a song I had been composing.

Music was one thing that always helped me return to innocence. Before it all happened at home, I had played clarinet and piano since second grade, every day after school. Practice, practice, practice. I quit in fourth grade when my band teacher grabbed my ass under my little blue skirt. My Mom had been in bed that morning with her drunk, and told me I looked like a prostitute as I left the house. After her grabbed me, I was flushed face solo in the bathroom stall shaking and told myself, *Guessed she was right, I look like a ho.*

I shouldn't be wearing that skirt. Really, that band teacher was a dickhead pervert, but I didn't bother telling anyone. That was minor compared to the other stuff, home. I just never went back to band, then. Too bad, because I was first seat clarinet in the fifth-grade band, but, 'You gotta suck it up and make a plan,' I told myself at age ten—there was nowhere to turn. Since I'd met Sam, actually, I'd found a piano. I had been starting to write my stuff down again, starting to let myself believe in my dream. Something you may not know, that people been touched funny lose sight of. Dreams become something for the spoiled brats of the world, or softees. Survival becomes key, fulfillment isn't something you even really consider. Until you start to heal.

"Told you last night about Jess," Sam called across the flim-flam at me. "I'm makin' moves for us, tryin' to get cash for capital case I hafta fly solo. Some suburban white kid for a few pounds of pot. Just don't answer the phone or door, babe."

"Dance, the music, the…"

Lately, then I'd been trying to write things down, make songs. I wanted to record an album.

Oh, smack, I heard the answering machine click triple time.

Mother's saccharine, bellowed, "Hello, my darling daughter, I just called to tell you I was sitting here in my sunroom watching these two gorgeous loons float on the crisp inlet pond…"

I am sure I stared at the two-headed tape in the machine, dead-eyed, and mouthing mother's words, verbatim. She said the same thing every time

"…And, ooh, how the evening sun is slanting just perfectly making shadows across the limbs of these northeastern trees."

I winced; *my massive occipital pulse.* Mom's voice always made me shaky and filled with questions. Slid my bony, slender fingers behind the green, silk curtain hanging window, grasping my half-drunk Jameson, soldier on demand.

"Cool, liquid sunshine," I crooned, cracking screw top.

Mother's words only sorta began to resemble poetry once booze hit blood.

"…I am so content just sitting here and wanted to share it with you," her dripping singsong droned.

Wumpbang, crash splash. I saw Sam's shadowy silhouette, arms flailing.

James and I moved to the upright keyboard against the back, brick wall. I perched, opened the cover, gently dusted keys. B minor four times to A minor, "Girl," I spoke some child-tone love words to my instrument; fingers a

17

haunting melodic impromptu. My face surrounded by black, white framed photos, Xerox newspaper articles, of my maternal great-grandparents, an old song and dance duo, Vaudevillian performers, Charlie and May Brown.

Crukslam. "Oh shit!" Sam's voice echoed like from inside an army barrack. *"May, May? Shit, hey!"*

Sam called me "May-May" from a moniker I went by then, when I wasn't in the club dancing. Seemed Charlie and May had born a baby who'd died soon after hitting oxygen—they'd named her Charmay. The little gone child had visited me in a dream when I was hitching across Cali, my teens. When I moved to New York, I decided to use the name for singing.

"Baby, do you know where my Afrin is?" Sam snarfled, stumbling in, scratching his nuts. Sam's right finger pressed his nostril, trying to blow air out through his beaked-to-the-left Cuban honker. Black spikes gleaming from yesterday's pomade.

Like a newly hatched chick-a-dee..., I thought, maybe said, probably curled my shoulders forward and giggled. I am often shy to show emotion.

B minor four to A minor, "Gi-irl, don't hide your face from nothin'," I soft lilt, D minor four to A minor.

"Deviated septum strong as the Hoover Dam!" Sam touted, zealous pride.

He said that about his nose.

"Where is that dang-nat—" he hopped ball-toe, cuffs up. "Man I gotta get back in the ring. Golden gloves, baby! I wanna coach kids and help people out the way they did for me back in Miami!" Sam went swinging at air, "Wham-bop-around."

I threw my head back, a distant kind of laugh.

Sam set to blindly moving about his couch entertainment jungle, grabbing and turning upside down every holy plastic-red-capped bottle of Afrin nasal spray, scattered.

Glass bongs, scads mobile devices on charge, lighters, purple, yellow, red twenty, fifty-, one-hundred-dollar empty zip baggies, an electric shrink wrapper, two scales (like the kind you weigh a frog in biology). Vases; there were several multi-colored, hybrid bouquets of blossoms, cards with sparkly hearts, written in Sam's scrawl. Sam did this surprise bell whistle shazam about a couple of times a week. I had gotten hip to—Sam laid these gifty-gives when he'd done something in the world he didn't feel good about. Sport in some broken finger, cracked rib: "Someone cut my line at the deli. I smacked a cabbie."

I figured, Sam just needs to get back in the ring. Golden Gloves boxer at sixteen, in Miami. And, it's true, some people do need to get popped in the face every once in a while. I admired Sam—*him real refreshing.* I saw myself a girl, spent life quietly sucking it up, leaving, taking care of myself. Sam didn't let anyone walk on him. Besides, it was painfully cute, him toting kitschy store-wrapped decorative glass birds; pink, purple jewelry boxes with mermaids, sparkles. Albeit, seemed a real distraction from us channeling resources to fulfilling dreams and passions—it played a little commercial break, in the middle of my Baudelaire-inspired, boozy, artistic unravel. Like, I looked up and suddenly felt I was starring in some 1950s sitcom; *maybe because he was Cuban, and oozed heart shine,* I thought. "Latin-heart shine," me and Sam called it, his showing love like that.

Then I eyeballed the thing he'd been on about, Jess: One large black duffel unzipped—three brand new pounds of pretty lime-colored Mary Jane, hanging brightly untouched.

That salmon phone cacophony blasted out for another try at getting picked up.

Sam put his hand on the receiver. It was September of 1999. We had caller-I.D.; Sam loved that feature.

"It's my mom, please don't…" I sashed my goose-bump skin with a silk black robe been hanging over the back of the stool I'd perched. Slipped my blood-red toenails into patent leather six-inch platforms, my house slippers I called them.

"Oh, how is Mom-Mom today?" Sam.

OMG. It was *her,* again. Mom clicked a second, bouncy message, "And, oh, honey, did I tell you that I was in my painting class and people actually told me I was good! I mean they were really impressed with my work! It was so exciting! I can't wait to tell you all about it…The teacher came around and looked at each person's work, I was painting a postcard of some fruit and he said it was a perfect likeness! I think I might be really, really good! I can't wait to tell you!"

"Uch umm, she's. Guess it makes her happy talking about the loons," I sighed, said, "Oh…if you're looking for that twelve-hour-pump-mist Afrin you bought yesterday at Duane Reade, it's under the coffee table, by the left leg closer to the couch. Other one's in the bathroom."

I was so embarrassed. I always knew where everything was. Since I was a little kid. My best friend, Alison's parents used to take me on fancy vacations with them, and if they lost a book or their eyeglasses, they always asked me—I knew exactly where it was. Not like I was going to steal it or snoop. It's like I took an eyeball shot of a room when I went in and remembered every detail. I hear that's like a thing. I mean recently in life, like kids been in dangerous situations become like a fly, watching to make sure they safe. I just thought me annoyingly detailed. Fact, started smoking daily pot when I was fourteen to stop being on the ball so much, and to stop myself from vomiting up my food every time I ate. Pot had benefits then, I guess.

Sam was on all fours peering under the couch. I was, "Fade: Mom out." Giggled to myself. Switched the mon-mute button on my Mbox recording device, audio became digital waves on a multi-tracking system, computer music program. Basically, a mic XLR or quarter-inch input, records voice or piano to my Mac laptop. Pro-Tools multi-track music editing software squashed live audio to digital file. That's like the top ten percentage of the actual audio wave. It's why people refute the digital era; though detail may be considered brighter, depth of resonance your body and brain receives is much thinner. At that moment, I wanted the depth of resonance from the outside world to inside me, completely zilch. Slid my Sony MDR V700 cans over my ears, shifting output from DSM3 M-Audio monitors, to hide all that real-world sound.

"May always knows where everything is!" I saw Sam's mouth moving.

"Da-ance, don't worry you're alone." D minor, A minor, I wove, "The music the…spotlight." Mom's voice clanged like metal, my inner eardrum. "Dancin'"—my fingers weren't able to move chords fast enough, to keep up with my lips.

"Shit, I shoulda recorded it." I sat slouched, staring at dirty window glare, sundown slanting, mumbling lyrics so I could jot them down, "Dance…the music, spotlight…shit."

Wouldn't be in this pit if you'd stayed home your whole life, practiced piano, you fucking slut—wicked voice inside my head. *You are shit,* the voice screamed, day in, day out. I was constantly riddled with an urge to get the Baudelaire-inspired, boozy music I heard in my head, out into the world. *No one is ever going to play music with you, have to skimp with this cheesy paste-and-loop program, charlatan.*

"What was that stupid line? Shit, where is that…" I dropped to my knees, fishing for ink under dusty pedals.

"Uch…"

Cock-a-doodle—doo! One of Sam's three cells squawked.

If you don't know why three—it's 'dealer life.'

Whackem, Sam hit his skull underside coffee table. I bounced upright, too. A double-dozen of red blossoms nearly tumbled onto his cranium.

We both gasped. The glass rolled south. Water and petals painted wood in seven directions.

Sam, satisfied, and in his usual unscathed way, lay vertical on the couch. He stretched his muscular thighs, crossed the lovely curved arches of his long-toed feet, and opened the red top of his Afrin. Snorted back. I watched oxymetazoline hydrochloride crystalline tingle spin *grand jetés* through Sam's cement nasal; blasting back wings, soaring wind down his neck.

My eye widened, *a wild breeze happening in me, too.*

Sam's phone jingled—both he and I shot straightforward again. I swear I felt his every breathing, vibing move like it was my own.

"Yea, idiot man," Sam revved, the moment he'd been anticipating all morning, "Jess, it's not like fuckin' rocket science."

I shook myself. Trying to get back into my own skin. Realized, sitting Indian style on the floor next to the piano. My right elbow on right thigh, chin pressed into palm. Left hand and eyes down to notepad, scribbling, *'The Spotlight…Dancing body…Naked.'* Somehow I'd been writing the words to my song whole time. If you'd asked me, I was inhaling Afrin and yelling at Jess. They say that's a thing too, I guess. People like me, with the trauma stuff, don't know how to stay. They call it "disassociate." We rather be in someone else's body and feel their stuff, 'cause it's less traumatic than our own. If you'd told me that back, then I would have laughed at you and called you a freakin' doctor softee who thinks it makes it better by knowing the reason why. I would have been half right—Knowing why you do what you do doesn't make it go away or make it feel better. But it does help you start to love and understand yourself, so at least you have some chance at healing the part of you that wants to kill yourself, and start loving yourself and maybe start wanting to live and feel and grow and find your dreams in the lightness of day. I don't have all the answers. But I can say, I'm not dead yet, and I know that. And I can say, all this happened and I lived to share it with you—and maybe you will get something from it all—and I too, I guess, some more clarity and perspective on it, by writing it out, so I can have greater choice in my actions rather than just reacting all the time to the trauma shit in me. So, yeah. Let's go. Back to Sam. Tally-ho.

I listened, Sam barking at Jess. "Yeah, you told me fifty times, got your story practically memorized like tomorrow's audition." See, Jess was Sam's then business partner.

Doodling my page, ears picked bits on "Little Lord Fauntleroy." Sam called Jess that. I'd named Jess the 'Candy Apple Kid from Long Island,' a while back. Jess had these golden, silk strands of hair all way down to his ass; a Boston U graduate; marionette-indented-cheeks like-Joni-Mitchell. I heard him sniggling on the other side of Sam's mobile.

Sam pummeled in recitation, "Yeah, you said some kid was supposed to meet you in Mayville with three girls," Sam was always making up name on any old town, to cover up possible phone trace, just in case anyone was listening in. They weren't moving major volume, but you never know. One guy gets beat, you don't even know about it maybe think he just left town for a week, but he rats to get himself off, you're on the fence and you never knew it 'til it's you in the tombs. Sam was careful like a church mouse, he said.

"So, Kid's north side, outside Starbucks; you're south, front Gap. Kid smack barrels you, grabs Goose running. You're a dumbass handing over Goose before he introduces you to the girls like that."

If ya don't get this lingo. Dictionary: *Girls* equal 'cash,' thousands. *Goose* (it's a vodka): really it's code for 'pounds product,' makes just like two idiots yakking-on chicks 'n booze.

Sam lectured Jess, "I teach you everything I know. Twenty years my hard-knocked. You pull me like that?" It was true. Sam was only thirty-three years but he'd been in the dealer world since he'd been eleven, actually.

My basic gist on this jig sawed: Sam had some white kid from Queens he'd been training to run side deals, little bike deliveries. Small retail thing Sam pulled together to stay afloat until he got payback on Fauntleroy. *Whoaz, wait.* See, Jess and Sam had been business partners, but hadn't been talking much lately then. Jess had tried to cut Sam out on a deal. Yep'm, back up.

OK, yep, see: Sam had met Jess, and for some reason, gone all doe-eyed. I mean, Sam literally taught Jess *everything he knew*, took him as a business partner. In my opinion, you don't make someone equal splits no matter what they bringing in as wholesale, if they don't know the business and don't have the smarts to pull through if the apples fall. Risk falls on you, in that case. They actually a casualty—that's why I say so no equal splits. But Sam went all in, and turns out fucking Lord Fauntler-boy, now that he had his knowledge and connections from Sam, seemed to be trying to cut Sam out of the picture on in-loads and pickups. So he could make all the cash himself. On this thing, that days, Jess didn't know Sam had set up deliveries with the Queens kid. Sam sent the Queens kid in secret to try to buy bulk from Jess, the Kid claiming to Jess he came in through a mutual friend, guy Bleu. Jess was high those days, some new crack addiction, so he was easy to get to 'cause he wanted money. Kid went to meet Jess and yanked the goods, took the bag and didn't give Jess the cash—secret gave it to Sam, for profit cut on sales turnaround, Sam—pinky promise. Jess was now, as Sam had expected, running "daddy," simpering to Sam, asking to help him catch the crook who'd pulled this conk. Thinkin' Sam didn't know he'd been cutting him out on the in-loads.

Up to speed, yo?

Now, I'm not here to teach you the drug business or smell you anybody's dirty socks.

Me and Sam both had been bumping around most our lives. He'd gone prison at eighteen, been in New York about fourteen years before we collided, which was May 1998, about a year and few months before the start of this story. I'd gone homeless at sixteen, seventeen—Mom had kicked me out—well, Mom wouldn't say that. I had gotten into some trouble, ya could say. I was at double-hitter juvie arrests, and a date rape between ages 13-16. I'd fallen in love, you could say.

My play-by-play: Mom had decided we should move to New Jersey, before that we lived on a college campus, upstate New York. Dad is a big professor type. In Jersey, my first love, high school beau, Drew, was eighteen. He had a thing for Grateful Dead and LSD. His dad worked for Malcolm Forbes and never home. Some local Colombians ratted me and Drew out for distribution, to get themselves off. We only had a few sheets of LSD and some pot but that was enough, they ordered big and Drew wanted the money. It's always the money. So, he got the load, I went into deliver it and the cops were waiting outside. Grabbed me, nabbed him for employing a minor, me and the rest was razors to his mattresses et al. After he got bailed for their snitch, Drew tried to pull some dirty snitch trick, to get himself absolved—but got caught and swam up the Feds bars quick. It's a long story. Basically, I had been at the place when the UPS delivery set-up Drew concocted happened, by accident. Red head kid Drew tried to set up was a friend of ours. I happened to be at the kid's house playing cards after school when the UPS came. Kid had no idea. I didn't either but I knew something was rotten when he opened package and it was the same six sheets of the Orange Sunshine tabs I knew Drew was toting around in his orange VW bug headlight cover.

Cops took the innocent to the station, he'd turned eighteen a week prior, Drew didn't know. Cops handcuffed me to a kitchen chair and said, "Tell us something, we know you're the girl from the arrest two years ago. We're going to charge you with distribution."

I said, "Drop my charges and I might." I slipped out on a few details and a recorded phone chat with Drew, with no record, clean slate. Drew got fifteen years. I was fifteen years old.

Eventually, I shaved my long model tresses, which had proved time and again only attract trouble over virtue, and found peace hitching the highways solo—Left coast, Canada, Mexico—sleeping out under the stars on the beaches; no belongings, no relations, and no hair.

When I got back to New York, I was twenty- three, I linked up with Sam on the random. He was with Jess at a nightclub I was dancing in. I watched Jess and Sam, their whole partner thing go up, down, between. Sam and I shacked up, and now there I was listening to him on the phone trying to pull the wool on Jess. Or Jess on him.

Sam dolloped paternal, "Jess, you always meet the girls first before you give 'em any. I teach you everything I know, and I specifically told you not to work with suburban fuckin' rich twerps. For that, son, you deserve to be swept. Hang on…"

Sam hung—flagged fast his other vibrating cell.

"Pappy!" Yelped spitfire Spanish/English to his main distributor.

"Yo, I got three goose for you. *Sí, hombre bro, lo tengo buen rey cosas mexi su i llegar a buen precio.* Wait, wait, hold on, man. I know, I know, you need more. I got 'em coming. Now. The best. Lemme call you back."

Sam, to his Queens Kid, "Sonny, my boy. You run 'em uptown tonight. I'm on the phone with the guy now. Goose, no floats—You come straight, me. Gots?"

Scribble-lyrics listening I was to Sam stoking business, I was happy like a harpoon rocket.

We finally had a plan. Together. See, Sam had a script. I had some songs.

"Got more talent in his pinky than most guys," this big writer/producer from HBO kept telling Sam.

It was true; everyone got jazzed when Sam pitched his story. Sam waved his arms, practically foamed at the mouth, acting each scene dynamic. It was all about his Cuban family—fleeing Fidel, parents rafting to the states with three kids, growing up in Miami. This producer guy at HBO said Sam could have a part on his show, *Oz*. But Sam kept waiting.

"Gonna go legit," Sam's bluster, "get my script made, play the lead." I don't know what you think about all this. Maybe you write me off as a criminal type. I don't know. I'm a survivor and I felt safer with Sam at that time than I had anywhere else. That was enough for me. Well, safer with Sam when at home. Outside, I felt safest in the strip bar. A little spot in the world where I could make my own choices, my own money, decide who could and could not touch me, and enjoy the primitive sexuality I felt transported me out. Apparently, that's all trauma victim shit too. Not making excuses—don't have to excuse anything in my life. Just brass tack real stuff: need to feel safe, control over my body, who touches.

I learned at a young age, my sex: powerful. Make a grown man weak and kill me if the wrong person fell victim to their desire for me. So, I learned that the real world was not a place to express attraction, but the strip bar was. And I always walked with cash—so I'd never be homeless again. More later—That morning-eve grifting with Sam sifting cash, I knew I was on my way to work. Been there till four, three nights flush. Three more shifts before a break on Sunday.

Pirouette: Let me tell you about Rex.

Rex

Rex was this guy I had met at work a few months back. New York Darlings Gentleman's Club.

It's cool how we can dress anything up with money and make it shine. That's what Rex wanted to do with me. Cindy I was at the club. Rex been coming in night after night, buying all my time, bringing me wine, better than the cheap champagne they served.

Rex would begin, "You were standing, long legs, bare skin in G-thong, holding that brass pole on stage; the glass reflection of your statuesque, when I fell for you." Dreamy eyed. *Yikes*-man.

Personally, I hate a person tells same stupid scene over and over. Like, *OK, it happened once, neat-o, and what, next.* Softee types like nostalgia, to revisit the, "oldies but the goodies," Rex would say. *Ugh.* Old Rex loved recount details of first night he and me slash Cindy met, like his favorite Valentine's romp.

His hat had caught my eye first. A cashmere hat with a black band, and feather. He was chatting a gal. She'd just danced for someone else, pulling her blue glitter dress on overhead. Looked like she'd met Rex before, casual chit. No biggie. I'd seen him around Darlings a few times, past months, Rex. Didn't know his name. Never stayed long, never chose one girl. I especially noticed his hat. Much as I liked the thing, I thought, *kind of cavalier, him flaunting it inside.* Gentleman's clubs don't usually allow brims worn, basic decency. *Guy dapper enough to sport that class, ought to hold manners, remove it*, I sussing detail to gauge character. His wrinkle-waist, *floppy-like Pillsbury dough*, I thought. *Rust-thick chin.*

My quick scan got eye contact mid-rap. Smiled right at him—*and how round those pink cheeks under his brim.* His hop toward me—

"Oh," I stepped to ascend from the stage. His hand out, to help me down. I giggled, flounced like I had a poodle skirt, curtsied, that's how Rex described it, twinkling. I thought, *guy smiles too much: softee-symp*

"Cynthia," he was singing. Fat man's taupe trench, double lemon pinstripe.

Said we'd met before, gave me his card once, but—

"Well, I'm so glad to meet you now!" Cindy-I laughed.

Rex Revan—pronounced like the bird, Rex's sur.

A Sade song came on. "Dance?" I sang.

His hat made me do it; I pushed him into a seat. Pulled the forest-green cashmere off Rex's top-bald head, put it on me. A seething, gay confidence that night, happy to be free—Jess feud had just heated up at home, left Sam in a snarl. His cash low; I liked an excuse to get back to the club: we needed woot.

For Rex, pulled my black satin gown down one arm, *like an '80s makeup ad,* my hands-on hips, spun slow-mo in his hat, and gave a wink, smiling big over bare shoulder. Satin gown to skin, sailed hips winding guitar, towering him bare in black rhinestone G-string, patent stilts, a floor dance. Leaned lips to graze fat black mole Rex's meaty flushed cheek, singing Sade his ear.

In my face, I saw a strangely pointed tongue. Mr. Revan licking the rim of that thick plastic shot glass, tossing back neat bourbon.

"Makers?" glittered waitress bustier passed over my naked dancing shoulder.

"Rather Bookers, m' lady," he chuckled, I mused the shape of Raven's tongue, pointing thing darting around. A fish tank of human study. Analyzing: *what the shape of his tongue says about him? Hey, a gal has to stay interested in the course of eight hours of strangers, eh.*

To me, a pointy-darting tongue read: *uptight, anal, horny guy.* May sound loopy, but I had a theory. Fair to suss, the way a person breathes illustrates their anxiety level, and how they relate to emotions. I figured, that then shaped their tongue and mouth muscles. So the tongue and mouth say a lot about how a person expresses their emotional needs in this big world. Pointing tongue and licking lips: *desperate.*

"I'm trying to get this Darling's manager to order me Bookers for the bar," Rex rallied on. This tongue darting in and out of his mouth like a skewer used for cows branding, "but they haven't done so yet. Guess I will have to become a reputable customer, Cynthia!"

"Cindy—" I sent heat into his ear hole. "Means a girl who is amazingly cute. Usually innocent and smart as well." Winked my eyelash on his cheek.

Rex pinched my own cheekbone, chide-corrected, seemed to perceive me: a "sweet innocent."

"My darling, Cynthia is a beautiful name, Greek: *woman from Cynthus.* This was an epithet of the Greek moon goddess Artemis." He twinked. (Twink: a wink with a twinkle. Yes, I make up words.)

"But my mom named me after Cinderella…" That was a new story I had concocted for Darlings.

So, I took a fast glimpse off Revan's jovial twink. Perceived that I had successfully titillated this man's desire to educate me.

What creates the makings for a regular patron, a regular customer of mine—rather than just a guy wanting quick peek and feel at my lady parts? Anything that gives him confidence, ego boost, a sense of strength as a man in the big world. My street smarts knew, Raven needed to feel superior, and wants to educate me psychologically—He had emotional needs and I had fed him the Revan's ingredients. I was always looking for regulars who spent money, it took a load off me for the night of trolling, out of the public eye on main floor and into the privacy of the lounge for Champagne and Important Peeps.

Alas, that first night together at Darlings, Raven quickly whisked me and my plastic platform heels, dropped his Platinum Amex on Darling's manager. Clomped we up the two flights of red plastered, no rug cement stairs, and huddled there, we, corralled in a dark corner, surrounded by shoddy red-mirrored liquor-stained, sipping Freixenet bubbles—which mind you had bubbles practically big as the kind you blow through a straw in one of those kids' bubble games. "No champagne should have bubbles that big!" I may have even scoffed aloud in dissatisfactions, to which Rex laughed. Dissatisfaction for one's surroundings is a wonderful way for a lady to try to get the man to want to do better. Or at least test his male instincts, suss whether he was a provider or a taker. This knowledge was instinct, my one main survival tool.

Within a few weeks, Rex had started coming to Darlings to see me on a regular basis, spending six hours straight in the Champagne dinge. He often arrived donning poetry books, talks on theatre, philosophy, travel, and perfume. He actually knew a good deal on theatre, made for interesting company. I had started studying at a small New York acting conservatory a year back

"*Hatful of Rain!*" I told Rex I was playing the lead at NYU. Big schools impress types like him. I had snatched up this script to perform, *Hatful*, because I knew the role from life: Girl finds out man is lying about a dope addiction, Rex didn't need to know that.

Rex beamed, "Ben Gazzara originated the stage lead before appearing in any films."

I'd blurted, excited, "Yes! And Gazzo and Cassavetes get credit for writing, but really all were written improv, rehearsal style!" I did love to read.

I frolicked over, Tenny W.'s play, *27 Wagons Full of Cotton*. Another play I had just finished, wanted to play the female role in, raving, "That movie *Baby Doll* was based on—" *Tsk,* whispered Cindy my head, *don't give him too much information on your personal interests.*

Rex galloped on, "Yes, the Williams play! Did you know that movie was banned by Catholic Legion of Decency from U.S. release due to overt sexual themes?" Then Rex hipped me to bitty *histoire*—"It was banned in other countries like Sweden." Rex had recently traveled Scandinavia, seen an exhibit.

"Oh my gosh, you are so intelligent!" Cindy squeezed his thigh.

"Let me take you out, shopping," Rex began to offer.

I pulled back, replied politely, "If you wish to buy me a gift, please bring it here to the club."

That wasn't good enough for Rex, so I offered, "Or you may give the store a credit card. I'll visit there, pick out a few things, you pay the bill." I'd had many men buy me gifts at the clubs; Prada crushed velvet jackets, Vuitton leather pants, Gucci watches. Never met outside. I had rules. That's what the others did.

This night—Rex laid out a plan. The night before the morning this story started. Sam was yelling Jess, Mom dripping saccharine, I writing lyrics, Rex's proposal percolating in back my mind. During our few-shifts-flush red-room Rex and Cindy Freixenet-Cuervo, fat hat man appeared with an offer.

About last night:

"I've rethought the situation, dear Cindy," Rex had…"I have this fantasy. I want to dress you up in a nice Chanel and a ripe Borsalino hat, just like Jackie O. I want to get you a singing show, at my pal Lucky's club. Who knows where it could go."

Rex always talked in rhymes when he drank.

I hadn't mentioned my dreams. Or plans with Sam. Rex chimed on how he had several clients in his foreign exchange business, someone a producer at the heart of record production, some club owners—Rex had heard me sing. I often sang when I danced. When I clicked into the rhythm, started dancing slow and hypnotic, felt the vibration of sound, singing, sex moving through my body, it actually made me want to keep living. That was enough reason for me. That and beating up on Sam. Well, trying to win. More on that later.

Rex ran on, "Rather than run the risk of getting you into trouble by bringing Chanel shopping bags to the club, or worse your stunning suit threads getting ruined in the ladies' dressing room, or worse…" Rex advised we do the exchange over a Grey Goose martini, 12 oz. pre-chilled glasses, three blue cheese stuffed olives served up at Hudson Restaurant.

—*Revan has a point*, my mind. A spanking huge black shine and white letters Chanel bag in Darlings' hairspray-stained and smelled of dead rats mixed spilled bottom-shelf-liquor ladies' bathroom slash changing room basement; could and would get stolen, vomited, spilled, trampled…

"I'll pay you what you make in one night at Darlings," Rex galloped.

"You would be getting a great deal!" sparkled I, letting him in on a secret, "You see, I only get a half cut of the $350 an hour in this bubbly lounge. Plus, extras from dances, tips. I'll only accept if you pay me directly exactly what you would spend on a regular night at the club." I bounced, like I had made him the best deal ever.

"Fine!" Revan brightened.

"Make an arrangement?" He wanted my number.

"I'll meet you wherever specified, you can count my word," promised me.

Six hours drinking, of course, I, a bit more friendly than I might have been others. Those days, there weren't many hours I wasn't drinking—so who knows what better judgment was. I was maybe sick of the late-night club grind and this would give me shorter evenings for the same amount of money. I knew there would be no sex or physical involved. This guy wanted me to string him along and make him treat me like a lady, not a quick thing for some cash. I could play this role for *him.*

So, back in the Lower East Side studio dive, see, when I was sitting on the floor, sundown glancing, listening to Sam spout Jess business, my root beer gazers (that's my word for my shade of brown eyes) rested on the sea of Crayola Sam-love; gifts of drooping blooms, half-written poem scrawled cards glittered vases; bling jewelry boxes, wallet mirrors. My thermionic current began to percolate boiling, an old familiar howling. This internal struggle that I had had since I began dancing at Gentleman's Clubs when I was 19 years old, just off the road from hitching homeless.

No interest in dating or being near anyone the years on the road. Date rape back in Jersey, and a knife in my neck of a man jerking off on me in a tent outside a Reggae on the River show in Cali. Or in Mexico offered a warm place to live a few weeks by a man in his fifties, wanted sexy massages in exchange for my keep, he announced once I got there. Nah, no men for me, I was solo with the sky and my bag. Free from the hell of four walls.

When I found the Gentleman's Clubs, so many men, always some stranger. Made me feel adored, yet untouched, like I wasn't that messy girl, that shitty child with my humiliated limbs strewn across mattress after trying to get the drunk boyfriend off of me. Some new man from another place, spouting another dream, dishing another problem. Each stranger offered me one reserved, private, protected hour or two or three. The Gentleman's Clubs had become my secret, semi-safe sandbox. I especially liked Darlings: "It's the old-fashioned way a strip joint's supposed to be—not some glitzed-out Disney World. Men walk in that place, usually have money, want hang solo with one

29

dame—two lonely people connecting in a timeless place hoping to feel better. I can get with that," I'd tell you, if you were cool.

Bubble gum my lolly—Sam was. More on that later.

This morning-eve, I felt split up over it—*How do normal girls do it?* My head screamed. This happened every night before I went to work, unless Sam wasn't home or I was mad at him.

Flip: my inner voice lashing: *I'm an asshole. Nice girl would stay in broke, be happy to order food in front of the tube with her guy.* I kind of wanted that, simple life. Heart pure for one man; Get a waitress gig…Same time I had this haunting, like an inner pimp turning me out, or a calling for freedom and independence, saying: *Nothin' doin'! Make your money, girl.*

I couldn't wait to get out of the sublet dive and into the semi-hell-safe-cash-paid fabricated and fleeting intimacy with strangers. Perhaps, it was a way out of getting too vulnerable, comfortable—meaning possibly fucked over by Sam, or anyone else. I mean, and then Rex dangling carrots.

"All right, Pappy. I'm the first man on your list, right, bro?" Sam was on the bark.

I dropped my knees, motored all fours across our wooden floor, picked up each gently fallen long-stem thorny gorgeous; admired each overturned luscious rosebud, petting broken petals. Green sticks spiny glistening, like silk oil swimming across the water in one strip sun left of the day. I wanted to show appreciation for my man.

"You won't be sorry, man, I promise you. P-R-O…" Sam barked the seven letters. I had heard him do so many times. Hung up.

My hippity-larking, "Lovely these flowers, baby! Thank you so much!"

Sam, settled into couch, gazing on me, "I just hope these ones don't die in three days like all the rest. If they do, I'm gonna return 'em to that fuckin' guy on the corner, I swear."

"You can't return used roses, baby." I climbed on top his heat.

"I can. Fuck that!" Sam, circled my ears his fingertips.

Musing…*he's right, if anyone can return used roses, it's Sam.* My face his armpit groove.

"Did I tell you you're beautiful today?" he.

Shook, no. He stroked my chestnut mane, pulled my cheek to the soft triangle curls between his perfectly sculpted pectorals. Bronzed nipples.

"Well, you are, baby. You are." Sam lit jay, puffed solo. I didn't smoke any much then. Dizzy. Booze anemic.

We two drifting under ceiling fan. *Tap-tap-tap* aluminum, the window.

Me thinking, "Why'd you go all doughie-eyed on Jess?" The question never got satisfied, I'd asked countless times.

"Took him under my wing. Taught him a simple trade pay his way so he could play music," Sam, zzz-'d.

Me: "Yeah…Jess is a kick-ass drummer."

Jess played table drums, too. Cool Middle-Eastern jive intertwined to soulful cat's jam sessions. Jess played tablas, too. That's how I had met him. I had been singing at some improvisation night jam at a club called Nightingales in the East Village.

Jess is how Sam and I met.

Limbic Resonance

With Sam, I felt I had met my match.

There I was squiggling half-time-trance for some guy, in a different club, under a new name—Angelica, I was. New York clubs are different from San Fran. This one was in a basement. Place felt like a subway to me, the way bench seats lined the walls with guys in rows knee to knee. But it's the same deal anywhere you go.

I opened my lids and spotted the long blond locks of the pretty kick-ass drummer I knew from that old open mic jam down at Nightingales I'd sung in at a few times year and change back on a quick model gig hop over from SF. Yep, there was good old Jesse boy. . He was standing the main stage staring up at some Brazilian girl; quite enamored, her flexing inner thigh muscles, as she moved hips above him, looking nonchalantly over her shoulder at someone else.

Fuck, I got no interest talking to him, this context. It was pretty late. I was pretty drunk. They'd kept the club open past four that night, few gals finishing lap dances in that crawl space they claim for, "very important people." Pockets stacked cash just fine for one night; I was thrilled not to be stuck back there. I wanted to go home, and figure out my life's problems alone in my bedroom.

I wove through scads of half-dressed leggy, silicon-breasted-drunken, foreign chicks in the lanky bathroom slash dressing room. Pulled my shiny, onyx boots over jeans, under my stretchy, black dress, arms through Dolce velvet overcoat. I cashed in club ducats—tipped out DJ, makeup shrew, maître d,' bartender. Hit the pavement.

No small feat finding a cab that hour, Times Square. Hubs of milling people, chatting. I never talked to anyone after work.

Looked up, the moon had disappeared. I figured, New…hate you can't see stars in the city…this time month you ought to see miles…

I looked down: endless rows of ruby jewel break lights, my twelve-inch auburn Barbie fall still secured behind my bangs—and there was Jesse, carving beeline straight toward. Beside him I saw—slender lipped, spiked black, hook nose, tat shouldered, smoldering—the 'I could go either way on anything at

32

any time and wouldn't show you for a minute which way that is or why, but try me' kind.

We two slid into limbic resonance immediately—*it's like I found myself in a male body,* me.

"Hey, Charmay!" Jesse, smoothly geeked out.

"What are you doing here?" Jess chirped.

My Colgate smile by day cover blown.

"Makin' money—you?" Threw my best sarcastic smirk.

All three jumped East Village bound in cab. Hit some rock haunt after-hours, you have to promise not to curse—owner's rule. Brownie's owner knew Sam. Scored some coke.

Hit the bathroom—faded into scrawled-on walls, someone else's raw poetic landscape…Sam and I were off to the races; deep connection, no words needed.

Bam—I'm in the middle at the bar. Jesse's yakking on, "I didn't know you strip?" scrapping paws all over.

I turned politely smiling, "Would you please remove your hands the fuck off?"

Jess slunk.

To my new cat-like friend, looked down embarrassed by my cheesy, fake French-manicured nail extensions stuck on with toxic glue—another trick to the dancer's trade; expensive as hell to pull off, on every night. Never-ending battle, fingernails wedged between me and my guitar strings.

I said, "Actually, I'm a total tomboy."

Yanked my trusty money-making wig to reveal my then auburn paige haircut. I'd shaved my head for safety when hitching the U.S. highways solo. It grew back, and then I'd chopped it again. Yes, battle numero *deux* was me and my Rapunzel braid. With Sam, I stuck the weave in my bag.

Night had struck a big April drizzle…Me and Sam did our getting to know you: shot the shit, did shots. Stared at flash reflections dripping slowly down the bar's picture window pane…Johnnie Red yakkin'…racking phenolic resin pool balls: Stripe, solid, stripe placed in plastic triangle on the dusty green felt.

"Kid grows up Miami, family fled Castro, Cuba, ya know," Sam.

I watched him, *somethin' beautiful,* I thought. Tall back lean 'cross table, breaking cue, pool, stick hand, scrape, blue powder; jet-black, long spikes pointing all which way…*this new cat's tongue turns staccato run-on, twisting some kind of melodic rubato,* I thought. I always listened to the music in a person's tone. Sam was pitching his script my way—said he was shopping it around with NYC movie bags.

33

"Older brothers beat him up a lot, his neighbor found him in a pool of blood—that's a scene in the script," he went on. Click-clack pool balls; clean split. Moved 'round table: ten-ball, three-ball, one-ball, down.

Sam: "By age eleven, Kid (Kid was the character in the story) had taken up training, boxing. Aimed fight pro-junior Golden Gloves—his job after school: lawn maintenance for neighborhood kingpin, Doug Lord." (This was the name for the drug lord in Sam's script.) Sam wiped a bead sweat, "Besides name switches, it's true, every word."

Ricocheted blue number two right side corner; roll, dunk left bank...

"Lord asked him to work sides gigs, run packages—dealing," Sam dropped fifteen-stripe, purple four.

"By eighteen kid wins Golden Gloves and making loot, gets cars, houses—'Course real dream this kid is to be an actor—" Sam and my eyes collided.

He clocked it out of the corner, nine-stripe yellow bounced off the rim of the table. Handed me the stick.

My leftie grip, lining cue for an easy straight down sides: scarlet eleven. Sam pulled a joint from his Marlboro pack. I sunk.

"Not bad," he.

I moved over, lined the six ball.

Sam trolleyed, leaned table: "Then some setup, kid gets locked up, State—gets parole, studies acting at Coconut Grove. Goes to New York to fulfill his dream, but he ends up hooked on dope. Then he kicks. Story finale, him in his loft writing about his life, sober—well, that part's true—"

Sam laughed, "Haven't touched dope since I was thirty-one, over a year, that's sober to me." Fired up.

"That's good," I said, rolling the tape of his scene in my mind while moving long stretch, lining up tip on brown seven, "Last thing I want is a cat living bleach-life," I covered him.

What I didn't say: Honestly, I was kinda struck dumb, *how much his person this guy just dished.*

I hadn't had much school. You'd asked me then I'd said that I was pretty much raised in the Gentleman's bars, and on the road, while leafing paperback novels like Kerouac, Nabokov, Shepard plays and Tenny Williams. One thing I'd learned early young, the house with mom, *keep cards close to chest, professing anything, especially love, is for suckers.* I guessed Sam had nothing to lose, or hiding something bigger. I hoped it was the latter or we may be in softee zone.

I blew smoke rings, said, "A real Tarantino, Ridley, *True Romance, Angel Heart.*"

These were flicks I dug. "Cooler, it has Cuban flair."

"I pitched it to Burt Young last month," Sam pulled back, dipped a key bump white pony and passed it my way. "Took him down Raoul's joint…" He picked up stick, drove the five down the table to hop the twelve.

"*Pope of Greenwich Village*; *Last Exit to Brooklyn*…Scorsese's young." I went on, smooth. I wanted to seem cool by spinning random Burt Young leads I'd seen.

"Yeah, yeah!" Sam chalked blue tip.

"Had Burt rolling on the carpet, laughing," Sam was saying, "I saw him shed tears when the main character guy's in prison, got all his inmates doing improv acting scenes like gangsters, instead of fighting for real." Sam growled.

Wow. This guy's really got it, I thought. I mean, I didn't know much about the in-roads of producing a low-budget indie film. I figured you needed stars involved to get the money, so Sam's thing sounded promising. I honestly figured it'd be all in preproduction and shooting celluloid within a few months.

Sam sunk lucky thirteen, piped: "Burt said mine was the first pitch he'd actually sat through! He's back in LA now, but, we're keeping touch!"—and spun black. Sunk.

Seven a.m.: We two-hit saunas at The Russian, East Village. Sweat it all out.

Narcisse and Stars

In going back through archives memory bank, I booted up this long-forgotten image. I do want to get back to me and Sam driving hairpins—fueled by some kinda love, plans for making it in entertainment, and a suitcase stuffed with pain and addiction—but I don't wanna be one who hangs on to only bad stuff. I learned a trust living kind thing bumping out of Jersey into West Coast gypsy style; black and blue inside, my starry dreams still covered with baby dew drops—from sweet Narcisse, this albino angel I met by a string of natural hot springs in the virgin woods, Oregon.

I'd leapt a ride from this Colorado Rainbow Gathering to a Craft and Farmer Trade Festival, and spotted a sprawling oak I wanted to sleep under. There was Narcisse playing flute for the breeze and trees. I camped near him solo like a fairy or wood nymph, listening to cracks in the forest at night, beating butterflies past my ears early dawn. Narcisse sang these high-pitched rhymes; tales of a boy who gazed his reflection and fell in love.

Narcisse only ate white food: rice, potato, yogurt, milk, ice cream, pasta. Wore white; crocheted veils over white three-piece suit over a white, button-down shirt, over white socks with white patent leather lace-up shoes. Got kinda dirty since he lived outside, but he was beautiful, a living moth. Looked like a fire halo when the steam caught sun's glare behind his porcelain hair, pale eyes a-flicker. Whispered, didn't speak boisterous ra-ra like those corporate-A keg guzzling yahoo ra-ra's back in Jersey can. It was incredibly jarring living in Jersey.

"Falling in love with oneself Child, it's an ultimate joy," Narcisse told me. Intimate with our inner truth, he meant—not that selfish self-involved stuff, which if you ask me is about fear of losing oneself. Touched me, what he said. These days when I first wake, I try to listen inside, stay with, long I can. Did when I was a little girl too, but lost it somewhere, the two-step shuffle things—or delegated it *for the flimsy.*

Lizard

Monsoon swirled inside that early April sunrise sky, after the late-night Brownies swag. Us newbie love-doves stepped onto the sidewalk outside those old all-night Russian baths.

Sam flipped open his vibrating cell and pulled his leather roll, cash. He swept me into the backseat of a Lincoln town. Peeled a twenty at the driver while yelling into his phone at who knows: "What, are you crazy, man? Birds are chirping, bro, get some sleep, we got busy doing tomorrow."

Sam then went on to tell me that he and Jess had just begun building some kind of business, he wasn't specific on what. Said he'd been staying at Jess's place for that time being on Thirteenth Street.

"Let's go to my place," I said. I'd been in New York about six months then, rented a room from my older sister Wanda, in her Upper East railroad.

"Subir FDR en la calle veinte y tres. Y sube noventa y siete punto uno, hermano, gracias." (Translates: Hit the FDR at Twenty-Third. Turn up Ninety-Seven point one, brother, thanks. The radio station.) Sam spoke smoothly Spanish, the driver. I didn't speak.

The car swerved, we slid up Park Avenue South. Rain like bright tiny diamonds hitting window.

Sam pointed in Union Square glimpsing a boarded-up commercial space. "Supposed to be called Metropolis. I threw every cent in," he glammed, meaning I think he was trying to impress me.

"Got a lease, gut the place, hired architects, building a club."

Galloping detail: "In the middle, one of my partners, real, good friend for years, went down Miami, never came back. Got picked up on somethin'. Other guy cut losses, pulled out. I was left with space, getting dicked left and right by money guys, trying to find more investors to finish—had to give up my beautiful brand-new co-op on E. Tenth—ended up living in this fuckin' rat-infested Metropolis basement for six months, all dark and scary. That's how I started this script. Sitting under there, shooting dope every day." Sam crossed himself. I had noticed him do that a few times. Mom raised him Catholic, he'd mentioned—and about God a lot, too.

I'd had my own run-ins with God-like, while trekking the Pacific Coast Highway; laying out my bag, sleeping rocks, crevasse on cliffs. I'd always kept a scrawl-journal, written to some God, I called The universe, or life force energy, since I was a kid, like six or seven earliest one I have today. I believed it all the same thing: vibration. My definition for God would be: That silent sound runs through our bodies, beings, universe, beyond maybe; connects all, its rhythm pitter-patter. Most, found myself thinking, *Life is one big funhouse mirror, reflecting spiderweb chaos.* Main thing nature showed me, "Everything wet gets dry, you wait long enough."

I *had* drawn some real clean line of demarcation: where a chap stood on level of trust and loyalty. People, three basic modes, I'd figured then: Softee, Orphan Misfit Survivor (OMS), or Softee Wannabe Posed as Misfit Survivor SW/MS. Oh, so ya know, I'm talking genderless character, so don't get all nutso on fucking gender politics, please. Anyway, Sam was sharing Jess freestyle only what one can learn through years of hard knocks, while he paced the white wall carpets like a panther.

I yakked the softee Jess earlier, let's get nitty.

Definitions: *Softee.* Never been left alone. Deep down scared shit; don't know if they could survive. Do by the book—though rules of morality slippery and undefined. Look for praise, from other Softees—not loyal to anyone due to no idea, so will sell you out if they're in jam. Sweet, long as you know what you're dealing with.

Orphan Misfit Survivor. "Us, who's been through the shit and we're out in the world trying to make it on our own, under radar." I would have said, then. Loyal only to other OMS.

Softee Wannabe Posed as Misfit Survivor. Not the orphan misfit he claimed. Weakness: SW/MS wants softee love, will do whatever to get it—no backbone—they'll turn on you, claiming their moves are based on morality. I found myself silently wondering where Sam fit in this Rubik's for Life.

Watched him launch on, to cabby: *"No, vaya a la izquierda, sí suben Primera Avenida hombre, no necesitamos FDR, olvídalo."* (Translated: No, go right, yea, go up First Avenue, man, we don't need FDR, forget it.)

Same time, was trying to recall what my bedroom looked like. I had spent eight days that week holed up alone, puffing opium, writing poetry and sensual songs. When Wanda's roomie married, I moved back from San Fran, laid down cash for rent. Attending a semester at Lubin Business School, where my dad taught. I didn't see myself a softee wannabe, but I was pitching straws for chance at finally making it right with my dad. I never liked school much and if I didn't do school, he didn't like me. I thought there was something wrong with me for liking stripping. Maybe there was. I've come around these days to hear that girls who like the sex industry and were abused, are just enacting their abuse; safe in familiar. I don't know. I hated school because everyone seemed a sheep with no new thoughts in their heads, just trying to be accepted and find a business that made money. Boring. Dancing gave me time to create, express, and pay my bills.

So, I got up, dressed in these horrid business casual daytime shirts and pants every morning for class. Even took economics, for which her dad was really pleased. Not one of his kids had ever done. I like business, I mean if you're a stripper you better understand economics or you're gonna get walked all over. I was raising my hand for discussions, acing tests. Played lead role Bianca, in their theatre department semester's production of *Taming of the Shrew*. I'd studied Summer Shakespeare, ACT, San Fran.

Dad never called, asked how I was, what I was feeling, if I was OK. That was all I wanted, accepted being me, and cared for. Protected even, from the vicious Mom's drunk boyfriend. That was really the crux. I didn't realize it then. I thought—suit up, show up, shut up and try to be good enough to get dad love.

All I was really feeling day to day there in the Upper Eastside railroad: pit dodging artillery by way of glances from cauldron bitch-called Wanda.

"Isn't it fitting, you come home, play the sweet hate-able Bianca," Wanda confessed one night, her tight upper-lipped huffiness after my performance.

I mean, she was still mad at me for being born. As kids, they said I was cute like Brooke Shields and Wanda was smart. She'd gone to private high school, four years of college—I'd dropped out and been homeless. Put down your gauntlet, give me a rest, I didn't say.

"I've always secretly compared myself to Kate the Shrew. Dad liked you more since we were kids, and now you are back," she went on.

Wanda had even begun dishing wisecracker jokes, referring *Whatever Happened to Baby Jane?* Bette Davis; Joan Crawford. Two elderly sisters, roommates. One runs the other down with her car, locks her in the house, pretending care for her, and tortures her to near death. Wanda seemed to laugh in such a way it made me uncomfortable.

Apparently, Wanda felt I was going to ruin all Wanda had done once I had split, to get Dad to like her best. *Whoa, weird, Dad never even speaks to me. I am pretty is all he responds to,* I didn't say again. Sister shit.

—Wanda even sided with Mom when the date rape happened in high school. I guess she had a crush on the guy. Met him through me a few times when she was back from college. He and I were always platonic until the one drunken night I woke up he fucking me, jumped off as I came to and ran out the room. I don't know. Wanda liked him, said he looked like George Harrison.

She was always crushing on my guy friends. Mom was always trying to set her up on dates with my exes. If kids compete, it's a reflection of the parents.

No worries, Wanda. I'd bumped into some guy, random, recognized from San Fran. Tossed me that poppy tar. I'd melted in, skipped school, burned candles to bone, locked in my bedroom, a bottle red wine by noon, writing music, lyrics, plastering erotic murals all over my walls. Strip by night for employment. Thinking, *what the fuck is the fucking point, stuck in a tiny apartment with a prickle prod lowbrow big sister; meat grinding my very life force rotting under fluorescent lights, buying into the institution, to do things they say will make them like me. Just do what makes me feel like living,*

Sam—was rapidly becoming one of my favorite people in the world— *"Aquí, mismo hombre, esto es perfecto,"* he piped across Lincoln at driver. (Translated: Right here, man, this is perfect.)

Up three flights, swung the old, heavy, squeak squawk door beeline through that railroad share. Wanda was dressing for work.

"Sure is raining cats and dogs out there, be careful!" Sam chimed as we two entered. 7:30 AM, I guess.

"I gotta get us some WD-40!" I made eyeball contact with Wanda, her fishing knots from a necklace, pulling on her pants.

"Where does that expression come from, anyway, cats and dogs?" I mused, trying to make light. Wanda rolled her eyes.

Sam harmonized melodic, toward Wanda, trying to make chat, "Well, you know that P.T. Anderson, that director, I was just reading an article in Hollywood Reporter about his next film, shooting now. He says, it maybe ends with a torrential downpour of frogs! Ha, ha! I researched that! Real-life articles about frogs being sucked into waterspouts and raining to the ground miles inland. Director got the idea from some plague of frogs in Egypt, some Hebrew script. Frogs are a barometer for who we are as people; we can judge our society by the health of its frogs, the texture of skin I guess. We're polluting ourselves, 'we're killing ourselves, and the frogs are telling us so, because they're all getting sick and deformed…frogs,'" I read P.T. said it himself.

Sam rambled on, "P.T. said, 'What the fuck, life's a bowl of six degrees of separation to malarkey-ville chaos. You get to a point in your life, everything's out of control; you're staring at a doctor who says something's wrong but has no way to fix you, And you just go: So what you're telling me, basically, is that it's raining frogs from the sky!' Hahahaha!" Sam let out a big yelp.

Wanda seemed annoyed—I was surprised because Wanda studied film in college, worked a day job at a TV channel, did stagehand work for off-Broadway Theatre. I thought Wanda would be interested in PT chat. Whatever,

Wanda never was a morning person. Me and Sam breezed into my backside bedroom.

"Ah," Sam gasped softly, turned quiet, rare for Sam. His eyes glazed black-and-white murals, Helmut Newtons, fashion couture. Helmut: beautiful erotic fashion nudes. I loved him since I was fourteen and discovered a book, library vibe. Sam, dumbstruck. *Wow,* I had never really seen my space through someone else's eyes, never had anyone over. Like I'd ripped my heart open and shown him what makes it beat. Sam was pointing at the floor-length satin "priestess gown," hanging on the doorframe.

I picked it off its puff silk hanger, held it out to him…"You like?" Swirled the black, V-cut beaded cleavage to lowest rung my sternum satin gown; onyx embroidered straps, train five feet past my gait. "Place is like *Alice in Wonderland,*" Sam looked kinda awe.

I, flame faced. "They're meant to be sequences, costume ideas for my songs, videos."

"Poof," Sam said, intently staring. My gaze drawn into his posture, *something, a Modigliani painting*; rounded shoulders, upper back real drawn in, his hook-long nose profile: his eyes from the side such I imagined a teardrop eye like liquid liner painted on a porcelain doll, from the front they gazed like a panther's. *His fingers, like sculpted Gothic,* palmed my demo cassette—1999, cassettes. His left-hand sort of dangled in the air flat, maybe like he had a cigarette but, no. Some kind of immersion, time space held frozen, blue-sepia *Charmay,* staring out in a leopard jacket, smoky eyes. My singing demo cover photo.

I watched Sam, staring. I was too shy to show my work to anyone. I liked the attention. I felt ashamed for liking it. Heard the lashing voice, "You suck at what you do." Mom always said I had no talent. It's just an excuse to be a whore. The demo I had just finished recording with the Spin Doctor's bass player, met at that Nightingale's improv jam. He'd taken an interest and offered to make me a demo. *You are just a lowly slut with no talent and you ought to just stop being so lazy and this creative artist bullshit,* I. Yet, I couldn't stop myself drive to explore eroticism, and create music. Seen and liked by Sam—and wanted out of my creeping shame, exposed.

Water falling heavy on wrought iron fire stairs,

"Raindrops hyperspace vertical style?" I tried a wild card to escape. I quickly stripped—peeled every inch of my clothes off down to the skin. Unlatched the wrought iron window over the futon, and climbed the fuck out. Left Sam alone in my bedroom. I climbed two flights of rickety rusting fire escape to roof.

"Are you crazy?" I heard Sam calling, behind.

I laughed over shoulder, "Coming from a guy like you?"

Sam followed up, appeared on the roof looking somewhat stricken.

"Lie down, look up." We two lay on our backs in half-baked sun staring up at sky. Droplet prisms flashing, throttle spectacular face.

"Pretend we're lying in water, like you're floating," I whispered.

Sam cooed, "Ooh! It's so clear; look at the rainbow trouties and minnows!" tossing pretend sparkle water, watching colorful cascades, he gaffed like a hyena, asked, "You ever gone diving?"

No, I shook. *Hell, I like this guy but he is a bit tangential, really it's kind of clanging*—I prefer people just be, not tell stories all day. Listening, his story got me. *Wow. I getting sunk.*

"In Miami, just after prison when I was twenty…"

Him being a dive instructor, in Miami after prison. Coke, pot—five to eight years State, out on special two-year fast-term to parole. "We took the keys, beers on the boat, night. Swam alongside three dolphins, way out deep, dark, real slow, alone; they gathered front around behind me for like forty minutes," he said. "So peaceful. Those dolphins, man…I mean, closest thing I ever felt to that was when I OD'd a couple a few years back. Flatlined for almost three minutes. Hovering above, looked down, saw my dead body there, white light all around heard fuckin' harmonies, man, angels singing," he said.

"But it wasn't, shit actually freaked me out. Enough never to touch dope again."

"Must be hard…" I lazed, about how hard it would be to keep clean, sober. At the time, I had never actually tried not to get high or drink. I had heard a fuck load about AA when I was a kid because Mom was always telling her drunk fuck to go, but I hadn't heard more than that. Losers who pissed on walls and touched kids are funny, and were the love of Mom's life, went. Or should go but didn't I guess. Anyway, Sam, *Shit, this guy has died and come back.* I realized how intense a life experience that must have been, something I had never had happened to me. I wanted to feel everything in life and, *dying for a minute…I really want to feel that,* all I felt. I admired to a tilt, Sam, then on. I guess, looking back, I felt like, *Shit, this guy can go through that and survive, he can protect me from anything and we will always survive. This is no softee. I met my match, and he's stronger than me.*

I guess that's another thing when you been touched funny as a kid. I wanted someone stronger than me, protect me. Sam was that, for me.

Back in my bedroom, we towel dried each other. Sam, me: Lay. Sam hit "Play," my demo. Rolled on top of me.

I heard my own voice, languid, singing my own song, lyrics…"Strange days quiet persuasion secret kisses."—Sam played his fingers on my navel skin, like I was a guitar. Wrapped my rib cage toward his, our nipples touched. He slipped inside of me, pushed in, up.

I had never made love to her music before. I usually hated listening to my own voice. My lips whispered my own words, into his ear. Our breath, eyes locked. We two moved in unison; earthquake our bodies shook together like…

"Hallelujah," Sam whispered, shined his watery brown winkers as he came in me; I came, too. He rolled off, looking at ceiling, said, "My Mom taught me to pray when something good happens."

Two lay there. Mouthing that Jeff Buckley cover, Leonard Cohen, *"Moving in you and the holy dove moving too…"* My nails twirled my hair. I used to listen to that tune over and over then.

Sam, whispered, "Y'know, whatever you been through, whatever you done, I don't need to know."

Shit, he probably thinks I'm a dumb stripper girl, thought me.

"It's not really that crazy, y'know. Just kinda make more money dancing, kinda seems the thing I do best sometimes…"

I hated talking about it. Thinking now, I don't even know if that's what he meant. He could have been sort of saying he wanted me to accept him and not ask, also. But I was just so self-conscious about the dancing job; I deducted myself into "this is all I am, a whore. But I love it."

Boys and girls, always the old "you should change" talk. Always ended up leaving whoever said I ought change.

Sam held me, whispered something I would never forget: "People like us, damaged from someone, shit, somewhere—we have way more heart than those fuckin' normies. Dance—do it, don't do it, won't do it forever, and if you do, you'll still be you—wusses don't get that don't deserve to know you."

Surely I must be dreaming? Somehow, he knew.

Sam pulled me to straddle, sitting up on him. He laced our fingers together. That is when Sam and I made our plan.

"Bill Esper's a great teacher," Sam, saying.

Guess I'd mentioned earlier, to him. When I had gotten to New York, I'd auditioned for a Sanford Meisner acting conservatory, William Esper, and been accepted to William Esper's private class.

"You'll get agents, work." Sam told me, a couple of his buddies were on an HBO show, *Oz*, about the prison inmates. He said they had studied at Esper. Sam blustered on then about a, "Producer-creator, Tom Fontana! He's a buddy of mine! Big fish!" "Says I got more talent in my pinky than most guys," Sam told me then, "I'm gonna get my own script made, play the lead. Me and you, we'll save money. Start a production company together," he.

43

"Yes, I want to get a New York apartment, or an old house somewhere, build a music studio, shoot music videos...we can produce films like John Cassavetes and Gena Rowlands..."

"And record you! One of these days I wanna be hearing your voice on the radio!" Sam's cherry.

My heart beat like a lizard. I had never experienced anything like that before.

It was an alliance between us two. Really it was uncanny that Sam had shown up in my life around then. During that springtime, I had been scrawl-journaling: *'I want my next guy to have done time, be a heroin addict gone kicked already, now making mass money dealing and owner/founder of an up-and-coming independent film/theatre production company...'*

I needed an underground deeply broken misfit heart who had survived; still drive with unkillable passion, talent to see his dreams true.

Seemed Sam fit all that—to a T. He was an OMS like me.

Gershwin

Sam showed up mid-June with fist-fulla roses at that East Side railroad walk-up. Instead of taking the carriage ride through Central Park, he'd planned for us—I packed a bag, left a month's notice and a wad of cash to Wanda. We two checked into our first hotel.

Sam announced to the manager at the Gershwin, "Newlyweds!" Scored a special two-week suite.

"Someday it will be true, we will be newlyweds," he whispered in my ear, spiraling staircase to the sky.

"Lay down on the bed," Sam asked me to undress.

He delicately placed thinly sliced orange and mango on my hardening nipples. Slice pineapple between my lady lips, drizzled honey. Sam ate each piece slowly making eights, starting at my ankles, behind knees, inner thighs, waist, nipples, back down again.

Springtime, New York: cool breeze cuts hot sun, Sam brought in fresh violets and daffodils. When the flowers started to wilt, Sam made a bath, blindfolded me. "Close eyes," gently said.

I, moon-rock shine silent, listened: "Now I'm preparing lamb chops on the stove!" There was no stove, but it didn't matter. Eyes clenched, I imagined Sam a bonbon-shaped cheery cooking show host, as he howled: "Smell the lovely rosemary aroma!" and "Voilà!"

Picked me up, dumped me splash into the hot claw-foot petal-soak. Turned the lights down. Climbed behind, wrapped his legs, arms around my waist. Tangled purple ribbons, gold streamers, silver bows all over my naked patches skin.

"Describe a fantasy, what you think of alone," Sam coaxed, rubbing my upper buttocks bone.

Embarrassing. I had never told anyone before. I was quiet but he got it out of me eventually, tickled it out.

"I want two guys to be inside me, on my birthday, same time."

I didn't know if I really wanted that or if it just sounded like it would feel glorious. I imagined some kind of power, exaltation, freedom by virtue of

45

being pushed beyond boundaries and made to open up my flesh; so touched in every orifice and spot imaginable. I was really shocked I had told him this fantasy. I felt so alive, wild, talking to someone I actually liked—not someone I was trying to excite pure their entertainment and my employment. Different, so vulnerable sharing my private sexuality, my fantasies, my truth with someone I wanted, physically, emotionally. No idea what that felt, until that moment.

Sam laughed, "Doesn't sound too hard to arrange."

Sam's thing: "It's just sex. It's fun, no big deal."

Yeah, I was an exotic performer. Candy for men, women, couples, one-offs, regulars, old, young, rich, poor, smelly, perfumed, kinky, sadistic, submissive. I'd heard, and told wild fantasies, night after night. My job. I was good at it. My private? Untouched, distanced from all. I was for sale—but not for touch by the riffraff of the world. The club people couldn't hurt me. The real guy—was definitely going to leave me roadkill.

So you can imagine, I had never been to an interactive crisscross. I mean, people you actually choose to be with for free. Absurd, to me. But, stepping out of the Gershwin Hotel for a café one day, I spotted that 1920s Parisian sign hanging in the breeze: A woman on a swing said, LE TRAPEZE D'OR.

"What's that?"

"Swinger's club, babe!" Sam goosed my ass.

Sam told the manager at Trapeze we were newlyweds. Slid through. Sam led.

Inside there were several floors, black lights, pumping house music, rugs on floor, mirrors on angles. Human sculptures in minute shadows, slivers of silver lights, sinewy through hallway corridors, door frames, dark staircase ascending. I thought they looked like the Kama Sutra temples I had seen in books. I had always had a thing for reading Sacred Sex Tantra books, reading about sacred temples from pre-Christian religions, matriarchal tribes. My favorite books I had read on that road trip to Mexico with the massage-want-me-man, *When God Was a Woman,* and *Sacred Dance.* I'd picked up in West Marin Library, right outside of San Francisco. I'd gotten grounded there for a few months healing from a fractured spine incident I'd thrown myself into. At Le Trapeze, I got really quiet. Watching.

Bright buxom-hipped ladies sucking each other's cherry pussy. Men, balls sagging, heard them slapping against each other's noses. Couples piled in closets. Hot tub bubbles lots of moaning. Made me shudder a little. Sounds similar to what I had heard as a kid growing up the house with mom, during her late-night parties, at the boheme campus. When I was nine years old, used to sit the top of the stairs, listen. Something about women over forty, moaning, banshees, primordial whining, cats in heat. My eyes hovered over skinny arms tied to walls, hanging upside down some triangle leather inside a circle. Three-on-one whippings, flogging. Legs hanging spread from ceiling fastened swings. Three to four bodies hitting it hard, slamming in on futons. Men painted green, five men spanking two men and three ladies meowing all fours.

All smiling at us. Wanting, beckoning me and Sam, *tattooed spike hair and lanky legs supple butt is all they see,* I thought. Winks, come hither their finger joints, their direction. I looked at Sam. We stood together. Watching. I heard myself, breathing. Saw no breath but the whole room, painting like: she. She. Lots of she's…I saw…

Perhaps I was overstimulated. I don't know. I almost fainted, *all going to tear at my clothes, my skin.*

Sam watched over me. He held my pinky nail, led me to a black-lit room. He sat on a chair. Pulled me straddle him. Legs on either side, my feet on the floor. He lowered me down onto him. His round fat cock head bulbous, pushed through my cavern, my wetness. His spit on his hand, on my lips. He got me wetter. He in me. Holding down me, in hard grasp around my waist. I remember that hard grip. It was the only thing that reminded me I was there, alive. The almost bruising sensation of his grip. He had me grinding. Circling. His eyes, his circling hip bone, his cock rod held me erect. His index cracking my lumbar. His hot gaze; Then I felt their eyes. Those people who wanted us before, had gathered. People watching us then. Gathering, all around us. Holding themselves, these people were. I could see them all. A circle of people around us. They were fiddling, stroking their own twats, shafts, nipples: their own flesh in their own fingers. Watching us. They, moaning. I heard them. Some began moaning. I could hear them, echoes like my ears. Was I a child at the top of the stairs at Mom's? Was I here with Sam? Who was Sam? Who was I? Was I being raped, molested or in love and exploring? I couldn't tell. My skin was hot. I couldn't feel my skin. I was skinless and vibrating on top of this man's cock, cumming and coursing on display for all of these people getting off at my sight.

I remember then how I bent my lips to Sam's ear. "Imagine," I whispered, "Sam, you are on a rooftop. Surrounded by high-rise apartments, offices. You are fucking, chugging—the ridges of my sugar walls; my sweet muscles swollen; my body convulsing orgasms. I up high, like everyone peeping out their windows, only they were standing right there. Standing watching while we're fucking. Sam, you and I. They are part of us. Me them." I had Sam then, all of his attention. Safe in our tunnel.

Sam rotated his hips. I came on him. Soaring together…I felt him explode hot cum inside me, he grunted long, he. We sat in eyes washing new, floating on river like through the Grand Canyon, Colorado rapids they together, morphed nature and time inside seconds, molecules inside hue, wave's vibration, inside rhythm, staccato, backbeat. We were in time.

Eventually, Sam said, "Tan tan." (Means so-so) Like the crowd wasn't good enough for us, to touch them. I nodded, silent. Grabbed his hand. We two left. Split.

Zipped up our threads, and walked out smiling on that sunny springtime sidewalk.

"One day, we'll have it all." Sam piped, holding my hand. I felt solid. I'd fallen to bits in there, melted, gone into time warp, parallel…Shocked, horrified, elated, expanded. Now Me and Sam were swinging hands, and stopping for a New York pretzel.

"And if our acting careers don't work out," he laughed, "we'll make pornos together, score a mint, move somewhere southern!"

I was starting to miss dancing. I hadn't worked in a while, danced. We had left Wanda's, Sam had money, he was working flow and starting to pair up with Jess. I was itching for the dance, my music, my ambitions. Dancing Angelica before all this, Times Square club, I had seen a client a few times, . He'd given me his card, said: "Skip the club, visit my hotel. I don't want sex or even to touch you, just dancing in my hotel room. An hour of dancing for 500 bucks." I had never done it. I wanted to make the money. I knew I could handle myself. I called the man to discuss. Told him I'd have someone waiting outside so no funny stuff. I knew the guy wasn't going to ask for more.

"Come along, wait nearby," I told Sam. "It's just G-string dance."—When I got out of the session with the man, guy been real fine, but Sam had been waiting solo in a bar downstairs. His imagination had freaked to wild.

"You don't know how important you are," he grabbed my shoulder.

"Why don't you just take a break for a while? Let me take care of you," he decided.

Uh-oh. Here we go. He wants to change me. He can't handle it.

Sam didn't have bank accounts, just a guy living. Spending day-to-day pulling strings. I wanted Sam to get behind me and let me make money. A team.

"I'm getting things rolling with Jess here in ten days, hang in, we'll be rolling," he insisted. "You're better than this."

I didn't think I was better than anything and *this* was just fine. *But OK— we compromise for love I guess,* I figured.

That night, Sam called his mom, in Miami.

"Talk to my future wife!" he said, pushed the phone on me.

"No!" I said, played shy. Actually, I thought, I like intimacy between me and my lover; not me, my lover, and his mother. I, silent.

Sam said, "You'll understand more, when you get older."

Yeah. I look back on all this and I think, well, I imagine, every human wakes up sometimes the night, not knowing why they're here; saying, 'What's the point? Who made us? We can all run around like a chicken trying to stuff it—the unknown. Or just be with okay with the emptiness, I figure. I mean, it seems to me, looking back on this story, that there is a point where even dreams will hold you back, like how staring too long at the eclipse can blind you to the rest of the world—make it so you don't have to be with that vast galactic space. Truth is, that's all there is; only thing finite, or you can depend on being there the end of it all, anyway. So, here we go…

Ammo

Sam and I began moving hotels every three weeks. Started up fast and went on a whole five months.

"Partnered up, this commercial production company," Sam deliberated to everyone we crossed paths with between stepping in and out of Lincoln town cars.

"Just shot a cable Mercedes ad for my buddies, got a dealership, Miami." All people with a dream need a B-job for a while and all subterraneans need a cover.

Sam placed a pair of *Breakfast at Tiffany's* sunglasses on me, whisked me silent charisma alongside his carte blanche dilettante up, down, around, all over this East Coast trade route. We were Miami, NY, A.C., Jet Blue. The exclusive Morgan, Palms, Nation, ZO Hotels. Sam shook hands left and right, folding baggies stuffed with hippety-hop-ups to each one's palm, from rock star chefs to red rope owners; movie-biz peeps to sports reps and veeps; always coupled in entertainment buzz convo, "I'm shopping my script…I've got Burt Young and few key players on my pinky ring," Sam told the next person over white table lunches, to dusk grim billiards, then blasts 'n lobster tails.

"One day, soon, they will all sit high on the dust of their own stars, watching me play the lead in my script," he whispered in confidence to me. We sat inside early light steam massage, sauna, and no bother stopping—so evening clothes shopping—and it's off to another dinner. I gleamed brightly powdering my cheeks with the Tiffany hand mirror he'd bought me.

Every once a while, Sam would murmur, "Miami cowboys…" about them fizzling his Metropolis deal. Then he'd disappear awhile; leave me poolside—rapping news on the import seaside loots, I figured. I didn't ask.

"I'm looking to build a softer life. Out the big rackets," Sam kept saying after he'd got off the cell, jacked, confided in me tidbits of talking with Jess.

"We are going to set up this thing in NY, these cats growing buds, out west: Sam wanted to do business with peaceful throwbacks from '60s—'70s who learned as passed-down trade…" instead of the hard-nosed cut-throat bulk pony imports. Jess was Sam's main Yahtzee, I mean he saw that Jess had the connection with the west coast growers, and he saw a new horizon, with his business.

"All artists need a B-job," Sam's voice chuckled, in my ear. I didn't look at myself that way. I thought if I had real talent, I wouldn't need a second gig. I admired Sam for letting him be him. I wanted me be me, but.

Sam had met Jess through a guy, named Bleu, hanging up in Harlem, carving a new connect for himself, some Dominican brick bud, bulk. Fuck knows why Jess was up there. Bleu was some guy Sam had pulled out of a conk some few years back, grabbed one man before Bleu made county tombs and lower—and that been made Bleu loyal for life, Sam said.

I knew Jess no way could survive that world without Sam.

"Yeah, Jess *was* pretty skint, but his dad's a fuckin' New York State judge for Christ's sake. He doesn't need me," Sam said, on that particular day's stroll.

Jess: I was sitting in some booth at Nightingale's writing poetry on a napkin. Jess walked over. I guess some gals go gaga guy spouts jive Eastern philosophy. His rap reminded me of my mom and my little brother, Aidan. Spouting on about how you should see the world. Always seemed like a way for them to hide whatever they don't like about themselves. Yeah, we hung a bit, Thirteenth Street roof, some yoga poses together.

Jess went off about, "The importance of letting go, releasing material for Zen living!" Blowing lines of coke to talking about his newest and greatest whatever the brand name, and his dad's old cars in their place on Long Island, whatever.

"Yo buddy, go out and speak the Gospel and if you must, use words," I'd split.

Sam, I told him, "Kid lives a consumer: car gas, plastic labels, suburbia corporate entitlement his whole life, never given up a damned thing."

"Jess *was* pretty skint," Sam twiddled his soda straw, repeated, "Parents weren't sending off cash so easy anymore, when I met him, he'd picked up smoking crack."

Cornerstone of the deal: Sam smelled retail. Jess had a lot of hippy-boy suburban-type friends, and they had friends of friends with dreamy notions of dealing drugs, and dating hot women. Sam was big glamour in their eyes.

"Boys watched too much fuckin' TV," I laughed.

Sam's eyes showed a real sweet nurture for Jess. I didn't know why, figured, *I can like Jess OK, if Sam trusts him.*

I watched the two boys make moves: They shared clients, traded herb only, all equal splits. Small deals at first. Sam brought down East Harlem pound, two brick; showed Jess how to break, weigh, sell. Jess revealed he had a few college chums who had migrated to Cali, "Hooked up with some-kind-crop hydro growers, dude!"

"They're looking to drive bulk pounds east cheap, monthly."

If ya don't know. West Coast strains, East Coast guys are willing to pay over a hundred bucks for 3.5 grams. That's over double what the growers sell it for, bulk. I knew the scene—hitching through Oregon, I'd shacked in a house with growers, hydro, outdoor in a huge house out backwoods Eugene, Oregon, for a few months before I shaved off my hair, and thumbed out onto the road, solo. Those Oregon guys had developed their own strains, seeds; guys' dad had taught him growing up, in Woodstock. He'd cultivated a few of his family strains, and started indoor hydro, and outdoor farm. We'd help clip, package— it's a business based on supply, demand; wholesale, retail; import, export. I figure, *on illegal? Whatevs*: It's about how you conduct your business, legal or no: Some thieves do the work; some do the work straight up. Like any business.

Anyway, me and Sam—it was all temporary, our minds. "I'm trying piece a solid gig into capital, catapult celluloid success independent industrial..." Sam, his film. My dreams—I wanted to hide.

Cali

It was all set: first-night load-in, Sam and Jess.

Morgan hotel, NY. Fourteenth-floor suite. Glass floor to ceiling towering views over New York's architecture. TV on in every room.

Jess lay back, silk Goldilocks hair flipped over the arm of the plush opal leatherette. Low-hanging, slim hips, skater shorts, red. Some pink button-up stripe collar dressed his gangly channels, limbs. I call arms channels sometimes because they are the connection from body to other stuff out the world.

Sam had put in first invest: scraped together fifteen-grand, a sweet capital dollar for thirty pounds at five K each. Jess brought connects, worth their weight. His Cali blokes were set drivin' 'cross the United States. Scheduled a roll in by nightfall.

I didn't bother to ask why they didn't pay mules to cart for them, just figured it was their first-time hooking distance and didn't have a crew together yet. I guess they wanted to meet eye once, too. I clocked (that means watched, in my dictionary) Sam was busy fastening Jess as his even-splits partner. I guess he was trying to cultivate trust with Jess by giving so much at the top. I don't know. Sam sharing every little nitty, every nili-nana-spec thing he knew about dealing with this type of bulk. If you don't understand business, it's the same no matter what the product: they were talking the score on directing, pacing, protecting a high-end quantity. All bud import. This was before the heyday for medical weed and THC oils, edibles, and hydro allowance. Oh, and "nili" means 'every single little darned-nat detail that not everyone should be taught, because some stuff in the business situation better left kept to oneself so they retain some power. Ya digz?

"What New York hotels are safe," Sam was schooling Jess, I was cooling one earphone Thievery Corporation: electronic Middle eastern with sitar. Leather Dolce strap across ankle on the opalescent pale tufted L-shaped couch. Curves my bare calves, hair up, a twist. One ear cocked: Sam and Jess.

"Elevator banks off to the side, no one's seen walking past the front desk; have alias tags on hand, book a few rooms all cash. It's a one-night yard sale, son," Sam.

"Yes, man," Jess.

"Main aim, get the big dog paid off ASAP," Sam lectured on, "Top buyers in first. I got Gallagher, Kiam, and Tyler on call." Resourceful—Sam had prepped three of Jess's college buddies: helped them build capital and clientele, be his top buyers. But meant all his hooks were through Jess. Not good, anything go south.

Few hours later, sun was lower than the ocean, I was sitting back, Glenlivet in hand. I love the languid evenings drunk, when nothing is expected of you anyway, so melting into forms, shapes, slurs, murmurs and visions is almost unnoticeable by others. My own skin was warm but I had no clue if I was alive or dead, or cared. My eyes and ears were Sam. The slight black hair tufting beneath his chin bone, hopeful light: "Once you're paid back, it's a trade-off. Big customers can wipe you, one fell swoop cash. But you turn bigger green with smaller retail. We'll ride a little both right now, son. Get our feet wet. We 'll sell it out in one night."

I pulled Sam's elbow, stuck own nose in: "Maybe Jess's posing misfit but it's shit softee. You're likely he'll yank carpet on you or he will just be stupid, fuck it up—just let him run errands, give a cash cut for supplying…" rambled on…, "mingling with those softee types…they want to play Misfit Survivor games, but deep down they want to win other softee love—got no backbone."

"They'll turn on you to get it, claiming it's morality…Really they're just as whacked as you, festering their own secrets, rather point the finger out!" I was a big talker drunk.

I mean, Sam did agree. "I don't even think Jess knows all that, he's in for money, I got this." Sam kissed my head. Guess he thought himself stronger than the kid from candyland Long Island.

After that I sat back, thinking, drinking. They say that's a bad combination. Sam said that. I said it's thinking and not drinking, problem. I was looming, thoughts, words, ideas…*I am a girl. I have limitations. Sure, I'm rather fiercely feminine. Strong for a girl…why I working sexprowess and puissance over a man's physical,* that analyzing and reflecting in the swimming tank of my wet brain. Enamored by this feeling. My eyes repeatedly traced the limbs, forms, slopes of Sam cracking his knuckles, sternum. His pumped lats flexing through tight black T each time he hit a consonant. His deep growl, gruff, commanding voice: "Most important, just know I got your back. Remember: people do weird shit, drugs, and money in frame, they can't help it. People have a low threshold for survival sometimes. So don't invite it."

Jess, shaking toe-head up, down: "Of course; yes."

Familiar *glurg* my stomach.

Sam made Jess repeat these rules back to him, three times, word for word.

"1: Never let guys picking up see or know how much you're holding. You don't and I don't wanna get robbed or set up.

2: Never let people meet each other. This is a major fucking key: They will try to cut you out. I think our California buds are pretty loyal, not like what I been dealing with, but dumbasses'll try to get supply somewhere else, steal your clients, sell cheaper—they just will, so always come to me you get bing something funny, I got you covered.

3: You always got to secure your turf, got have a few dogs guarding everything, separately—.

"Promise me, bro, you got all that down. You lose, means I lose and I'll paint your blood all over the inner rim of your mother's fat thigh," Sam lingo.

"Trust me, Son, we'll be in flowing in no time."

I heard that, "son" and I wanted Sam to look at me like he looked at Jess. Desire: be seen as a solid partner, a comrade, a soldier. The way boys are with each other. *I am so easily shiftable, so watery, so independent, never formed a tribe or group with anyone…I want to walk into a room and tell people what to do and they will listen…Like Sam can…*

Sam brought in three backups, his chosen team: his people.

Cider: smooth-haired gal greeter armed mobile in lobby, escorted buyers up and down from main-exchange suite.

Dux: ex-pro wrestler stationed on guard in major stash room, trained to make pre-weighed sets if needed.

Sebastien: Sam's main right major, loyal. Looked sixteen but Sam swore twenty-four. Sam trained him to be ultra-cop savvy—"but not so smart he'll palm profits," Sam told Carlotta. Sebby ran cash and deliveries.

Sam fed everyone seamless plans, so all around everyone was protected. Anything turned south, they knew exactly what to do, say, and who to call.

"Otherwise," Sam told me later, "They'll pee their pants and rat."

Examining, I was.

Two guys arrived. Cali guys in T's carrying huge sacks duffel.

Observing, I was.

First thing in, cheery "bro" hugs. Sam introduced.

"Break bread, for good luck!" The sweaty growers just off a long road haul, wanted to get high.

"Gotta toke to know what we're selling!" Sam and Jess chimed. *I cringed: Basic, you don't get high on your own supply.* The high school rat fest, with

Drew and me. Tripping liquid LSD the whole time made us fuzzy for watching our own backs.

"Man, hottest Bubble Gum flavor! Chewy in your mouth, sweet," blah-blah, words for how to sell it to buyers. Cali boys a few different strains. "And the Blue Char, Apple Plum, infamous Purple Haze."

It *was* the best crop I had seen around New York, with Sam. I knew fluffy, dank, orange hair, Indica, Sativa, kolas; living with those Oregon growers. Me, I could take or leave the green, really. I understood the delicacy of strains, tastes. Same as booze, but—I'd rather drink anything from grain, grape or potato brown any day. Different mentality, too, far as I had scoped out. Smokers and drinkers. Boozer: Solo fixture. I wasn't into groups, other people. Sure, I'd knock back at any party, work, bar, whatever, but my relationship was with the booze, not the group experience. I had kept hard liquor in the bedroom since I was fourteen. By then, always kept a nip in my bag, closet. Mom's drunk has always stashed it around the house. I learned from him, I guess. Jealous of his power, wanted to be like him, really. He was the one in the house with all the power over Mom, and eventually over me. To this day, I still have to remember I am giving him power by letting what he did rule my emotional life, my feelings, actions. *I've always been a wanderer, in search of fuck knows,* that hot Mary Jane hawking night at the Morgan. Laying back cool. Sipping booze, watching next room puffs smoke…they in a cloud of candy smells and yak. Scribbling journal: '*Me, I'm so solo, never meld with anyone like that…Guess I'm mutable—Changing, how I've changed since I met Sam.*' No, I wasn't putting the drink down. I kept musing: *pot plants.*

Mary J has different sexes. Female plants (chicks, girls) make the bang THC—stuff gets you high. They reap demand because they are rarer. Male plants have almost untraceable THC—produce twice amount mass paper, rope, oxygen over our average tree, shrub. Thing is: *If there is even so much as a trace of one male plant in the room, the female plant will automatically turn male.*

Shifting, I was. Couldn't control that—same time kept having that pop-thought, I'd learned somewhere in the seventies, eighties feminist lit, Mom had that book, *Why do I feel I am Nothing Without a Man?* I got the idea, remembered hearing somewhere that: "Women have to hold their own form, not lose strength with a male."

Pondering, I was suddenly starting to think, *Maybe something's natural to shifting…Is this a beautiful, feminine kind of malleable? A girl's instinct when safe in her man's strength—is it weakness of mine, am I a dumb submissive girl?* The reprehensible thought that any feminist and my own inner lasher would have scolded me for, but I was thinkin'…*If I go with my wish to meld with Sam, change some, will it actually make me stronger?* I wrote. *Would I let myself depend on Sam? I have never thought about giving over to this kind of mutuality before. In my mind, a woman who does that is ultimately weak. I hate weakness in anyone. But am I stronger for it I trust?* I didn't know the answer, *but I'm always up for a new experience.* Early September flowed copacetic. Green buds did flips: small stacks Benjamins. Sam and I focused on acting, writing, and ideas making legitimize cash. We settled in a four-room Stuyvesant Town sublet. Sebastien, Sam's loyal-like-little brother showed up from who knows where, and crashed a futon in the living room.

"This is different, babe," Sam twirled my hair.

"We are starting something *together*. Gonna finally get what we really deserve...the life we dreamed since we were kids..."

Makes me think of a black-and-white cartoon I'd drawn, at ten years old, for *Elementary Gazette*. Mom gave it to me in some box, in lifelike recently.

It is a mouse wandering Christmas alone and I wrote a bubble above its head saying: "Just looking for a companion with whom I could share my thoughts."

I guess Sam was that Mouse for me.

Stepping Out

Now, I don't wanna lose you, all my jumping around. Present, past, present. I'm not here to teach you anything. I heard from a friend that Native Americans said, like, "past, present, future, all happening at once, inside us."

I looked it up and read a letter in March 1855, Einstein wrote to his recently deceased friend's family, "The distinction between past, present, and future is only a stubbornly persistent illusion." Einstein died a month later.

So, let's get back to it—fast forward from where we just left off, back to where we were.

Lower East Side studio sublet. Sundown evening slanting. Tally-ho—

Naked. I was staring into an antiquated black frame boudoir glass hanging low on the shadowy bedroom wall. Every inch of my 25-year-old face appeared as though reflecting back in broken fragments, and each was 3-D magnified. I had on black silk stocking, red nails; fingers straightening back seams. Beth Orton, Portishead's "Numb" droned through my stereo. Exasperated, 'this loneliness, won't leave me alone...' Orton sings from her journal, I read somewhere, loved that. *I want to crawl inside her curdling cries.*

My palm-wrapped around a Stolzie Revolution stem. My mouth downed Penfolds Bin 389; cherry beet plum subtle oak-fused dark chocolate cabernet Shiraz—Rex had brought to Darlings as a gift, a few days prior, insisting: "I wish educate you further on vino, Miss Cindy." Sweet bouquet; dank earth; made dressing for this event more enjoyable.

Hows and whys of old Rex getting me to say yes, stuck like tiny pinpricks in the layers of my unsettled mind. *Challenge old Revan to a duel,* I guessed, told myself. Downing a gulp. *Accepted his offer on the stupid blue Chanel suit over chill martini, Hudson's. . .*

"Yes," she, Cindy had said—I couldn't quite settle on who, which one of us, me—had said, "yes."

My hair half up a Bardot pump, twirls down breasts. Up down. Down. I couldn't decide. I could barely glance the glass.

The slow clucking of Sam's breathing, snores from that red couch, TV across beige tapestry. Silhouette curled-like; boy sucking thumb. He was sort of sweet like this, penetrable somehow. Churning, turning under a blue-knit Army hospital blanket.

"I always get a bad cold in December," Sam had shrugged.

This cold was lasting.

Sam had been yelling on the phone a lot, then, and not coming home till early dawn. I didn't know what to do with that.

My mind whipped, brushed more powder on my face: *I'm a greedy person, scummy...cheap move, resigning dining with old Rex. Shithead, lying to Sam...*Flopped: *I dunno why Sam even likes me. Flapped: Even Rex is too good for me.* Forked: *I'm doing Rex a favor. If he didn't have me, where would he be? Stuck back in the club flanked by some strange Russian chick*—and, Damn some of those Russian dames are really hot.

Pulled sparkly sweater coat to floor over evening slip-dress, my pointed black Enzo Angiolini spikes, I was getting antsy. Turned five years shy big thirty over six months ago and still, I've got nothing. Ought to take what I can. Shit, I never even had socks. It was true. In fourth grade, I had been on the boheme campus, went to small-town Red Hook elementary. Teacher scowled at the sight of huge holes in my heels and toes. Scolded me, "Go get proper care." I got sent home from school, for gaping holes in my socks. Embarrassing.

Mom was in the city with a boyfriend. She was always in New York City those days. Four-night a week on the regular. That time, I waited three days at home before I got socks and back on the schedule. A long time for a nine-year-old.

"Make do with what you have!" Mom had barked, when she did show up with her drunk Polish boyfriend, the one.

Touching finishes on my freshly painted face in the mirror—felt a familiar riddled rush to my hyper-sensitive lymphatic system, about Rex, about the drunk, about Mom, I don't know, my answer: *There are negotiations in life. You've always known that. Suck it up; do what you can to survive.* This plan with Raven, well, I could taste it all working out in my favor. Rex said he wanted to get me a record deal with one of his big foreign exchange clients, he'd mentioned it several times. First, he wanted the cronies of his to see me sing at his friend's Lucky Strike joint, which scared me because I hate to be seen unless I'm naked in a room with strangers, dancing; an artist who hates to be seen is an atrocity. I trusted that eventually, Sam would get even with Jess. Jess the softee who had pulled the rug, stopped calling Sam when the Cali guys delivered. Cutting Sam out of the in-loads and the sales. Just as I had predicted. *We'll put this all behind us,* my mind fueled resolution: *Rex is a chump who is asking to be taken care of by me; I must dangle his carrot right back. Say whatever I need, he needs to hear; rotate me and Sam's plan in motion. Make our dreams come true.* I can't say I even knew clearly what those looked like, but I knew I wanted to get out of wherever I was, as soon as I got there. Another piece to the spectrum of the bruised and addicted. Nothing is ever good enough, or feels safe. Everything is a plan for survival and escape. Until you start to see this for what it is and learn to feel, heal.

That night, I inserted the tiny diamond studs Sam had gifted me for Valentine's Day two weeks before.

I slung mink collared cashmere, cover my clothes. Dust rolled low, dark corners the room, last few minutes lowlight sun. *Move smooth past sleeping beauty,* I was. "I love you, baby, give me a kiss," Sam called out from under that blue blanket, arms wide.

I wrapped him. "Loves, too. Darlings, I am late." Smacked Sam's kisser, my lying lips.

Double unbolt door.

Sam flipped fast awake. "That guy gonna be there?"

"Who?"

Sam, "Who, you owl. That Champagne dork you told me is on your court."

I smiled like I'd just recalled an old friend.

Busted, flip, "Babe, this sunny side eve, I am betting odds old green-eyed Rex will be waltzing my way near nine—dangling one big old carrot." I had mentioned this regular bloke a few times when counting cash after work. Unclear if Sam liked Rex laying all that dollar on me, or he was jealous. I guess a little deuce up on the flip flop there.

"I will pick you up at four, baby," Sam called after me.

"Might get off early. Text u."

Sam, "Don't let those guys touch you up there." *Lip about her work lately? Get your own business straight, boy,* thought I. Sunk guilty slash thrilled to be hitting a five star for dinner.

"Think celluloid and recording artist success! One day, I want to hear your voice on the radio!" I heard Sam call out as his cell cracked up.

"Pappy?" Heard him, "Right there five minutes man." Broke off—spitfire Spanish.

Sitting in the cab back, I wondered about my decision to take the shift off that night.

Oh, if you don't know, strippers are like roving concessions stands; like yellow cabs working within confines the club. A dancer plays a C-note to house, shift pay, you start your shift. You dance, peddle cash, all in pocket, no splits. If you glide in late on a shift time, you get taxed fifty bones; If ya slide in after the 8:00 p.m. "Dream Team" kickoff: this is when each plastic-platform-cleavage-wazoo gal clomp together, tiny stage, DJ blasts '80s hit "Girls, Girls, Girls—" mufflerless motor revving—and the club announces each lady by name and her like, favorite sport or fruit or something. Humiliating, but it is a good opportunity to get the quick-dash commuter cash, before the heavies come in for late night.

That night, I didn't have to think about any of it. Dinner at Hudson, set: 8:00 p.m.

As the city whirled by, lower east side junkies turned three-piece business suits, thoughts of my Italian grandmother Grace, on Dad's side...*am I falling into a state of, or falling from.* Grace had ended up with Alzheimer's; years of loyal and dutiful marriage to a drunk, abusive husband. I, wrestling exposure of the red wine stains only Chanel girl red lipstick could hide, thought, *Well, least you could say I'm always up for a good martini.*

Hudson

Spinning through revolving mirror paneled entrance doors, I smacked right into the host at Hudson Restaurant. Name tag read MAX.

"You must be Cynthia for Mr. Revan?"

I flashed a wide smile, thought, *How the hell does his garish swarthiness know my name?*

May sound racist of sorts, but I had a kind of predilection for men who strike a vampiric beauty: gaunt bone cheeks, onyx sapphire stars framed by shiny midnight curls; thick scarlet lips, gleaming longish fanged cuspids…that was thrown to discord by my soufflé of suspicions.

Max pulled my elbow through mishmash shoulders jostling. We carved a narrow parting around a circular island bar, central to the room, weaving between channels and hands clutching Hudson's alleged thirteen-ounce swimming-pool martini. Ornamental golden chandeliers illuminated *multi-award-winning scotches, cognacs, liqueurs,* I was bit drooling, while stock tickers flashed and football boomed out of flat screens, Bose speakers over bar…and from somewhere I couldn't spot, *strange jazz music drifting. Nice break from Darlings, tinny techno-sleaze, bad sound gear…*and cut by the bits of raucously delivered conversation that was not so different from Darlings—

"Such a drag, Sun City home remodeled, kids on Saint Bart's,"—*stresses of a CFO,* I pegged as Max led me on toward some staircase.

"You must try Versace's Dubai Hotel, worth the low-intelligence hassle over there," what I assumed a tired lawyer grumbling to a slick Armani…

"Nice pout to your lips, baby," one aimed an arrow on me, his warm breath spittle touched my ear. I suppose these days, since the MeToo movement, this would be considered harassment. To me, this was normal in every crowd, men thinking women were there for them. And I always wondered if we secretly liked the attention, lewd as it was. Did it make us ladies feel young and wanted at least? And in charge, because we can always turn our nose up and walk on? These questions always loomed in my head. I glanced down fast at glinting gold wedding band choking his hairy fourth finger, and clutching icy amber cocktail.

Hmph. Hudson Restaurant; supposed to be a high-class joint. *High-class men,* I thought. I figured, majority of men here have their black Amex, leather Coach, high-end private diplomas, name probably on upper-level credential business cards; most of them probably have a wife in Westchester, and attend some type of church on Sundays, traditional holidays with their families…all a bunch of wannabe Donald Trump homogenized assholes…(um, this was actually written before he became the president, and I did think it back then.) Went on to deduct: These same men's several pairs beady carnal eyes seemed yearning sex, burning black holes the crisscross seams of my black ballerina twirl dress, is the same look I see, day in out, gentleman's clubs, zagged my mind sharply. Familiar *Glurg* in my gut.

Torn, I was, about whether I wanted to be in mainstream society, or I liked and felt more at home in the subterranean underground of the sex world. I had told myself at nineteen years old, after a few years hitching the road looking for peace and safety from what I was told to call home as a child; when I first walked into Lusty Lady in San Francisco, that I had just taken a wrong turn, falling into stripping. That's what they tell you—you're fallen, woman. Fallen into the scarlet life, when if you had grown upright, you would be pure and lily, married and playing the church morality and rules. *Mendacity.* We all buy into it one some level, it's impossible not to—and of course, there's the question. Is it instinctual to want to be pure, married, living by social morality? Or is it told to us, by way of the church wanting to keep order in society so we can work and survive as a well-organized team, all following the same rules? Well, as a young stripper, just off the homeless road, I said, *One day, I would straighten out; develop some kind of normal career that these upper-societal-corporate folks could respect.* The kinds of people my father claimed to be— and made perfectly clear I was not, and that I would never be. My father and his wife hadn't spoken to me in a few years then. He rarely knew me growing up, and often told me he felt I wasn't going to amount to anything but a teenage mother drug-addict on welfare—and so not worthy of his attention. Yet, the more I went out around the high-class establishments where these "socially respected" lived, the more I saw that everyone was doing some version in their own false way—and the club was just a distilled version of it, and place where people didn't have to pretend and could just ask for what they wanted and see if the girl would do it, for proper pay and maintenance. It was honest, to me.

I had spent ample hours as a child climbing trees, contemplating in their branches. Innocent, naked legs crouching in a little skirt, high grass brushing knee, skin. I loved to touch the veins in flowers, blossom. Mom and I used to walk together once a week, down around Anna Road on that boheme campus we lived. Mother's long-legged gait. Up the winding to my piano teacher's house, Margaret. Means "pearl," Margaret does. Margaret's grand posture, flanked in long purple knits, silk skirts, and pointed-toe heels, down a long spiral case from upstairs to greet. I always imagined that she'd exploded from a blazing white cloud to appear for music, a pearl angel. Her great big white diagonal walls. Windows for ceilings.

"Play what's in your heart," Margaret's soft, gentle drawl spoke in my ear as I practiced scales. Her knotted fingers touched my little hands, on black-white, pitter-patter. I would practice four hours a day at home, up and down the keys memorizing "Für Elise;" lose myself in the wind's song alive. As the bliss of kid life faded, I started to see everyone as *wanting.* I saw people everywhere, that are dead inside. Most unable to even make eye contact without having some kind agenda. All just fishing to get fed.

I would have told you then, tell you, "Strength, this world is about its survival of the fittest—and I don't hate men, I understand why men are drawn."

I'd have said to you, "Women have an intuitive connection to life force that is incredibly magical to be around, if the gal's in touch with hers." Men in the man's world: have to be the strongest thing walking Earth—knowing you can kill anyone. That may be true, on instinct. But no one seemed to want to really learn communication with anyone, to go deep into intimacy, instead of power. Ladies hanging seemed to seek one fast climb up a food chain ladder; Guys, knew that if the woman got under their skin, they could just pop off and find another.

I didn't have the answers. Couldn't say I was so perfect at communication or intimacy. But something was lacking and I could feel it everywhere. I had thought about it a lot when I was hitching the highways, before entering the urban world with my songs, trying to make a record or some kind of profession that people would like me for. Back on the road, leafing those old used books, some Freud, Jung, and that religious history, I had decided to blame ass-back morality: It seemed to me, simple: *Sex urges are confusing, so marked as bad, yet they are the most natural thing in the world. Then anything you stuff under comes out in the weirdest of ways.* I was haunted for trying to figure it out. It was the wildest conundrum around, to me, dealing with other peoples' sex urges, and how we survive in the world with them.

I had lost my head on all that, because swerve: my au-de-confidence turned anxious. *Huge pound head. Socialized world is fucking marshmallow fluff liars.* Yes, I have grown to appreciate that level crass honesty at the strip club. Guy wants to be near me, feel my magic, sex, get to see breasts, ass—he just asks, pays, leaves. Drama-free money, protection. What haunted me—*if I chalk impressing these upper-level duds aside, designate them as paying clientele—do I spend rest of my life an artistic, social outcast, sex worker?*

Sounded lonely. Flip: far my life then, strip bars, gentleman's clubs, wazoo was the most similar thing to primitive nature, the jungle, the planes, the land, the survival of the fittest strategy balls out, that I had ever found. Resting note on that wild mind race, I said: *It is close to the primal forces that I feet most alive.*

There we had arrived. Hudson's mezzanine. I eyed Rex's bald head glowing bulbous in corner, over white lit-candle, reflective silver; rising like full harvest moon.

"Brightness blossoms," Max yanked me, presented: I curtsied.

Rex in full view was employing a noticeably sharp, silver dental-hygienist-looking tool to extract filbert meat his nut.

Greeny hazel winkers, glassed where the whites ought to glisten, loomed ever-more dehydrated yellow than I had recalled from the club. "The bottle now, please." Rex offered no hello.

My own eyes then landed Day-Glo Chanel caps shining huge print; glossy black shopping bag resting aside Rex's auburn wingtip lace-ups.

Max pulled chair; pressed sit; pushed me in. Pulled a side table for my purse.

Stuffed in the upstairs corner, I eyed the culprit on the jazz: simple tulip white-tank, long skirt 'side piano. Hair slicked sparkling garnet. A soulful twist on old Ethel Waters's *Honey in My Honeycomb. She doesn't need Chanel to sing, you slut*...I scolded me, *Oh, wait, Max, please don't go,* my eyes trailed onyx*; Stupid girl, getting so attached*, I barked at me.

Suave. Hawking eager over-tall "Frank" waiter shimmied silver cart spread: dried apricots, figs, raisins, Roquefort, select olives, smoked nuts, Dom preserve. Fingers handed both Rex and I a menu etched Canadian Islands, Alaskan fishing boats.

Rex's silky, baritone. "Order whatever you wish, dear Cindy. Or I can recommend for you, a dish."

Rhyming again.

Frank the waiter appeared, a spitting image of Giants owner, John Mara— gray curls, glasses, big nose. Popped, poured bubbles. Tasted, Rex.

A raisin dropped in a glass of champagne will rise and fall endlessly until the champagne goes flat, I thought of an old, poet friend, Miller painting watercolor in a little town, Inverness, West Marin. I had camped beach there for a while before hitting city...*If I drop a golden one from the assortment tray into mine,* me zoning...Miller had died in the bathtub. Swallowed his own tongue. *Oh, zoom.* Rex had placed his champagne down and picked up menu. My dark eyes studied menu...*broiled sole, enflamed hearts*...Words seemed spiral, explode her face...*artichoke must be here somewhere...tender baby* *legs…What are the chances I will be able drink before my proverbial raisin's second descent…You're being paid to dine, idiot…*I barked at me.

I did know the rules: *You may not drink until he does.* I wasn't raised with much outing, in general. But I understood the rules of dining, speaking, fashion, respecting the man. I knew I'd be leaving the house by the time I was eleven, stuck with Mom and her drunk boyfriend. I had started studying Marylin movies and Scarlett O'Hara—I figured I'd be a sex worker of some kind at least until I met a nice man—would need lady skills to get by.

My inner voice started barking rules: *1) You will sit, listen, be interested in all he tells you. 2) You must act wide-eyed; like he is the only man like him you've ever met. 3) Tell him everything he shows you is wonderful, reference anything he has taught you in the past, as having helped you greatly—because deep down he actually feels he invented it. 4) Don't reveal much about you. No one wants to hear the truth, and when they say they do, they are looking for ways to look down on you—treat you like garbage—or put you on a pedestal, that either way is about them. Makes them feel better about themselves. 5) Simple: a gal like you must be Ivy League, just dancing for a few dollars to put toward school or some such. 6) No mention father, it stresses them out to be reminded. 7) Make like you've never been to this place he's escorted—but drop hints that you've been sought after by many contenders. Sparks of competition speak wonders; makes him think he has to do better than the unknown others. 8) Game on, play Cindy.*

Then Rex pulled the stodgiest move. The man actually produced a small stack of colorfully hand-scripted index cards from his left olive-and-woolen breast pocket. Placed the pile beside that silver sharp dental-hygienist-looking tool he'd been employing to extract filbert meat.

I blinked.

Rex then picked up card #1, and announced, "I have a few ideas of what we might discuss, dear Cindy. First, I would like to say that I thank you for taking an incredible risk in coming to meet me here. A lot of girls in your position wouldn't have been so brave. I thank you." Tucked that card into right breast pocket.

I triple-blinked. Eyes fluttered, then shook forehead tizzy-like, eeked a sigh like a hot summer day, and tootled his way: "Well, I do want to tell you, I've never done anything like this before. But you seemed like such a nice man," Cindy giggled.

"I'll go ahead and take your words as compliment," chimed, he.

"Well, you ought," smirked she, back to solid.

Rex picked index #2. Cindy sat back and watched as his plum lips aspirated: "Wellfleets, bluepoints, Kumamotos, Miyagis, and Totten Inlet."

Rex likes to spout knowledge, any subject, I remembered. The walking-encyclopedia routine often appealed to me, I like when it was retained info—not read off index cards. *Yawn.*

Shut up, slut, you're being paid to listen.

"Olympias being the only West Coast native!" Rex wolfed at me.

To which I laughed back a nod. I'd told Raven one of her many club backstory lies: "I am a native San Franciscan." Secret: One of my favorite things about being a dancer, was that I was allowed to create any life story. I could be anyone I wanted to be that night. Got a little confusing when a man became a regular. I had to recall what the hell storyline I'd tickled his particular psychological fancy with. Inner laugh at Hudson: *I ought to make my own index cards for reference, tee-hee.*

At Frank, silver-waring shellfish cutlery, Rex nabbed, "C'est le fin por l'huître, monsieur!"

"Huître," Revan tossed I, "is how they say "oyster" in France!" I noticed schizoid eccentric's meaty filbert stuck between lateral and central incisor, as he pulled card #3, went on, "Germans say auter, Spaniards: ostra. Russians: gigantskaya ustritsa. Japanese: mugaki."

Spat inside softened, Cindy gaily giggled. *Perhaps this knowledge helps him secure his client relations in Foreign Exchange.* Exhausting laborious lectures from Rex at Darlings, late nights after I'd asked, "your art, money trade…" Resulted in Rex's two weeks straight Champagne Lounge chat, delivering PowerPoint presentations on his hand-delivered Dresdner Kleinwort Foreign Exchange (his place of employment) Internet printouts, "Yen, to euro, pound to dollar New Zealand; predominates Australia; US. Franc to krone, krona, karuna to peso, real, shekel to South African rand, Zurich, foreign currency swaps…"

"And of course, my dear," Rex chimed lesson plan across table, Hudson's, "the root of all language: Our Latin word for oyster is *crassotrea gigas.*" Revan grappling at the right word, boomed ever so loudly at Frank, raising his arm like some kind of el capitán heading to Rome, "Add European flat oysters!"

Honestly, I had never been all impressed by food. I liked ice…my mind wandered a memory…*drizzling cubes from a juicy hot mouth and rubbing the nape of my neck. I liked Sam, his lips, wandering the inner rim of my lady parts…around the center…up my ankles, calves, behind my knees…Fantasy wandered…Maybe I can teach Rex to do that—oh, Not.* Wake up: Old green eyes yellow rim leaned his round head toward my face, lifted a glass, "To hopes we may voyage across the pond together one day…"

Ew. Boarding a plane with this unsexy daisy…

"So, are you a dirty girl?" he briskly grabbed my fingers, whispered.

Frank's horse jolly.

I swiveled, "I have a real problem with anyone who bruises liquor; I'm a pure spirit kind of lady." Smirked.

Frank waved, "Two Grey Goose, martinis."

And there was Rex: boingo. His stubby fingers raised his crystal flute of circa 1978 Dom.

Ah, warm...Soothe my stomach, brain, toes, blood..."Oh, I don't think I have ever even had champagne this good; my little heart is aflutter!"—*Naïveté strokes a man's ego.* Really, I had drunk Dom for breakfast many times.

Revan grinned.

I suddenly felt, *I can't feel my own lips.* Blood sugar dropping; fingers frigid. I, —*shit.* Looked down to see if I had any on clothes at all. Spending half your time hanging around in a G-string, while making casual conversation with fully clothed people can confuse a girl. I often felt naked when I wasn't.

Game back on, Cindy, I commanded....

So, somewhere, over oyster guzzling chit chat, I let my red fingernail extend to Rex palm, drawing stencil hearts the lines of his small fat hands. *Draw lightly on skin, look into his eyes...*I watched as goosebumps sprouted on his forearm skin; this meant he was resonating raw inside. *Technique always resulted in melting him jelly.* I'd discovered this in my days sculpting, *Rules of the Seductress,* a mental understanding from all that I had learned through this thing called life. Ultimately, that's what people want: to be entertained by a lady who made him feel alive. That was what I was training myself to do for these guys at work every day. Wake them up from that eternal deadness of adulthood. I loved that.

Rex Revan bounced in his chair. "You did that exact thing, dear!" Revan relished delight, regurgitated the story of our first meeting, *again.* "You put Borsalino on," Rex in his chair, glee, "Turned your back to me, spun in a circle, like Cindy Crawford in a lipstick commercial! Bravo! And you sang dear, first time for me, while drawing fingertip hearts on my neck.

"You're ruling my every move," Rex sang there at Hudson, his own version of the lyric." He sighed like granny. I blinged a Mona Lisa. Raven burst in cough-wrestling some stuck schmew in his throat. Bubbly gave him throat scratch, he'd told Cindy once at Darlings. Actually, it was sugar, but he ate it, anyway.

Sugar cow, I sniggled; *doesn't he know I gotta be inventive stretching long hours with some stranger man stuck inside those gritty walls.* Fuck if I remember what I do—does it have to make his stuck history?

I watched Rex pick card #4, and his fingers went to fiddling the silver latch of brown attaché case; initials embroidered in Victorian monogram, script: RPR.

*What's the P stands for...*I toyed name games my head, *Pinocchio, Pee-Wee, Pamplemousse...*Air traffic control alphabet...*Romeo Papa Romeo. Alpha, bravo, charlie, delta, echo...foxtrot...*I had learned along the way...*hope to learn French one day...*

"In order to make you more confident," Rex clumsily handed over a paper file, "I want you to show you, I am secure in positioning my offers."

Revan Rexibauld walloped on me a fresh copy of his most recent year's W-2 forms. Moist saliva glands in my tongue. My winkers scanned: gross, spending. Crossed my leg, clenched and unclenched my calf muscle. My foot arch rise, fall in the slip of my stiletto heel. Suddenly, I couldn't help but glance a glare Rex's way.

Wanting spit venom the fat Elroy's lame face. *Huh?* Rex's net equaled only a small bit over mere one quarter million duckets per year.

Frank rolled up, parked like standing on tiptoes: "Cracked Eastern Canadian and steak, martinis, Côte du Rhône."

RPR's W-2 my fingers. *What's the angle? Is he just a chump? Why would he reveal bad cards so quickly?* I quite preferred: 'Don't ask, Don't tell' policy. If I hadn't been told, I'd easily played along; believed Rex was in the high millions. My inner lashing voice railed me*: Of course, Rex's paycheck reflects that. Rex had been throwing bits of cash on me, but guy is a softee-symp.* I knew from what he had told me of himself: Rex showed up for work daily; had bosses. I recalled a mongo difference between worker bee and entrepreneur head I had observed in the world: *Workers get fucked on taxes; they look to their bosses for answers. Starters have no cap on income; don't have bosses.*

I held developed a molten respect for the ruthless trader and self-starter business guys I danced for at the club: they had to be savvy sharp to make it their world. I certainly didn't want to date their socialized domestic persona, but when we were in the subterranean, primal environment of the club, I knew we had something in common: We both loved blood and bone—thrill of the hunt; thirst for the kill. With Rex, during those Champagne nights, I knew what I was dealing with a guy who'd been academically pruned and of course, worked hard, but never self-started or went into anything that wasn't totally dependable. He was a safe guy, a softee.

Rex threw me furrowed brows, sad puppy face. I tapped my red fingernail on my black stocking-knee—Dug into my, *Rules of the Seductress*: *Rex reeks desperate and this often equals generous. Take what he offers, awhile. Who knows, I'll assume he has major stock portfolios, banking scads in the Caymans.*

I passed the docs back with a conviction, crooned, "Lovely, your generosity, to share yourself so candidly."

Rex, "Trust is important." He ferociously stabbed a very large, jagged utensil into a slab of bloody meat on his plate. "Kobe beef—my dear," he said.

"Japanese calf. Hung in slings over rafters in the barns from birth, massaged with sake, fed beer daily, so its muscles don't form tough." He bit in and his teeth glinted.

"Well, as a caring lass, objectively reflecting your W-2 scores, I must offer a twenty-five-cent cap Lucy-type word of advice: An endeavor like myself is simply just not a good investment a man like you, who clearly works hard, with a soon to be ex-wife, twin daughters in line for education and remuneration." Rex had told me weeks before, that he was in the midst of a divorce with the wife of twenty-five years. This was his reason for being at the club so often.

Rex read from card #5, gnawing his sanguine scathing slab: "Well, you know all about me now. I'm from a great family, Catholic school, Harvard Law parlayed into Foreign Exchange. I'd like to know more about you, dear."

I double blinked at the sight. Blood dripping down the side of his lip. The endless fucking hours I'd spent corralled in that red-mirror-liquor-stained lounge-sipping Freixenet bubbles listening to this entitled fuck-cod chime on, "For several generations, my family has been members of certain private clubs and alma maters."

My eyes gazed off, watching the tulip singer, "Lilac Wine." dipping into my personally concocted through years of being female, *Silent Seduction Rules[1]*: Feigning blasé, even dreamy and romantic keeps a man on tenterhooks, while gives me time to hide my internal disarming self-questioning, and find a next move.

"Well, you know I sing, write songs. I am a Theatre major at NYU, most currently playing the lead in the play *Key Exchange*! A girl who is in longing for family and marriage is dating a boy who won't give her keys to his apartment because he is commitment-phobic. I feel it all so deeply!" Truth, training at that Meisner conservatory, Bill Esper kept handing me housewives who cringe and iron. Then telling me I sucked at playing them. I don't

---

[1] These *Silent Seduction Rules* I mention, just my own musings. I had devised mentally back at the clubs. I have recently been informed that a Robert Greene wrote a book. I hadn't been aware of it before then, or of course I would say that I had based my own methods on his. Nah. I was just living it.

understand these types female roles, or even care to—I wanted to yell at Esper every single day. Yet, I guess I had done so well at keeping my broken past shut down, Colgate smile America's Sweetheart cover-up for my teacher, I was afraid to blow it—thought they might blacklist me from getting an agent if they knew the real me.

I was Rainbow Girl turned Little Trash Girl. LTG is how I saw myself after Dad left and Mom's Polish drunk. I'd tucked secret Little Trash Girl; chiseled away ruthlessly at becoming the untouchable heartbreaker—black widow type by the softee. My street savvy knew better than to tip Revan or Esper off to the angle.

Rex like Eeyore hee-haw charley-horse voice sometimes he sounded, chirped *Key Exchange,* adoring, "I know you are that kind of vulnerable. Since I have gotten to know you thus far, I have seen you as having the heart of a wonderful mother, caregiver in a home." I nearly fell off my chair. "You never mention family, doll, other than your sick mother from time to time."

Mother isn't sick—just makes *me feel* sick. Not protecting me—then crying that her loved life role is the gift of being a mother. In high school Mom finally found a new husband who gave her home in lovely Connecticut, and a new kid. Nine years later then, Mom had begun suffocating me with phone calls, talking about her loons and more so how she hates her husband. Mom doesn't love me at all, just uses me to fill her own fucking void. Alas, I was so confused about what motherhood really was. Would anyone ever really admire the truth of *me*? I had tried to be real with people before, who *I* felt was on the *inside* In my personally, mentally concocted *Rules of Silent Seduction,* telling Rex, or any other man, my sick mother stories deemed a cash ringer.

So, I blinked lashes at Rex, "She is doing better thank you, just a few more surgeries and they think her issues should be cleared up. It isn't cancerous, thank the Good One." (I probably even crossed myself to make him happy).

"I spend a lot of time with her, visit her lovely home in Westport, as often as I can, and pray every single day that she has at least fifty great years ahead of her, at least." On imagining dealing with Mom for fifty more years of my own life, I lost my *Seductress* manners. Slammed back a huge drink. The red goblet and Goose martini and champagne, whatever was left in a glass near me. My weakness then: old wounds, resentments. Big ones. Yes. I remember how Rex leaned in so close, I could see the length of his horny eyebrow hair. "Well, we, dear Cindy, you and I share a common bond in understanding. You know about my folks."

I grinned, *yes,* masking bitter. Rex's laborious lectures at the club, the same stories twice, thrice, on praise and gratitude: "My parents are proud Irish, from New England; married over fifty years. Residing happily in our original family abode. When my Father's health weakened, I realized how he had been such a rock of support in my life."

All the praise Rex had received from wonderful Pa during Rex's tough times at school. Father had helped him become the same successful man and Rex, "Finally, through all of his health challenges, for the first time in my life I was able to ascertain this reversal of roles. To demonstrate appreciation, repay all he'd given to me! Little Rexy!" (I'm sure I almost vomited then.)

"And for such, I grant my sorries with your poor sick mum—Let us sit together now, dear. Revere together just how wonderfully she has given to you!"

My alley-cat hide spiked. Painful thing to understand——assumptions from people who haven't been through it, that everyone has had the same kind of family love and values family in the same way, is experienced by the "un-healing survivor" as neglect and shaming. Then I would have said: *I abhor douche bag crass cold shits like Rex; completely unaware that not everyone has whatever cushion he's had.* Rainbow Girl turned Trash Girl, dove deeply into drink.

Rex, completely unaware of my response, and only too happy to fill my glass with more booze, went on as though he found himself the wisest most compassionate man on Earth, "And my own mum, my own dear mum's family from France, they are. You see Cindy, my poor mum, while we always summered back in her homeland, and held welcome doors any time, Mother always felt so far from her family, raising us here in the States for Pops..."

I wanted to spit right there in his blah-blah-blah face, grab his shirt collars, scream red-hot faced and thrashing across the white tablecloth: *Until you been homeless, alone, no fallback, a fear of getting swept away and disappearing, and at the same time wishing you would—we will have nothing in common. Do not assume we do.*

Another part of me knew that I was just pissed because I felt in order to survive, I had to lie about myself. Rex's treatment of me was a testament to what a good job I had done so far of covering my Trash with a pretty face, sweet persona. *He is buying this, not the real you. Entertain him,* I reminded me. *Reveal nothing. Let him see himself in you.* Cindy tilted melodramatic, looked at the singing tulip doing "A-Train," hoping to create that dreamy romantic face for Rex to gaze.

Silent Seduction Rules: a good seal the sympathy deal for these male softee, sugar daddy-want-to-be types, I said, "Father and I lost touch a long while back." Eyes down picking at my mini fork.

Oh, if ya don't know: Men like to hear that the Dad failed, so they can be the hero. Especially the older ones, if Dad is not around, they don't feel so perverted for hitting on the daughter. Additionally, they just can't stand the idea of another penis in the picture. So, to tie it up, I added my sister. *Silent Seduction Rules:* Men love to believe that unmarried girls are at home with their sister and mother; my psychological-stab at understanding: This makes the man feel safe: She is soft and helpless in the world. Plus, she isn't out with other dicks.

Nailing this performance, "I share an apartment with my sister who is in television." My brown eyes cast down, long imploring sentences all the while nibbling the sweet tail of my lobster meat.

"While I'm working on a demo to get my songs in front of a great producer and label to promote me as a singer-songwriter! So, my dear Rex," I turned back my face up Rex.

Rex pulled dandiest yarn. Picking card #6, he grabbed my left hand, rubbed my fourth finger: "So why aren't you married? You are a vision. Unfurl; let yourself find who you are without having to work so hard. Personal security can do wonders for a girl! I understand the needs of a woman, I can assure you, Dear Cindy. You possess a sparkle I wish give light."

I would have rather assumed Rex was just drunk talk—this the first Revan had dropped the M-word—then he deliberately pick index #7. "I am not an abandoning man. I seek a flourishing, giving, youthful woman with whom I can spend time," gallop on, Rex did—like a bull in china.

"I am willing to take vows. Oh, Dear Cindy! Call it, sowing oats. Antidote to fears I may burn days till death behind a desk. Or alone in a hotel room. While my bank account overflows and my stomach does the same!"

I wanted to rip his warped face, shove bloody scalp down his gangly throat. Aghast, so, I actually forgot that moment, that I already was married. Sam and I had eloped to Vegas somewhere in there. Not a boring story, but I sliced it out in the edit.

Rex clenched my fingers in his sweaty palm. I inserted a "one eyebrow raise." (Another *"Gal can't present herself to the world without a little glamour,"* honed at eleven years: Instructions on how to learn: Hold one eyebrow flat; raise other until you can do it without holding. Side effects: Paves little brow wrinkles over raise-brow.) But, really, I was offended by this man's baiting marriage as a means to get me ga-ga. That marriage, rub the fourth finger jargon chat was a well-known male trick. I'm sure it's in their own: *Seduction Guide, E*very woman is just waiting around for a man to marry them and make their life right, and she will melt the minute they bring it up. Not. I wasn't interested in being bought, and shacked up with someone I didn't love. I was entertaining the man. *This Characterless buffoon with no inkling what it feels like to search for some kinda love, to have no one He ought be grateful* *for my presence at all,* I went on my usual then resentful rant, *Doesn't know what it is, people use the word love, throw it at you, yank it back, then yell your face for your being upset—and walk out on you.* Rex was a vapid candy in my estimations.

Alas, on a crystal tray; one golden cigar gal bounced over displaying an array of Maduros, Robustos. Rex pointed his stubby index. She lifted a Corona, sliced his tip. Lit his puff. I took my hand back. Rex stubbed his fingers in his dirty Goose glass, whopped back two olives, "Cindy, one must think highly of oneself in a world such big. It's dangerous not to."

They're spice, not food, I silent. I hate it when people eat the olives. Order a goddamned dessert if you're starved.

"Cindy, please," ragged his smoky tobie, "Accept my condolences for being a mere mortal. As you know, my life none so interesting. None so able to match your character strength and luster of spirit."

Could have at least offered me a smoke, damn. Really, who wants to talk marriage when we could kick back, smoke a chill.

Instead, said, "I may as well have claimed I was Mahatma Gandhi or recited red leather yellow leather…"

Silent Seduction Rulebook: Boys *cow-tow* if you shame them. *Turn up your nose and act like he isn't good enough.*—My psycho-stab: Something in each person always feel ashamed, and dirty. For boys, it is something to do with their primitive sexual desires crossed by their desire to please their pure mother. They are always feeling dirty. It's why they have that Madonna-whore complex. One side feeds their needs to be pure, the other gives them the opportunity to feel totally accepted and primal. Women have it too, the urge to be both. Hence my always upset over being pure and being totally free and wanton. Is it instinct or taught? My always question.

I downed a last puddle of the third round Goose.

Rex threw tie over shoulder, unbuttoned collar, wallet out, tipped gal. Crossed both arms, fat rolls. Silver pepper tufts beneath green-stripe button. Cigar in, he faced me, "Well, Cindy, dear," abruptly.

"You certainly are adventurous. Carefree, alive. Able to scale large buildings." His pointer and thumb grasped and slowly turned the emerald Harvard ring donning his fat left pinky.

A tell, I clocked; *sign of trickery my book.* Another *Rule:* Christopher Walken's line to Dennis Hopper (*True Romance,* movie) just before he whacks him dead over the stolen suitcase of cocaine: "A guy's got seventeen pantomimes. A woman's got twenty, but a guy's got seventeen…but, if you know them, like you know your own face, they beat lie detectors all to hell." (IMDb)

"Dear, Cindy, mea culpa," Rex moved on.

"I offer this gift as a first of many. It's your Chanel. I took the liberty."

He picked the glossy black Day-Glo lettered bag from floor. "I chose the Borsalino myself. I thought you could wear them while we are together, dear Cindy."

I preened glitter. "Well, I can't wait to wear it on our next rendezvous!"

"Now." RPR shot.

"Don't you like my clothes?" I looked down, my simple ballerina slip.

"Why, of course, you can make any old thing look designer." Rex waggled his buff-gloss square manicure. "I've simply had this mad fantasy. You suited in Chanel and Borsalino. I must have you in it now. Or out of it…" His pink cigar-stained lips snorted, bemused by little Rexy jeu de mots. Drained Côte du Rhône.

In my best Bond girl, Brit: "Would this entail sex?"

Rex checked index #8.

Dump drink bald head. Glazed my fingertips his jowl: "Perhaps, you have an envelope, our agreed upon for the evening, before we commence."

Winked. "A lady who knows what she wants. Gratuities will be waiting, Miss Cindy."

"I want it now." My voice shook. Like it did in preschool when my little brother Aidan and I had visited Macy's Santa with Mom.

Giant gray 'n' red rolly man stood, greet them, "Hello there, why don't you sit on my lap?" some kind of Santa lingo. Aidan sobbed for fear of the man.

I felt protective, stood up to Santa, said, "Sit back down in your chair." I just remember how my voice shook like that at Rex.

Rex-cow's bulbous greeny hazels, yellow rims. His, caressing my vacant finger space. Pudgy fingers slid inside his suit breast. One stacked envelope shifting.

I was satisfied. Chanel shopping in hand, made my way off to Lady's. Over my shoulder, I caught Rex's small devilish grin, sniveling tooth—*not a sliver of the elegance in vampiric beauty.*

'Za

Ten o'clock that same evening. Sam had dropped in cold on Jess's Thirteenth Street second-floor prewar. Sam saw lights on. Called on mobile from stoop.

"Hey, I got urgent new leads on the guy looted you," Sam told Jess—referring to that suburban kid that had ripped off Jess, at the top of this hokey pokey.

Jess him-haw squirreled on the other end, "Can't come in now, just got up."

Sam slid into the foyer when the neighbor was exiting, *knock knocked* Jess's, 2B.

Jess peeped the hole. Sam mentioned Bleu through the door. Now, follow me here. Sam knew Jess knew Bleu—Jess didn't know Sam and Bleu went way back. Bleu knew scarce 'bout Jess and Sam partnering. Definitely didn't know that Jess had just fucked Sam over on an in-load. Basic OG biz: You don't say, "Hey I know him," to no one, for the most part—it's hush business. You don't want people knowing your strategies nor having anything they *may* use against you. Crux: Sam had pulled Bleu out of trenches, bad scene is all I will say, so Bleu was loyal to Sam for life. OMS's are loyal like that. Bleu did know Sam was looking to score bulk, because Sam had called him around for connect. Bleu had tipped Sam that he'd be waiting on a pickup that evening, sayin' he'd found some good product cheap, and may be able to hook Sam up—Bleu slipped in that he'd scored few sweet hybrid Cali grass bulk pounds cheap off Jess in last few weeks. Sam knew Bleu was headed over Jess's that night. Sam went knocking Jess' door uninvited, figuring he would walk right in on the deal.

So, silk butterscotch Jess, grazing his usual shirtless dangly arms, low-hang slim-hipped skater shorts, red, and dead-like bloodshot aqua eyes, opened the door. Gave Sam some sweaty hug and story about waiting for 'za (pizza). "I just woke up, man."

"I have something I need to talk to you about. I want to help you get that kid that ripped you off got a plan" Sam. Followed Jess through Mary J haze down the long corridor three bedroom flat. Fish tanks, plants, fountains. Wall-size poster-prints, Alex Grey. East Village dwelling artist. Grey had a background in Medicine at Harvard, and got into meridian lines; subtle energy fields. He and his wife took lots of LSD and painted psychedelic rainbow man inside an orgasming woman, a baby morphing out her rufulus, flame womb. Colorized Pranic Ayurvedic; Chapel of Sacred Mirrors.

Jess plopped Indian style on orange meditation pillow in front of his five-foot Buddha sculpture. One aluminum foil open, covered in snow. Seventy-eight inch flat-screen TV, flashing porn. Jess picked up his tabla drums.

Now, follow me fast.

In the room:

Bleu: Afro American, purple hue his chocolate skin, stately king-like forehead, puffed magenta rimmed lips, gold links.

Skinny: young Latino, sports basketball gear.

Sally: the red-nosed pit bull, howl now again.

All hypnotized on the 90s porn: One woman with incredibly flopping boobs pulling red thong over cooch moves slow on another chick rubbing oohing orgasm to house music.

Sam crouched in, clocking scene, "Hey, Bleu, man. What you up to?"

"Yeah, man," Jess.

Bleu: "Haze."

Skinny: "Waiting on some 'za."

Jess, snake sculpture purple glass bong; stuffed fresh white pony. Amber flame. Yoga inhale: One long hot inhale...exhale.

Yoga breath is real handy for coke smokers, if you don't know like that.

"You listening?" Sam barked with a half-smirk, "We'll ride a little both right now, son. Most importantly, just know I got your back. You lose, I lose and I don't stand for that shit."

Jess passed glass to Sam.

Sam hit, no inhale: Blend in. Passed Bleu. Packed up.

Bleu smoking crack. Sam gave down mouth. 'No matter how you love him, can't trust a cat on the chooch. People do weird shit when drugs and money are in frame,' I can hear Sam say right now.

Skinny, scratched dripping pit, "Man I'm hungry. Where's that 'za, bro?"

That was all a dab-knackered lie: Apparently (Bleu told Sam later) while Sam was knocking, Jess sketched, push scales back behind the bookshelves, picked up the pot seeds, stems off his Persian rug, and squawked: "I gotta deal with this. Back me up, bros, we're waiting on some 'za, 'til I get him out."

Sam (told me all this later) said: "Got any toasty comin' with that? I got guys waitin' all over town. Ins?"

Jess, index, middle finger on leather rounds the flat drum, tap-tap-double, "om Mani Padme Hum…" humming ecstatic.

"The spirit of Buddha is so high today!"

Red thong flesh TV swivel, oohhh, lips pursed, sigh, "Baby." Her hands under panties moaning like beast.

Skinny, rappin', "California bud. Man, I miss the hot Bubble Gum! Chewy mouth, Plum."

Jesse, yowling like migraine but joy, "Some chic I called last night, man, she was filled with the spirit. I gotta get you her number man, bro Sam. I will totally hook you up. She is fresh and mean. Got up on my lap, grinding, purred, smelled like kitten! Meow!"

Sam lost it. "Shut up, pansy! I'll spread your ass like mustard. Listen to me very clearly. I'm doing you a fucking favor here. Don't let me down."

Jess, "Tibetan Prayer, blessings of Chenrezig. The embodiment of compassion."

Sam, "Jess got that the back of a Cracker Jack box?"

Bleu, "Somethin'."

Sam, grabbing Jess's neck, "Calm the fuck down. Jess, what the hell you playin'?"

Sally starts howling.

"Now let's get this straight," Sam skipping record, spit, "I love you like a son, bro, but you ain't makin' it pretty. You waitin' till I get something on you, bro?"

Bleu, "Why are you playing him, bro?"

Jess, whimpered floor, popped bloodshot, "With Bleu, Skin, my witness, I love you for all you done me, bro. I will come up with fifteen pounds for you by tomorrow."

Jess threw a shirtless sweaty hug, Sam.

Sam's eyes rested the girl spread with a dildo, playing her pussy like finger paints, panting. "Rockin'." He trying chill. "Gotta go pick up my girl."

"By next, week, I promise you, bro," Jess called out in the dark.

Serpent

I was 2 AM, gingerly winding back up that old rickety Lower East Side sublet staircase—I hadn't expected Sam to notice. Over Hudson's I had forgotten to check my phone; Noticed in the cab: Cell blinking, missed calls; texts marked urgent: 11:00 p.m. *'Where are you?'* 12:00 a.m. *'Baby call me!'* 1:00 a.m. *'Baby come home!'* Sam knew I didn't carry my phone at work. I often said I'd be off early, and ended up staying. Sam *never* texted urgent.

Desserts, *framboise* heavy in my stomach. Snippets Rex dinner jive my mind. I'd thrown the nice, new Chanel boxes in garbage cans; rolled the suit and shoes up and tucked them inside my jacket. If Sam found it I planned to say, "A gal at work was selling old designers!" Actually, in the ladies' dressing room, was one haggard obese woman selling her stripper-wear gowns: two velvet triangles for boobs sewn to a mini or full-slit spandex or velvet thing— I think I was scared I might get used to Chanel and learn to deal with Rex, against my own will.

I'd stopped by Ye Old Tavern down the block on the corner from our building for few Jameson. Sirens screaming. Truth is, my mind kept meandering back to final scenes at Hudson. Sitting with Rex, dressed up for him in Chanel and Borsalino. Masking my gut whapped walloped feeling, I used to get sometimes, since kidhood. *Like inside of my body, the delicate tissue had been rip-yanked, wassooied irreparable, and I was oozing puss internally.* I always imagined it looked like the snot-jizz that comes out of a cockroach when you mash it hard. This wasn't about booze. Booze made it feel better.

Rex's little table charade, my initial humiliation turned his fuddy-uncle woo-woo marry me to slimy-eyed undress in public requesting I suit up Chanel for him on premises—had curved prickle hairpin feasty, me feel meaty carcass. Shot spin me in one drop dime, and I was back in the kitchen with Mom's Polish, *Clammy hands my forearms.* It was during the super-man quick change into Chanel upon Rex's request. I'd found myself leaning against the cold Hudson bathroom porcelain. Frigid I felt under the blowing fan in the ladies' room stall. The old whisper hush-bubbled, triplets on snare half time beneath my skin. My eyes went blurry, all dimensions went flat in front me, like the diorama of life fallen to pieces. This kind of blurred out dissociated, frigid happened a lot, or whenever something threw me back to the memories, and I was not prepared to defend against their entrance. I was vibrating raw. Skinless, alone in the stall. Touched on sideways slam, that particular way Rex's glower had penetrated me, like a perverted old man who wanted to fuck me. I was used to that—of course. But every once in a while, in a particular moment combined attitude, it shot me, my mind, body, into orbital, elsewhere.

"Stupid girl." His voice—after all those years, still echoed my, him, Coarse, sopping sloppy hands, cold. How he'd pulled me, pushed me, bed. Straddled my baby face with his smelly crotch, my erect-from-fear, eleven-year nipples. Slimy fingers in my delicate nectar lips, his tongue my mouth. And the hard, shivering cock, enervated by the thrills of naught, or was it purity, was it damaging another that was the hoax. I have never found answer lurking snakeskin through sensations that never leave.

Serpentine, my mind and blood were churning. Rex bullshit—*got right here, back to that, what.*

Only thing that soothed this shaking, I was back against the stall, a fantasy. I wasn't aware of, did not, I, conjure it. My mind had a way of rescuing me back to someplace, the same place, it is always the same place in time that I land. Nowhere I had ever been before, or remembered. Never know if it makes me feel better, worse. Just went…

There in the stall melted and I was candles flicker, a lilting Bach concerto. Persian carpet, my feet, slip python peep-toe. Dainty fingers, porcelain. Gold, powder blue on chiffon-draped flesh. Ears picking sounds of passing giggles; convoluted temporary promises—My satin, cleavage breasts highly paid to receive. In this fantasy, I serve a parade of nameless faceless men, waiting to see me. I know they'll be leaving, and I'd remain untouched, within. Unmoved. This was happiness. Until I came out if it:

Gasp—and I was on my back: a man handling my skin; his clumsy fingers on my waist, shoving him against my dry, vaginal lips. Rough. He pumping his hips, his skinny ass; *inside my flesh.* I see his wedding ring on his fourth, covered in dripping from whatever moisture he'd gotten from my own pussy. Nameless, faceless man, rank breath sputtered my ear, sweaty armpits mashed my nose:

"Come on, baby, tell me I'm the best." His phone vibrating, probably his wife calling. Man quick, always came hard in the rubber begged cum on my face—this is what pulled me out.

In that frigid, porcelain stall I stood, alone. I ripped open Rex's envelope: money. Why the fuck did this make me feel better from the memory of Mom's drunk fuck fingers, me? It did. I didn't decide to think these, they happened upon me in moments of total anxious meltdown. The boudoir fantasy seemed better, safer until it wasn't.

Cold cash. Reality check. I counted. *Thirty crispy hunnies.* I fished an airplane from my purse: Dewars. *Twisted; Drained.* Yes, I carried airplane bottles of scotch and red wine in my purse, discreetly.

I found my way to powdered cheeks, sink. Two ladies piling brash orange, lips. Sweet Rosa, the bathroom attendant turning on faucets. "Chanel suit pants," she had handed the threads to me over the bathroom stall.

"Fit nice," Rosa touched me; fastening the teeny zippers, up the sides of my waist.

Little boxy in hips for a girl my age; Nice silk leg lining, I thought. My mind was slipped into this dream, high class lady Chanel. Rosa attending: Chanel jacket. I guess there were shoes. Three-inch heel? Yikes. Navy leather? Librarian—*Not my fave footwear for feelin' foxy...*I laughed. *You'd probably enjoy dealing books,* I laughed back at me. The usual two-way talk in my head. Oh.

I heard the ladies talking, "Soprano, Met production of *Lucia Di Lammermoor!*"

"I love Lucia...Several times, globally," I burped out to them. I had never actually been to the opera. Had stacks of vinyl at home, that I had dragged in from the streets, New York finds. I'd listened to Lucia over and over again. Rainy days, I would lay on the wood floor and read librettos. Float in the rare lilt. Lucia waiting by the fountain or her love. I always cried after Lucia knifed her bridegroom...the ladies were gone. Rosa handing me a quilted white patent, black typewriter key C-H-A-N-E-L, chain strap handbag. Borsalino hat on head in glass reflection. *Shady fatale, nice look for the hidden ones.* Tucked my cold green cash in its purse folds. Handed Rosa a hundred. So, tired. I was. *So tired.* I wanted to curl in a ball, sleep on the floor there with Rosa.

Spiraled my feet in those three-inch *yikes, no heels ought be so small,* back to Revan at the table, Hudson had quieted to a din by then...

Rex's after-dining brain wheels. Left alone too long. Perked little big man to tossing several even fatter carrots from his mouth. Upon my slipping back into chair, donning his fantasy garb, the navy Chanel suit and Borsalino, Rex spent the rest of that shady hazy evening painting promises of the singing performance he planned secure me at one of the most popular jazz speakeasies in town, Lucky Strike!

I spent the rest of the evening spouting lies about my incredible, magical childhood, over Sauternes. Raving to Rex, "My family trips to the Royal Opera in London, as a youngster."

—Lies felt so good in the sandbox. Though, reminding me for the millionth: *Why are some people are born with the yearning to play major league ball but just didn't get born the arm or the sprint?* Meaning, you may want to sing but you suck at it.

During the final Rex spiral down, fin de soirée, I had been transported back to my trusty *Silent Seduction Rules:* Men like to negotiate, especially with a chick they want to fuck.

How I had slipped my hand around the nape of Raven's medulla oblongata, and hissed, "I want you to know how much I appreciate you tonight, Rex. I mean that." And I socked on, "But," I probably even giggled to myself; *I really need a white glove on my hand to wipe the perfect little tear that has made its way to the outer rim of my lashes.*

"I will give you opportunity, to make up for this evening's foibles. Asking me to change for you in the Ladies Lounge, is just beneath your manners and my own sense of pride. However, I did it for you, because you are special. However, so that I can feel good, and to secure my trust in you as an honest God-fearing man." I whispered to Rex the exact amount I wanted from the cash machine, as thank you for my gratuities. Surprised myself, he'd acquiesced.

Max the vampiric damoiseau, wrapped me in my sparkly sweater coat for night.

Rex paused by the ATM near the entrance bar…"Ms. Bond? Hm. Which one are you? Pussy Galore, Jinx, or Amy Good Enough. I guess time will tell." Raven slipped dockets into my new Chanel purse.

I said to Rex, something to the tune of, "Some people make decisions for the heart in their mind. I am a person who is led by her heart. Those people often end up happier." Rex recounted that moment, later.

Universe had busted a cracking rainstorm. Rex stayed behind, for dry. Max wiped, gently wet a finger his mouth, black blurring beneath my eye, and said, "You're running, baby, better look at your reflection." Kissed my cheek. Shut the cab door. I removed the Borsalino. Gusts blew my hair wild, *like a princess on horseback.*

I had successfully lassoed five grand total for dinner…that felt *good.*

Fuck Me

Stiletto finally landed top floor five, that old Lower East Side sublet. Door C. Stair 45, I had counted many times.

Keytop lock; turned, pushed, chain: stopped. *Shit.*

"Now let's get this straight," I heard Sam through the bolted crack, door.

"I love you like a son, bro, but you ain't makin' it pretty. You waitin' till I get something on *you*, bro?"

Thank you, Jess, my dunce-cap brother. An ear load on him will shed focus, me.

Sam...blue solitude beside rotgut Cuervo Silver fifth, silhouette in muted TV glare slumped over coffee table. Jay-Z rappin' low, maybe "Run This Town." Blueprint 3. That album, just come out.

Sam doesn't usually drink. New behavior always makes me suspicious.

"I'll murder you mother fucker, spread your fuckin' body on your mother's doorstep," Sam threw his phone—a few healthy bounces on the hardwood; bike shop guy down the block, employed him making rubber casings out old knobby tires.

Guy ought to go out for more acting roles—Now, who the hell knows what exactly happened. I was in a blackout, for most part. What I do remember, sits crocheted in the middle of my dang blasted hippocampus, which is the sea horse looking middle area of your brain. I've read up on it—no one remembers everything that happens, usually the only things you do recollect for long-term are of significance. A normal bus trip, you will probably forget; someone tripped you up on that bus, you are likely to fix in your mind for some time.

It's like this: Sam turned, his raccoon eyes on me. Unlatched door—walked back to couch. I beelined bedroom, pretending I had to pee. Flung Chanel garment bag high in closet. Stripped down. Purse-stacked cash: I wanted to share it with Sam. 1) I had a thing for this 1960s sci-fi psychedelia Italo French coproduction, *Danger Diabolik*. Dino De Laurentiis and Mario Bava. *Suavo* thief comes home from a cash score to his blonde bombshell sidekick. He takes the loot, covers their round shaped, slow-spinning room-size bed with stacks; they get naked, romp hard. 2) Sam and I had invented this game.

No—go to bed. But I hit "Start": game. We'd made this pact: No matter what was going on, if one of us started game, the other must drop whatever, play. Game was on rare reserved we said; otherwise, it wouldn't work, like the boy who cried wolf.

Game was based on: "Fix me a drink," scene—that Albee script, *Virginia Woolf*, George, and Martha. Me and Sam had acted it in together, six months back at Stella Adler's studio, in Chelsea. Was after we went to Vegas and got married, starting to achieve our dreams. I don't mention the marriage thing, 'cause it was just a thing we did for love. Didn't make a thing of it, or tell anyone.

So, that night, well, let me tell you.

Rule 1: Person starts by asking for help searching for an item; secretly they want something else—from the other. I wanted: a lie down with Sam, and feel him inside me.

I stretched a sexy hang off the flimflam tapestry, my cobalt and periwinkle lace thong, demicup set. Posed like 1950s pinup doll. New white chain Chanel purse over shoulder; cooing:

"Honey? Do you know where the electric bill is?" Secretly I wanted a drink—then a Sam fuck in green cash...

Rule 2: Partner has to help search—ask questions, look; while figuring out what the partner really wants.

Sam. Shirtless, legs spread sitting; bandana round his head sprinkling bud into an E-Z Wider. Looked at me funny, "Why would I know?" half-smiled to my gaming.

Me: "I put each bill in a certain spot as it relates to its appliance, so that I don't forget to pay each month, but the ConEd isn't with the bedside lamp!"

That was true.

Rule 3: When partner susses it, they have to give it to the person within twenty-four hours—within reason.

"I think it's over here on the AC," he.

"Nope, no, nana, not on the metal human froster!" *Hint.*

"Check the VCR," Said he. This old sublet still had a VHS machine.

"Nope, no!" I flounced over, sticking ass in air, "It's just not there!" Checking laptop, under couch, flower vase.

"My God you can swill it down," he said flatly—That line was "Game" signal, means partner 2 had figured exactly what Starter wanted, and was ready to call it. Line is also a direct steal from the Albee scene. Sam lit his joint, kicked back said.

"Maybe it's by the juicer."

I opened the freezer. Blue-lit frost cascaded. Grabbed chilled tumbler, I left in there 24/7. But no bottle. *Fucker's playing me*—"No! Maybe it's over here in the icebox!"

Sam slammed the table. Erupted, *"¿Por qué estás actuando como una perra loca mentir cuando estoy tratando de estar aquí, hacer lo correcto por usted?"* (Translated: Why are you acting like a crazy lying bitch when I'm trying to be here, do the right thing by you?)

I threw myself on the floor in front of the TV.

"Baby, you know I can't understand you," lolled up at him.

"I'm so lonely over here playing all by myself in this sandbox. Come!" Glass toward Cuervo.

Sam pulled a hit off that joint; "Calm down, talk to me," he said.

"I really am getting tired," drawled I, shaking glass.

"I just wanna know why I couldn't find you at work tonight. I stopped by, spoke to Bobby the door guy, wanted to spend quality time with you. Maybe go to dinner. He said you never came in. What you did instead?"

Sam reached right over me. Shut off the tube. . .

"Look how much money I brought home!" Threw my money in the air; splayed like feathers after a pillow fight. Then struck some erotic-porn-girl pose—knees bent open, hands caressing inner thing, cooing.

"If I had my real druthers, it's not a drink. Let's get down to sexing in it right here."

"I don't care how much fucking money you make, babe, a lot of people in the world making a lot more money than you and they're not taking off their clothes for it."

My right hand flung up, a tinging sound his face. Happened so fast—His heavy double silver ring sharp slapped me back, broke flesh under my cheekbone; blood drops rushed my mouth. I smacked him back, kicked him in the chin.

"If you want to keep acting like a tough guy, I'll treat you such,"

Sam had warned me in the past—Last time, we'd scrapped he'd said: "What separates the men from the boys is to learn harness, focus your anger; not squash, run; you can be powerful yet solemn"—next time I wouldn't be treated with kid gloves. This was next time.

His eyes dead; left forearm flat against my collar, locked my shoulder, chest, neck, slid his knee between my thighs, pressed my crotch bone-hard: "Why the hell are you lying to me?"

"Why don't you get your slimy hands off, go and look in my bag?" I hissed. Weaseled up, through his legs, slid under the coffee table—he grabbed my waist; threw me on my back on the couch, my head cocking the side of the table slightly

Burnt sienna of his left eye, rage-blazed: "Where are your clothes?"

My cold defeated stare back: "Life's been rough, Sam."

His knee tingly in my sex; Trapped, I felt. My teeth filled with blood. I wanted to crumble into his arms, collapse. I pushed forward my chest, his fingertips pressed harder my wrists, black-blue; I flung side to side, couldn't get leverage, *fucking couch,* there was nothing hard beneath me to push off. I moved my pelvis forward, tried to lace my thighs and squeeze out; He wrestled-held me. I started arching, kicking, contorted; Whirly spiral colors in my eyeballs; Fight or fuck?—rush of brain chemicals. ephedrine, serotonin, oxytocin, adrenaline; *give it to me, I can take it;* Found his wrist, sunk my teeth, bit into his skin—heard break snap tear tasted blood—His teeth on my shoulder. My skin, *Ow. Pain*; or was it ecstatic power, exhilaration, rejection, depraved, awed, determined, lust-filled, fascinated, superior.

And blank: We two both laid out. Like a beast in the jungle waiting for something to happen, but nothing.

I came to: "I hate you. I hate you. I hate you!" Confused by the exhilaration of it.

Sam stood, looked down, spit in my face.

"You crazy, trash bitch. Why don't you take off all that makeup and see who you really are?"

Whirling around blood in my mouth all I could think, *I must be sick, caught in a cycle, I can get out of this, I don't have to be here, don't have to come back.*

I grabbed sweatshirts, sleeping bag, boots, song lyrics, journal; pink velvet pillow I'd used when playing May in Sam Shepard's *Fool for Love.* Favorite role I'd ever acted. Dancer gear: shoes, dress; one overly maxed-out credit card. Bankcard.

I knew I was good at one thing: ditching and moving. Since a kid I had always kept a suitcase stashed or duffel under the bed ready to jet if need be. Little brother Aidan and I used to make plans to run away. I always knew I'd end up alone, running. After Drew in Jersey: Oregon, Mexico, San Fran, every dark bar—

I'd tried to leave Sam before. He just always said, "I don't want to leave. I love you. Leave if you want to."

I stopped, eyed five grand hunnies on the living room floor. Sam on couch examining his wounds. I wanted out: *I can make money in any damned city.*

Sam, "You're gonna end up a whore at this rate."

Deep down I felt he was right.

"I'll be fine." I always was.

Sanitization trucks clanked, lousy racket. The rain had left the streets slink and blue. All I could do was sink to my knees, and I screamed. A wild banshee in the night.

Streets

I once drew a picture of a girl, I was ten. Standing on top of a mountain. I had screwed up making her nose and eyes. I scribbled brown crayon all over her face, and made it look like the back of her head. Girl, like she was walking away. I called it, "Good-Bye Girl."

I remember, Mom sat me down, face cold, eyes beady, they often were when she felt put off, she asked me, "Should I be concerned?"

I shook my head. I didn't know if she should be concerned. I didn't know if I wanted her to know me at all.

I look like that girl I drew before I blacked her face, made her look leaving. Cool winter, early dawn, sauntering down Avenue D. Fat lip, bruised swollen cheek, half drunk and full of oyster.

Frazzled. Stood on the bank of the East River; body quake, shoulder pound where Sam had broken skin, spine throbbed; inside my hot blood, a zigzag pulse, shuddering…*Sometimes I hurt so bad in the core chamber of my heart; I might bust wide open…scrambling for a thing, person; never comes…*

My mind rambled a high-speed index. Cortex raced: magnified data like electronic numerical integrating analyzing device for solving equations: Searching random access memory trip; Sepia images: family, friends; voices, like chains on old railcars rolled. *It's not a person I want,* or anyone. Quasi-coma Rolodex flip list search: *Shelter—nah.* Cockroaches and diseases. Since sixteen, I had been in homeless swelts, slept sand dunes in San Fran, sidewalks in Tenderloin, crashed under highway overhangs, ridden hours on end with truckers.

Wanda. We hadn't talked, she said she was mad I had married first, guess I told her at some diner visit. Wanda was dating Jess's friend, met through Sam one night out. She, a silent sniper, in my book. *Bertie's* (old friend family on Columbia campus) She had a red room with a typewriter and endless red wine. She had one of her sons there now; I wouldn't show up bruised, blue. *Dad—dad care if I were dead? Why does my heart keep beating?* Dad was still friendly with Wanda, Aidan—heard he'd built a four-floor Mc Mansion somewhere, Westchester. I wasn't invited. Hadn't spoken to me in a few years then. He'd gotten married, but I wasn't invited. I didn't have many friends I put any time into. Spent all my time with Sam, or making songs. No one I would admit this kind of fight to. *Maybe Aunt Jemima's unconditional love, endless pancakes—well I hate pancakes and she's not real, anyway.* Mom and her Connecticut domicile. I was aware that Mom having a home I could go, luxury. *I sound like all the entitled people who moan about all the therapy they've been to,* I thought—*attention afforded by wealth: Some people would die for that much care for their feelings.*

Mom never feels safe. I couldn't get through a few hours Mom without running to the liquor store a mile down the road. Too many unsaid things beneath Mom cornering me, dumping her marriage problems, picking at me for drinking. Then, paper fucking walls, I'd hear passive whisper, phone gab, Mom to some family member or friend, about me: "That girl just can't get it together. Don't know what her problem is!" Then she'd cry balls when I left. Something about Mothers who need their children to be sick, to feel better about themselves.

Rex, only a few hours earlier donning Cindy Chanel, making offers any nice gal wouldn't refuse. I would rather be Cindy right now.

They'd all call me trash.

I unzipped my old goose down. Untied emergency flight sack; twelve-gallon drum garbage bag tucked, bottom; laid plastic on a bench. Stuck my pack inside sleeping bag to keep dry. I knew the surviving outdoors well. Staring at early light crossing, *like a lightsaber.* Soothing: *No one is kicking you out. No one is trying to fuck you.*

I scribbled wet marks into my journal: *Wish the whole world just stop a minute; drop facade, weep.'*

Wondered, *Darlings. Was I disloyal, dating Rex?* Darlings felt more like home than any else I could think of. I'd walked out of that hole a bunch times. Try to get straight, waitress job—few months later:

Waltz in, see my favorite manager, an older round man with a salt pepper beard, jovial twinkle, he'd sing: "Cindy!" like it was Christmas morning. "You know, customers you started relations with, came looking for you, I didn't know what to tell them."

I'd smile, "They'll be back. If I were here all the time, they wouldn't want me."

Manager say, "Why don't you stick to it, put some serious money away for later? These girls have goals." A blonde Brazilian, her late '30s, with a child, "She's about to buy her own home!"

Frosty birds eye morn sky. My bottom line always spooked me out: *If I fold hope on Sam and our plan, then all I got is, me: I'm not safe in my own hands.* Illuminated water ripples, like sugarplum pixies. Sam's blazing-ray eyes like honey-dripping sun onyx sex on me; pain in heart, froze zing-zang bruises, probably bloomed rose petal. *Sam. No matter what: He'll never leave…*

Few joggers passed, motorbike started nearby in the frozen morning air. *I like the street lamps this time of day; turn indigo blue.* Passed out on that bench, awhile.

A song I scrawled in red ink, on a page, when I woke morning, that December rain.

> *'The streets are cold and I don't even know your name*
> *Oh, won't you please just take me hand, I'm so ashamed*
> *I'm all alone, mister, I hope you understand*
> *It won't take long but I could use a little change*
> *These are my little girl's eyes for you'*

***

People judge girls who go back to guys who hit them. I used to—before I did.

Sam had left the door open. I silently ripped off my post drunk, pee-stained clothing: winning marks of a sleeping drunk, if ya don't know. . .

"I had nowhere else to go."

Sam wrapped my shaking ribs, gently. Climbed into empty tub. He turned the shower. "Rinse me," we had done this before. Sam put his palm on my bruised kiwi shoulder neck; my hand wrapped his gashed wrist.

It was one of the most intimately fragile experiences with another person, I had ever had.

Daffy

When I woke later—Sun-glare screaming. Dog's tail, whale weight, banging on floor above. Tongue felt teeth fur. Crusty, swollen lip; caked mascara. Hair seemed dried like a sea hag.

Sam was hopping on the bed hailing a fresh vase stuffed perky roses.

"Wake up, my princess! I've gone meditating in the sun on the pier!"

Mother was leaving her: "Perfect evening…You know how it looks when light is angled just right over the horizon, inches of purple, blue, pink, perfectly placed. Truly awesome and I mean awesome in the truest sense of the word. I can't begin to tell you how happy I am honey!"

Sam piped, "We just need a fresh start, baby, a lucky break!"

Sam shoved a shiny wrapped orange square box, and like the Town Bard, read:

'My sweet angel, light of my life. Without you, I would be nothing.
But I am not as stupid as I seem—because I love, love, love and cherish you and want to see you grow like the flower that you are.
Love forever, Sam.'

Sam clambered off tossed empty Cuervo I had polished off, without a mention, "You don't eat enough, baby. It's why you get so drunk."

Thank you. So not in the mood to fight for the right to be a drunk this morning.

"French toast smothered in Nutella, whipping crème. Chocolate-dipped strawberries."

"Baby, I just feel like talking," I wasn't sure what about—

"Why? The fight? You're an actress, have to get it out somehow, it's what makes you great."

Scampered. "Open this while I get food. Please."

Mom, "Oh and the lavender-grayish texture-toned branches that you have to squint to see when the sky becomes the same tint…"

Sam yelled, "Why don't you just forgive her?"

I: "What? Why?"

Sam, "We might be happier." Shrugged.

I: "Why?"

He was right. Sam had been through more recovery influence than I at the time. He wasn't alcoholic but had been to detox a few times for things, and sat in on some NA meetings. I didn't know that holding on to all these memories was killing me. I couldn't see beyond my own day to day survival. People who don't get trauma might say, just change your perspective, but when you're getting hit by memories, resentments, suspicion, distrust, and anxiety from every curve, you do your best to survive it. If you're drinking to soothe, it's impossible to get off the hamster wheel, until you truly sober up. Start to feel it all. Feelings do transform over time, when you don't push them away. Only way out is through. You gotta die to awaken, warrior.

People ask—is forgiveness ever totally possible when you've been sexually abused. Most people say you have to forgive to heal. It's different for everyone. Worst is when people think they got all the answers for you. I can just share my own experience. Me, I still get pulled undertow, like a black hole, sucking air, disoriented at times. I am more aware now of the feelings, what they are signifying and what triggers them. This helps me from reacting, and gives me the opportunity to choose my response to my feelings, and choose the circumstances I put myself in. I try to have compassion for myself. For me, I know the guy who did it was an alcoholic, the others guys who did stuff were messed up too, but it doesn't make me forgive. I just try to learn and identify in myself the parts that need healing. Really, I try mostly to trust God, or the Universe I call it. I don't know why these things happened to me in my life. My Mom would say it was because I was drinking, or acting too flirty, which basically means I deserved it. I don't think so. I do think that, and maybe this is crazy talk but it helps me, I think that the Universe has a plan, and for some reason, I have to go through what I go through in life to become the best version of me possible. Really, so I can be of service to the Universal Life Force, to others, to you, to me. So I can be the best I can at whatever I set my mind to. I don't know what or how I learned from all this. There is so much we don't know about our own selves even. I just try to trust and heal. I definitely do not get urges to do this to anyone else. I do often to this day think people are trying to hurt me when they aren't, which have to watch. I can try to understand my mom, not being emotionally able to have empathy and my dad's disinterest in knowing. I don't have to like it, and I can choose how much time I want to spend with them, how much trust I have in them, and how much I share about myself with them. Some people just don't have much capacity for love and empathy, and everyone tries to, so they just do it the best they can.

I guess part of healing the sex stuff, is reminiscing happy times from kidhood, to remember to cherish the innocent inside, not beat up on her or him. Back then, like that morning with Sam, I mostly replayed—that dirty broken record, images flew at me, reflections like cut glass, flashing hot, hot, sounds I couldn't erase: *My rainbow legwarmers...I had been in the boheme road schoolhouse, Mom was somewhere. I wanted to look at the pictures the dresser her room. She had one of the family before Dad had left, on the beach. He came in, followed me, shut door, started touching. I was frozen. He was touching. I hadn't even bled there yet...And it was, until it isn't—And all he did was giggle..."slut, cheap girl."* And when these crept on, my lashing voice, words, long, long, hollow, sailed: *Don't count on dreams they are just going to lead you wrong. Got no talent, can't sing.* Mom's voice. Maybe that voice was there to save me from something worse coming into my psyche. All I knew, and hated. Burned-red cheeks hot neck. I hated myself for something like sex made me feel better; made me feel like dying all at once. Pure; ashamed. I often wondered, *then why the heart in my body kept beating.*

I felt so weak, I called Sam, "Please make love to me...make love to me...takes the hot flash away...there's so many things we, so many things we don't say..."

"Baby, unwrap your gift," Sam.

My fingers shaking, unwrapped the orange paper, bow of silk and fancy cardboards. One large round glass snow globe. Golden-white angel on a green ornate platform base, gold lamé swirls. Silver windy key; angel spun, white flakes fell. Music maker plunking "Amazing Grace." I let a tear. I loved old windup-kind music boxes. Sam knew, and had never bought one before.

I had a pink spinning ballerina jewelry box when I was a kid, played "Für Elise;" I sat in her blue gown, winding the thing over and over, watching the ballerina joy, singing the tune's minor melodic, "*Da da-da-da-da.*" Soon after I'd started piano lessons.

Flowers with Mom

Someone asked me recently, "Think of a good time you had with your mom." I thought *great*, then almost doubled over at—not at the idea of something happy, the fact it took me so long to boot up.

Mom used to stick me in her purple Hyundai to Nassau County, Long Island, see Aunt Goldy, her older sister with the flame red hair, on holidays. "See the house I was raised?" The thing called "mom" would be cornering me in the car with her joy-filled memories. Mom would grab my shoulder, point out the window. Perfectly lined-grid suburban streets, *pretty weird*. All named after tree types or bird species. Like we two were on some dreamboat, Mom was acting.

"Isn't it all so wonderful, honey?" Big white toothy smile blazing, Mom did have a very pretty smile: "My elementary, senior, football, baseball fields, town pool! I went there every summer with my girlfriends! Oh, honey, I had such a big group of girlfriends!"

Dairy Delite Ice Cream, Baseball; Dodgers, Brooklyn, Mets fans, Yankees. What her first car looked like. Her prom—I was made to suffer every detail; the dress she chose; sweet honeysuckle, gardenia her wrist. She even made me get out the car, smell one just like it was off a tree, gushing, "Isn't it so beautiful?"

I never understood, knew why Mom did that. Chick displayed zero concept that she had an inkling that by my ripe age of fourteen, I'd been negotiating shit much huger—Mother and I had nothing in common.

By the time I had turned nine, Mom had just stopped raising me. There were few family photos taken since then: Maybe old disposables, school year pics, and when I hit thirteen there was one color glossy that will always imprint my mind: Christmas breakfast with the Drunk Polish. I looked really weird like trying real hard, bows stuck all over her head, make it all appear striking happy.

For me memory lane was an unwelcome guest with a baseball bat.

Eventually, a hallmark shone though. Me and Mom. A field of flowers. Me crouching in a little skirt at about seven years old. I always loved flowers. Mom and I walking home from my piano teacher's house, Margaret—means pearl

Margaret does. I always loved that—she'd gait cracked soft leather heels long knits tulip skirts down white spiral case leading to the second floor of her great big white diagonal walls and windows for ceilings. I'd never been up but always imagined she came from a blazing white cloud. Hands were always warm.

"Black-Eyed Susans," I was always searching just for them. I wanted to take them home for my dad. I liked the yellow, black next to his green library light on the desk in our living room. I loved my daddy. Mom be standing aside, the sun, hands in her denim short shorts pockets, transparent grasses grazing her freckled thin calves. Arched back looking over shoulder, out toward hills behind Hudson River, squinting, she. Always reminded me, this wooden carved sculpture Mom and Dad kept in our living room. Woman's head bent over, arms scooping baby, breast. Something how her back was curved. Her distant kind of pretty way, sometimes Mom would bend down, legs straight, feet crossed, "Pick a yellow sweetie," she'd say. Mom loved daffodils. I'd pick everyone I could find.

Kind of made me think also of Quaker meeting my parents used to take us to, when I was little. We'd sit in a big circle, talk about praising God in nature. Blades of grass knew better than people. "Grow slow, simple, honest, among the other blades," Friends said. "You can do anything in this world, long as you don't hurt yourself or anyone else," parents used to always tell me. Funny…

Think I told you this, how my daddy played guitar. We'd sit together outside, front some fire someplace at night. He'd laugh, make jokes. Times I'd catch him gazing long, somewhere else, and his eyes looked real nice then, like the water. He would just gaze out and look real quiet inside, almost mystical. I understood it 'cause I felt that same way inside and never knew how to put it into words. Something about the music, the fire that helped.

The last I'd seen dad, then, wasn't so nice.

Art of Gifting

"Time for gift giving!" Dad announced. That particular Christmas, 1998. Dad made a real careful lot of nice. Invited me, Wanda and Aidan, to his two-level condo, Bedford Hills—a classier part of Westchester—for a brunch. I had just moved back to New York, twenty-one. Dad asked us each special what we wanted. I hadn't been around for a holiday in a while, and said I just wanted a small wind up piano, from him. Reminiscing childhood I guess I was. Really, that gift thing always made me real nervous. I'd had troubles with Dad and gifts before. This year he had asked me specifically what I wanted. I had said just a wind-up miniature piano, something special from him.

In high school, final days, Jersey with mom, I'd seen Dad around Christmas. I'd taken to skipping school and leafing Kerouac, Nabokov, Shepard solo in the city, off Washington Square, scribbling poems, swillin' Foster's. Rappin' fast-life eternal. I thought the conga guys had more knowledge over showing up for Jersey High English class, finessing crusty class debates on the underpinnings of upper-class Brit or standard AfroMeri lit. *Caged Bird* and *Color Purple* were two of my five greats—but I'd always hung at the boheme college library, read them both twice by sixth grade. One day, skipping school for New York streets, I'd picked up a few DVD's from an outdoor vendor. A gift for my dad. Meltdown: Dad wrote me a knife-nasty letter, "The gift you gave me is cheap and doesn't play in the DVD. It means you don't care about me"—said he wouldn't speak to my anymore, plus wouldn't teach me to drive, pay for college, whatever else he'd give to the other siblings. Mom told me not to answer him, that I could just read books, get educated for free. Plus, she added, I didn't do the dishes enough, and she wanted me to move on out as soon as possible. I ditched all my stuff but that box old journals, and hitched west a few months later.

Seven years later, year, upon my return to New York to try to make it right, I'd bought Dad some more upscale stuff. I'd learned the trade of dancing, had money finally. A few days before the Christmas Brunch event, big sis, Wanda, had pulled out a Macy's bag, flipped her feathered head to one side, and turned singsong saccharine: "Sweet sister!" I honestly don't think Wanda had ever actually learned my name.

Wanda had a few plaid shirts for dad, said he loved this style, but she had bought too many. Offered I could pay her for few and give them to him myself.

Under dad's Westchester gold and fake green tree, Aidan got a new Sony DVD. Wanda got a Taylor 314 acoustic guitar! Dad actually tuned the thing, and started strumming, even though his girlfriend of 13 years, Bridget, who wasn't there and I had only met once, disapproved of his guitar playing. Dad had left Mom for this Bridget lady when I was ten years, and she'd been clear that she wanted nothing doing with his kids—I got a T-Shirt from dad's university and a calendar.

Why the hell do those lousy, idiotic, posing, fucking siblings of mine get so many big gifts, and cars, and colleges, and all your praise—I wanted to yell in his face. *Ow.* It was like a mini mainstream society, to me, you follow the patriarchal rules and you get stuff. Me, I was living in my own world; a lonely world, and getting smaller by the day

So, that Christmas morning, post-gifting, Professor Dad folded his hands, opened yet another grave intellectual abstract. *He sure has changed.* Last time I really knew him, was before I was ten. These days Dad had even picked up some faux British accent. *Dad, you can't become a different bloodline.* He always hated his guinea from Brooklyn blood—wanted to be upper crust. Somehow it seemed he had gotten the idea, that a British accent would give him clout.

Dad's topic: "*The Bell Curve: Intelligence and Class Structure in American Life,* by political scientist Harvard man Charles Murray. Its central argument is about how intelligence is influenced by genetics and environment." Dad thought it, "brilliant research," and read bullet points on his fascinations, ending his lecture with…"*Bell Curve* proves, people with blue eyes have higher IQs than brown."

I was jaw-dropped. Dad was the only blue-eyed guy the table. Me, Aidan, and Wanda all had brown, like our mom and like my dad's mother, Grace.

Creepy feels. Minutes earlier, I'd been walking around dad's dining area viewing displayed photographs—*Close-ups of his girlfriend Bridget* and her three grown sons from a previous marriage—one cop, one advert exec, one finance—They all had blue eyes. Even one glaring 8 × 10 glossy: Dad holding the blue-eyed first grandchild. Dad looked real proud. *Not one single image were of us, his own kids.*

When I had seen him during high school years, Dad often did this ponder brag, *(Definition for ponder brag: Passive-aggressive: Combination of exploring a thought and shoving something one didn't want to say in another's face.)*

"I've become so close to Bridget's sons; they are much more similar to me than any of you kids." He'd tout. "They look at me like a real father. And they look like me too, with blue eyes and all. I still can't believe I had kids with that woman and they all came out brown-eyed." *That woman* was my mom.

Wanna-be loved Aidan jumped in real cute-smart on the *Bell Curve* topic: "I wonder what was in the original gene pool that would give the cause."

Weirdo Wanda, "I've actually read some, and I finally understood why my best friends have always been light-eyed!" She'd tested genius as a toddler. She'd gotten out of the house by thirteen, and sent to private high school. Me, I had never thought anyone who reads books and writes papers for grades all that smart—*Put that chick in the world to figure how to get by, she'll fold, run for the nearest bank loan, book back to a classroom*—. But, competing with Wanda was never all that interesting to me. *Symp Fluff.*

I was appalled by *The Bell Curve,* insulted, "It's a stupid test obviously structured by a pompous idiot trying to prove the blue-eyed yahoos have the right to slaughter and enslave due to intelligence." They all three looked at me like I was an idiot.

"It's just my opinion, I haven't read the book, but," I said.

"The trait for higher-level thinking ability would get passed down recessively. Like stronger body types and interests get passed: DNA is chemistry, core vibration, mutable based on influence, repetitive experience. So, Higher education has been granted for a longer amount of time to people with blue eyes due to sociopolitical economic history; genetically higher levels of learning capacity, memory of data through trace DNA may have become recessive."

Silence. I was the high school drop-out—an underachieving louse, to them. I was still mad that my dad's university, the college I was trying to attend at the time. I hadn't told him my feelings, some people you disagree with their beliefs or institutions they never talk to you again—Pops was that. But I had been in this class they called World Religions. I figured that they'd go way back, spiritual worship—reverential commune, one of my greatest fascinations is pre-Christian Yoruban African tribes, dancing, drumming to ecstatic trance to bond with higher life force and receive messages from gods. How Christianity crusades traveled Europe slaughtered, enslaved women. Goddess worshipping communities, where females were shareholders in power. I hadn't yet read the Old or New Testament and was looking forward. Thought they might cover the basic words of Jesus, the prophet of truth. I even had envisioned myself raising discussion with classmates—how I had heard somewhere that Jesus had travelled to India, disappeared awhile in the Bible stories. I wanted to know if it was true. I wanted to learn Eastern philosophy, Yogis, Hindus—Chinese Communist regime: The People's Republic of China, the government of Tibet, Dalai Lama.

All I got from that business school religions class was a stodgy lady professor talking Judaism and Catholicism, like they were the only ones worth learning about; "popes, kings, knights, crusaders, archangels, psalms, holy battles," she even told us what architects built certain churches.

One guy even joked and teach, the whole class laughed—"Seems before they learned to irrigate water, folks couldn't think straight!"

This inspired me to read up on the history of US education. Apparently, churches started schools—so all curricula was designed by the oppressive church (es). They controlled what history people learn, wrote books to flavor social view.

My problem was emotion. Once I started talking and the emotion got me, I couldn't stop. I was like no talk at all, or like a waterfall. I tried to pull reigns my wild horse, and present more pragmatic, for this crew. "Take two bags of marbles: one brown, one blue. Now figure: Since its established existence, higher education has been granted to those who have money. The blue marbles slaughtered a majority of the browns centuries ago. A larger percentage of browns than blues have been in service positions for the past few hundred years. So, I deduct: for centuries, a larger percentage of blue-eyed people have collectively had higher educations. That would result: traits of the blue's brain have been developed, sharpened, and passed on. Now let's talk biogenetics: It has been proven that genetics, interests, and chemical balance is passed on in DNA. Not to mention—brown dominates blue, so there's more interbreeding, so not so many forces having to adapt to one another in the DNA of the blue output. Besides—also, climate: blue-eyed people are from colder climates so historically they sat inside, talked and thought about shit; brown eyes are often from southern hotter climates, so—they ran amuck outside, fucking and building a lot."

Bottom line, anyway: "Who the fuck cares? Body vs. mind—which one is ultimately more intelligent? Neither one is better." I full stopped.

Aidan, "That's ridiculous."

Wanda looked happy to see that Dad looked fiercely annoyed at me. They all shrugged.

Dad said, pointedly, "It's an interesting hypothesis. What are your sources for these thoughts?"

Later, Dad revealed, "I'm planning to marry Bridget this spring. She and I have discussed it at length, and decided to invite each of you."

This was why he called Christmas brunch. "I want you to make a special effort to reach out to Bridge before the date; send her a hello card, a special gift."

Someone has to let loose truth, I thought.

"How come she doesn't reach out to us?" I asked. "It's Christmas. You were with her this morning, seems a perfect opportunity to send a gift basket, card, call the phone to say hello!"

Dad retorted his usual, "We decided to keep things separate years ago."

Ridiculous it is to have penalized poor confused twerps left unprotected to fend off Where the Wild Things Are mongoloids, in our home.

Instead—I tried to make what I thought was a levelheaded statement that I felt informed adult feelings, "It makes me have troubles respecting your fiancé, as a woman; the way I see, a woman can help her man be closer to his kids if she reaches out—why she isn't willing to do what you clearly do for her."

One week later, I received another three-page letter. Father never wanted to see me again. Reason: "You gave me flannel shirts for Christmas that were made for women." Apparently, they have small pleats where the sleeve connects to the wrist cuff and shoulder.

"Which means you do not care for me," Dad concluded.

Good, old Wanda. Girls' shirts? I'm an idiot.

Dad's final sentence—"and due to all this, I have decided I don't want you at my wedding."

Father never answered a single of my letters. Or calls—even after I apologized.

At the wedding, Aidan was the Best Man. Apparently, Wanda kicked up her heels dancing with Bridget's three sons. For ten more years this went on, Dad didn't speak to me a wink.

With Sam then it had already been three.

Ribbet

Tra-la-la, flapjack. Weeks after the Millennial bang up, 2000 celebration. Same old Lower East Side sublet, Saturday early eve. I plunked back at that upright piano, reworking an old tune, "Hush." Mind a half-lit malaise; life's lost too many tequila nights, fog—Tweaking lyrics, drum fills; arrangements, effects. I was peering ProTools pink, gray, white menu drops laptop screen, fleeting images, grey to brown, to black whirl-surface. Me, listening to my voice through new Bose headset:

"I've had two weeks of silence, the knocking's seemed to cease…Hours of distant drumming brought me to my knees. Everywhere I turn now, reflections in the trees. I'm walking on this path now…faded memories. Hush…" my voice, *What do those words mean?* I,

Rex had recently communicated a springtime booking for me at Lucky Strike as promised. I couldn't even think about it. I'm the Looney Tune's frog, sing sweet at home, put me in front of money guys, I'll ribbet.

Yea, Rex's lime double pinstripe and Borsalino had become a fixture my world those past holiday months. The V.I.P. room graduated to Hudson's and Chanel. Been outing number 5, by then. Manhattan's Fifth Avenue, West Fifty-Seventh Street. These Cindy Rex-ings were like a disconcerting dream I didn't recollect when returned back to the LTGirl I called me.

I had come clean on Rex to Sam. I wanted to be partners with Sam, not liars. Sam was impressed by Chanel.

"My three sisters all have Chanel suits and million-dollar Miami homes! But what's he got a fetish for *9 1/2 Weeks*? Does he want you dancing on windowsills, baby?" The Borsalino.

It's a 1980s flick. Mickey Rourke dresses Kim Basinger like a Wall Street suit and hat; she does a strip on his windowsill to "You Can Leave Your Hat On." Over and over again, he asked her to do it.

Then Sam-eyes went dark. "You like this guy?" Sam took my hand, "You kiss him?"

"No!"—I *hadn't*. "He's all money for just company—I was clear no sex. Seems lonely. Spends a lot," I laughed. *Guy must just be crazy.* "I mean, all he says, 'Just like Jackie O!'" I told Sam—how Cindy looked just like her, "You could be her daughter!" And how he'd dreamed endlessly of buying Cindy: "Classic Chanel suit, just like hers, and a Borsalino hat, just like mine!"

Sam glimmered hard scowl.

"I'm sorry, baby, I didn't tell you…never done this before. Wanted to test waters first, see if Rex was real, before I stress you out with my idea—it's a way to get out of the late nights at the club, really."

Sam looked cut, lashes down. *Did I hurt him?* Maybe deep down I really did want to slice Sam. Busting my lip, eye. Testing him to see if he'd leave, if I cared. Conflicted.

"Maybe Rex could help us both—'til you get things straight with Jess," I offered.

"Would you help me?" I asked. "Teammates? All Shared?"

Sam perked, "Lots of actresses have rich guys help them out before they make it!"

It's true, sugar daddy thing in my world. Most girls who dance have an older provider, and a boyfriend at home. It's a thing.

Sam laid out some ground rules:

(1) Cindy only meet Rex Revan at Hudson Restaurant, Pen Bar, or Chanel.

(2) Lunch: Home by 6:00 p.m. Dinner: by 2:00 a.m.

Main thing Sam coached: "Keep your mouth shut, women don't have to reveal anything about themselves and they never have to give specific answers to any question—especially not about sex. And don't fuck, that's surefire way to lose a guy."

(3) Rex can never know Cindy's real name, where she lives, any phone number, nothing personal about her. It is only about what he can do for her. She does enough by showing up.

I did promise Sam I'd get a bartending job at one of his friend's clubs, *Etoile*—means "star" in French. I did sort of want to be a "good girl" in the world. Thought I'd figure out what was wrong with me, and learn to want marriage, monogamy, kids—respect. *Why am I such an exotic? Will anyone ever love me? Women who marry or share their lives with a man, get fucked over by men; Is Sam something I can trust, have longevity?* Felt I'd be giving up a lot of my own strength to be with one man.

I followed Sam's rules. Bustling Chanel bags in tow, home by 2:00 a.m. Hudson Rex dines paid 3k, no touch.

I still only wore the Borsalino and Chanel suit when we met, as Rex requested. I chalked that move to Rex's *Territorial Retardation.* That's when a person can't handle knowing you know, or have ever known, or even been anywhere that wasn't fabricated, orchestrated solely: by them. *Rex fears I might wear a frock with him, that another dude had given me; which, in his mind, meant he'd stepped to less important.*

I didn't mind all that. It's the whole strip world premise. Girl materializes from nowhere, to be whatever makes the guy feel the king of the planet for their short commune. For Revan, I was always pretended she'd come out a Jell-o mold just that morning…fresh for *his* feasting.

. Chanel had become a pre-dinner ritual. Had almost the entire Chanel spring collection by then. Rex picked out what he wanted. I tried it on. Lady fashion clerk hopped around with measuring tape gasping, like I was incredibly important. Old dried puff Rex Revan touting, "Chanel, the designer made only for Cindy!" Me, swirling in Chanel's three-way glass, thinking, *all for quality, upscale hot-lookin' clothes,* but *I could pay for a lot of singing classes with that dough!* While Pimp's voice barked, *"Don't dare rock this boat…"*

"I just can't decide which is better!" Cindy cried, twirling three-way.

Rex always exclaimed, "Get both!" I had never heard that before.

Oh, and on the kiss, I loved that kind of swivel. Often Cindy picked out Chanel's primrose plump kiss lips—"In case I might want to smooch your sexy lips," she'd tease, as Rex bought. No plans of kissing Rex. I threw hints and played Cinderella turning pumpkin—2:am each outing, it was only a matter of time on this one, *and then what?*

My mind kept wondering, *And why did Sam agree to Rex? Maybe Sam understands, something I don't even. Sugar daddy comfort and boyfriend love. I mean it's pretty okay acceptable in European cultures like Paris, right? Maybe Sam knows he can't provide, wants me to have what I need. Maybe Sam doesn't give a shit, doesn't really love me. Maybe he has another lover on the side, just wants to use me. Maybe Sam just wants me to go out and make the money, be the bird that whistles in the house, while I provide for him off Rex's dime, and my own virtue. Maybe Sam knew he really doesn't have a choice, and is cool enough to climb on board rather than ditch. Haunted, what would happen if I live my life forever just as I am, some weird quiet girl whose songs no one understands, an exotic girl, with sugar daddies and sexual power. If I do that, will I also figure out a way to stay happily married to the celebrity drug dealer—or single? Can I have it all? Do I want all that?*

Meanwhile, Sam had his own end of our plan in the works.

"Eric has some good sample on the high ends!" Sam hyped brightly one night as I ditched Chanel in the closet. *Yikes, Eric.* My glowy high-hummed gallows to hear Eric's sticky fingers in anything.

"I'm gonna get a good deal on a scooter." Sam's voice cracked.

Why does he sound like he's sucking helium? I wondered.

"BCs?" I said, nougat nonchalance. (British Canada hydro-harvest, if ya don't know). Something high end to replace the Mexican brick he'd fished in East Harlem while eating Jess's shit—Still hadn't dealt with Jess, but it was clear as day he'd cut Sam out on in-loads twice or three by then.

Sam's plan: Old Bleu had called up Sam on a high ride a few days before.

"Cheap stuff supreme," Bleu said.

"Woo-hoo! Jess is getting some big hook-in bulk Goose cheap from out West!" Jess still had no clue Sam and Bleu went way back. Bleu had no clue Sam and Jess were once equal splits and Jess had fucked the in-loads.

"Little Lord Fauntleroy, fuckin' weasel-boy drummer with a newly formed call girl addiction pinky lie talking lips had nerve to stick the same story he's been saying last two months: 'I swear on my mother's grave. The plants are all dry over in Cali, something's off with the hybrid strain. This crop all turned male. It's gonna be a while, what are we going to do, bro?'"

A complete low nasty scum-of-the-earth lie.

"He just pulled a royal suicide jack," I said.

Sam didn't want to lose his retail clients, he'd worked hard to build them up, and they relied on him for supply. Soon as they went somewhere else, it could be over for Sam's business. But *Oy, like a kick in the tits: Eric—*

I hadn't seen Eric once since he housed beneath us the at Chelsea tenement basement the June, before almost a year back then—just before we moved to this Lower East Side studio sublet. Eric was an old friend of Sam's from Miami who was studying for bar exams, Fordham corporate law. Coy Eric had this cliché caricature neo-cutie pie boy attitude toward me. Sam always claimed utter oblivion to this whole charade.

One Chelsea night, Eric, Sam, and I had been strolling the street arm in arm past ReBar. Some corner drunk jeered at Sam, something about sucking Sam's dick. Sam saw red and cracked his forearm over the guy's head. Eric and I were stuck together on some bumpy plastic doctor's office chair—*Yuk fluorescent lights,* sifting my ass, waiting for Sam to get his boneset.

Eric, with this hairpin eyebrow like Grinch, threw skillfully sharp at me, "You know why Sammy always hangs around my apartment, honey, don't you?"

"*Simpsons* and getting stoned?" I.

"No, no, no, honey doll," tsked Eric.

"Soo much more than that. Poor Sam gripes all the time…You light candles and sit in the dark. How do you expect to get to the core of the man in Sam. Girl, you will never grab his true guts, honey! You've got no sense of the beauty in laughter!"

"We're thinking get cards with my old name Buddy Greene on them, and bikes!"

Sam grabbed my waist, prancing ping-pang staccato-like target-practice in a rabbit's-race-on-a-steel-drum: "I used to pull in eight grand a week making deliveries, man phones, train a couple of street scramblers; bikes and beepers."

Nice numbers.

"Are splitting the money with Eric now?" I asked.

Winter sun low, we two sat talking, dreaming, laughing, "my music, his script, our careers…"

After a while planning, Sam and I decided to fuck.

Rex. One night kept creeping back through the haze. That night I'd taken risk and tried donning a Chanel black glitter dress. Breasts, cleavage made me happy. I liked all the dressing up. I slid my knee under the table, between his legs, to fit beneath his floppy-like Pillsbury dough belly.

He'd brought me to Neue Gallerie; the Egon Schiele exhibit. "*Friendship,* my favorite," I'd heard my own voice, revealing to Rex, flipping glossy to androgynous twins in backpacks, holding each other. I'd always loved the Viennese painter's ripped legwarmer ballet girls. I even told Rex how I had always loved staring into the diamond-shaped hazel eyes, emerald torn sweater. Something beating louder through the cage of my fluttering heart. Not love, I didn't have words for it. Rex had seen the Oscar Wilde exhibition at Morgan Library, too. I had just studied Wilde in an acting class, and the time period he had written. I even found myself taken over to tell Rex that night, some of that I had been pondering, over dinner, "How many heartbeats are there in a lifetime? I wonder if we can feel all of them…" That's when I slid my knee between his legs, and it felt fat, flabby like I didn't want to touch him, but it felt warm, safe, somehow, calm.

I remember that night how he had grabbed my bony fingers in his star-shaped hands. "My dear, you don't understand. You are poetry, beauty, romance!"

These days, I guess I would say that I felt understood, seen, by Rex in a different way than I was accustomed. Sam, my dad, my mom, no one really cared what I liked or what moved me. Back at the piano, plunked, I was still—Cut, Copy, Paste. Pulled my silk robe tight against early chill. *Shit. Fucking Jameson,* I had finished the bottle. On way to premix down on Mbox hardware Pro-Tools multi-track editing music, software. Music, my voice, my poem in the Bose headphones my ears: "Visions linger lullaby in blue. . .Velvet melody climbs spiral stairs…" Lashing my head: *Chintzy poor excuse for drums, look at you hacking stupid midi sounds. Stupid girl can't even write fucking charts;*

has to translate by ear. Ice. I got up to crack another James. Bottom line: *I want to find a producer. Hire musicians.*

Mother phoning—blip to muted message. *Mom.* I was side-swiped by some-pang that quickly swerved guilty...(Is guilt a cover for something else we don't want feel?)

Just be nice, I told myself. Decided to take Sam's advice, call her back.

Radio Shack. *Ugh*...portable plastic against my ear. I hate the phone. *OK.*

"Hi!" Answered, she—on that Saturday evening. Tennis pong, mom.

Funny love-hate twinge, I. "How are you?"

"I'm really good! Oh, wait!" Sounded like Mom dropped the phone.

Society of mind: You shouldn't speak or think poorly of your mother. Living isn't easy. It's not like she's an ax murderer.

I found myself staring at antiquated portraits on my piano old Charlie, May and the strange ambiguity in their daughter, Florence—Mom's mother. Flo's sad eyes. Mom never talked about her Mother. Few times she had, said her Mom mean to her. Didn't like her hair or something.

Dad had trashed Flo with abandon, "Pruned to become a world-class actress while her parents traveled Vaudeville. Stock Market crashed and beauty ended masquerading poorly as a Long Island housewife...singing quietly herself old Cole Porter standards; in a dreamy haze of scotch and arrogance."

"No, it's great! Couldn't be better!" Mom launched anxious high-pitch on phone. "Just in from a wonderful sunset drive! A perfect evening...inches of purple, blue, pink, perfectly placed. Truly awesome," Mom squeam-meandered, "and I mean awesome in the truest sense of the word. I can't begin to tell you how happy I am, honey!"

Mom forged on, "Did I tell you...?"

Mother had finally started painting. My whole life she had touted herself loudly a painter. Never actually picked up a brush. She claimed herself Academic, but never created a career. Mom did sit on her couch spouting tangential philosophies.

Just be nice, I scolded.

Mom bubbled on her latest rant: "Trustworthy, friendly people in modest homes, with simple needs!" How people should live, and her definition of a good person. Connecticut town she lived: "Wave to one another's neighbor when they're in their yard taking care of their children, coming home from work." She'd even started going to Sunday church.

"That's all great, really..." I. Vehemently revolted by Mom's abhorrent conviction for domesticity in its prescribed formula. When I was a kid she waved her flag high and mightily defending her tilt-a-whirl world of jobless residents, shacking with us and Dad's monthly child support checks. Guess this socialized tasking, rituals, behavior jaunt is her way of assuaging guilt.

Mom's revolting "And Julian?" I asked—my half-brother, then seven years old.

"How's he doing in school?"

Mom chirped, "He's having a great time…playing sports and eating pizza, just like a little boy should!"

"Great!" I responded, monosyllabic.

She wanted to know about me.

"Nothing really to tell," I sang. *All this pontificating kills spontaneity's creative juice,* I didn't say.

"Autumn in full swing. Sam's production company is successful!" Half-amazed, how easily fabrications slipped from my tongue.

"Wow. Incredible. What a guy," Mom gasped.

I had never attempted to explain to Mom about her dancing. She wouldn't get it. That there were parts I actually liked. The energetic transformation that happened in my body; a transference of sensual force between myself and the customer. That the quiet survivor inside me had finally found solace. Naked. Moving. Alive.

Ancient wisdom from an African dancer girl at a club in San Fran, "Move as slowly as you can, feel the spaces between the music. These men are lucky to be with you, it's not the other way around," had changed my life. Engaging in arousing conversation with interesting men from all over the world about culture, travel, business, private longings. I could finally afford some of those things herself—without being dependent on a boyfriend or husband.

"Music. That's about it," I told mom.

She never asked more about that.

"And where is that wonderful boy?" She asked for Sam.

"Out getting dinner fixings, we're having friends over." Lies. "Isn't he a doll," raving saccharine through plastic. Mother found Sam simply adorable.

I swear if she could marry him, she would…

Actually, Sam really could cook. I would sit the kitchenette counter, laugh my head off chopping veggies; he singing punk rock versions of "Hot Legs;" "Born to Be Wild" making every pot, pan, utensil cha-cha-cha like in that flick *Fantasia*…Magically, mangled wrapped dead pulp pieces from Balducci's turned lightly broiled fresh-ground garlic-stuffed sole, sided virgin oil marinated dill blanched asparagus.

I stood clinking ice cubes with an arm ache, against the window frame. Eyes staring at swaying Delancey Streetlamp: *green to yellow to red; slow, stop, go;* and again…

107

That evening, only dinner guests Sam and me were planning to entertain: Miss Mary Jane. Weighing her purely crystallized pounds of one of a kind supple, hydroponic, fluffy green strain to profitable ounces and eighths—distributable for the hungry, needy, desperate, and willing all over this small island. And probably hitting Blue Ribbon for lobster and cocktails at 2:00 a.m.

"Of course, we all have different skin tones but I see one color!" I heard through Radio Shack, plastic ear.

Spiraling whirl trance orbital, I was halted. *Oh shit I'm still on the phone with mom.* "One color?" I got the gist. Mom's next rant: hubby trashing. I had listened to Mom dish that skin tone proclamation before.

Mom had wedded an African American Ivy League-educated graphic-design college professor bassist-for-a-reggae-band. He'd pulled her out of Jersey, I'd split, bought her a house in Connecticut, and given her a child. Julian was in the third grade then.

"He doesn't even eat my cooking anymore!" she wailed.

"My fridge is filled with *her* Tupperwares! She gave them to him to bring home on Sunday. Seven-day rations of *her* fried chicken, her mac and cheese, her corn hash, her grits…" Clearly, by way, the Mom said the word *her*…Mom had turned Lenny's mom Evelyn into her nemesis.

"Comfort food?" I said, meekly. *Lenny might want that food because it's what he was raised on?* I silent. *It's called culture.* I held tongue. I mean, *Race is a tough walnut*, I often thought. Flip it around different angle viewfinders eventually, casing becomes transparent, inside exists a dilemma that just is. It's true, we all have God's light in us, suffer the same internal conflicts. Each human, at any minute, is capable of going any which way—and *we're all born, raised with different interests, tastes…Fuck do I know.* Probably some massive marital curveball slap, when a man stops eating his wife's food.

Listening to her rave on an on, drinking the ice droplets my James…suddenly, my new perception of Mother's flag-waving: "all one color" propaganda jingle seemed to soar, clear as a bell through a crisp blue sky in my mind—and transfixed itself a velvet pink settee. I did know that Mom had never budged from making him eat her homogenized all-American 1950s Mrs. Cleaver-land, love-our country, apple-pie-and-baseball, frozen food, cardboard boxes, white bread, powder oatmeal. Probably what her own mom, Flo, made at home when she was a kid. Hissing: *Not one color, like treated equally. Sounds like she wants all people across the board to be exactly the same, and that means: just like she is!*

I had no inkling why Mother would want everyone to be the same. Control: fear of the unknown. Some people's cases: if it all appears like one sum illusion, it equals safer.

"He threatened me that he would get custody of our son due to racial differences if I try to divorce him," Mom lurched.

"He said that?" Hip to Mom's 'he said, she said,' gum-flapping: she won't reveal what she nasty she said.

I didn't dare suggest, *mom, race a possibility at the core of your issues, and one of your differences.* I had tried to discuss this once. Mom got tight-lipped, "We," she said, "people of the world, Do not have race conflicts or differences, we have human conflicts and differences."

So, I offered some psychobabble, "Maybe Lenny threatens that because he can't get vulnerable to talk—feels criticized. Wants you to listen. Doesn't feel you accept whatever he's feeling, so he threw a threat."

Mom swiveled snooty, whined: "Now you're sticking up for him."

If she wasn't my mom, I would never call this chick, I often…

Denial. Oversize bee in my bonnet, prancing like a polka-dotted rhino pregnant with a grenade—*Mom sweeps all pain under carpet, and tells everyone: "Hop around, people, we must act happy!"*

Sure, we might all be human! I wanted to scream. *But we sure as shit have had different experiences!* I wanted to jump, rant, scream at her. *Some people have been beaten down since childhood for no other reason than their own skin color when they walk into a room—I don't claim to know that experience. But, I do think it has got to carve a gash; an undying hurt lurking beneath all things.*

This is not a pity party.

Seemed to me, they, softees, Mom, live—riding atop a float: shiny people who got treated valid and important all their lives. Seem to act all perplexed, looking down their noses, wondering, "Why don't those people behave! Let's kick them in the ass!"

What they don't see is, sometimes there's just not enough hours to sit down, heal the shit before you gotta get out and start proving yourself the world. And sometimes there's just never enough love to get it straight ever again.

What it would be like, for me to sit down, yank the scab off the pussing time bomb, and actually converse with Mom about the things that happened to me as a girl in the house?

I shut that thought down with quickness; Mom was punitive. "Well, I don't plan on divorcing Lenny anytime soon. I'll wait until Julian is eighteen! But the man I married, or maybe I should just call him my pet for Christ's sake…he doesn't even sleep in my bed with me."

I had no idea back then, that I could simply excuse myself from the phone.

She went on…"Sleeps on the couch…a fully Mac graphic design and music studio in that basement…entering, exiting through the garage…"

Introverted artist myself, I got lost, swirling colors of my mind, swaying curtain in breeze, the lyrics…*when will the words come…where did the words go*…Marriage bullshit bored me. I had heard a lot of fizzled white knot grimes at the club. Most guys who came in were married, an outlet for kickback: Stories: "All kids, stress, her weight." Chat-dancing: "Woman on side hacking my plastics, accounts…My wife eats so much she has to be stapled…She only thinks of herself. I support everything, she still acts like a queen. Never wants sex. Isn't the woman I married;" Then the late-night projections onto me: "You are the perfect woman," and on…Funny old world. Men liked a gal with intellect, and no responsibility. (Definition: Chat-dancing. Stripper stands over a man, swaying hips in man's face, lips close to ear, and talking.) Made me think of Rex, when I first met him. His sad, twinkling eye sunk in round pink cheeks under brim. Rex wrestled stuck schmew; the old man's hee-haw charley-horse half-baked clamshell busted-up marriage party:

"We were married after college. Wife worked hard, we both did at first. Obtained together a costly Park Slope brownstone She became a great stay-at-home mother."

Years passed, she turned: "You're never home, not enough dollars. Somehow, she decided I must be with another woman," Rex hands moving as he spoke, rather like he was delivering a presentation: "No evidence!"

Gosh his wife is a flatterer, Cindy thinking, *Rex isn't nowhere near hot enough to just pick up another gal.* I had met three-hundred-pound high-powered hip-enough guys suave-ish enough to get chicks hot as models—Rex just wasn't one of them.

Wife got emotional—found a lawyer gung-ho to help.

"I arrived home one night and she had locked my personal belongings outside with a restraining order attached. My daughters witnessed the whole charade through their bedroom windows."

Fuck, I sat on Rex's knee. Daughters sitting their bedrooms, watching daddy taxi off, never to return again home. Heart skip—I topped our bubbles.

"Where did you go?"

"Hotel." His verdant eyes big.

"Eventually a nearby apartment, close to the daughters, twins…Still negotiating final divorce details." *Single tear bulging?*

"That's what led me to you. Well, this place. I couldn't understand what I was looking for but I kept coming back…Cindy Star." That was his name for me.

Rubbing my waist, sliding it down around my ass. *Oh smack.* I got feline curved-up back like hissing.

Rex flipped subject. His plan: Promises: "Lucky Strike, A&R reps. Profitable investment portfolios!" He had the promo line. "Cindy Star..." He wanted to make my dreams come true.

My chess mind went: *Every gal who's ever made it has to fuck or not fuck the right people, right?*

Gab-Ooze

Sam busted in dripping stuffed duffel bags, grocery sacks from every limb and orifice. Every time that guy walked in a room, I heard applause, breathless. I glance clocked one sporty new swollen knuckle, some open flesh, a few drops of blood. *What's the story on that?* He shoved one silken blue-bowed Bloomies box my hand. I placed Radio Shack in his. "Hey, Mama! How you doin'?" Sam blazed.

I wanted to tell him about Lucky Strike, but. Huge kid smile, grabbed me around the waist with one arm, whirling circles, and smacked me another double dozen bouquet exotic multicolored hybrids. Mom went gonzo through the earpiece; I could hear her questions, his work.

"Yep, one of these days it's all gonna pop, Mama!" Referring to his cover story commercial company endeavor. "And I got my sweet angel fresh roses to prove it!" Sam pranced about phone in hand, his usual presto chango: bright lights, AC, TV: Action.

"Wow!" I lifted powder blue Nike spandex from Bloomies wrap, whinnying verbosely. Matching latest Nike Air, exposed spring heel—*great sneakers, but Fuck, be sexier if he brought some piece of techno music gear or a hot pair of heels...*The internal bicker. *Something must be wrong with me, staying home in the dark. I ought to get with the wifey gifty shit. Lots of gals yearn for this kind of attention.*

I was willing to overlook any disconnect. I wanted Sam's protection, whoever that girl is that fit into the picture to make it work—*whatever.*

"So when am I going to see your big beautiful smiling face?" She listened, Sam pipe mom...candy land cooing happy hippo drone.

"You bring Julian in for a New Year visit; our home will be all bright and shining for you!" he yak phone.

TV blared evening sit-com. Rap blasting. Weed smoke the ceiling fan swirl. I dug my platform into tile, put on my best appreciative good wife interpretation. Situated fresh-cut springing palette in midst of dealer mayhem on coffee.

"Love you, too!" Sam told her.

I kissed his cheek.

Handed me the phone—"Love you, Mom!" I to silence. *Mom hung up.*

Sam picked me up, "Come on, baby! I feel like doing something crazy today!"

"You don't feel like that every day?" I smirked his hand; his gravel melted me every time. Kiss.

"Babe, I just got this cash, 'n big deal set with Jess. Just had a meeting with this big-time indie film producer I met through some buddies recently. He had me over his space, babe, Tribeca, just now," Sam was racing.

"Five thousand square. Five thousand bucks monthly he'd charge me. Wants me go business with him. Hydro-growhouse in the back of the space, we figured out how we can make it work. Rake it in and pump film and media out front. Babe, let me take you on that boat!"

Hopped another favorite game of ours—Sam picked up red couch pillows, threw 'em on our living room floor. I lowed lights. We had actually gone outside rowing a few times at the Central Park Boathouse, when we were first courting. Both hated the general public: lines, stares, can't toke or drink public. This was our "Big Easier," we called it.

Lie down flat back. Nestled my head, inside his mountain pectoral inlet, bicep cradle. Me and Sam, gazed up: *Blue sky.*

Sam made pretend splish-splash in sparkle waters…

"Look, the fishes, baby," Sam said. "So pretty. Like you." Like our first night, the roof.

"Yes." My voice trailed, *floating.*

Tickled my legs, arms, waist—his script. "Babe, I started writing a new scene for my script"—

OK, tune in:

Sam, cleared throat, changed vocal tone, each wally-gingbrat: "Scene 1. Miami. August." Hands like camera moving, "Longshot slow focus, sprawling Coral Gables mansion grounds, *Grrr,* like a lawnmower. Kid's hands on the pusher, white tank, dirty jeans, red bandana."

The mob boss, Doug Lord, he mows for invites him inside for lemonade and offers him work, in his business, shuttling messages and errands.

(Narrator) "Cut to: Interior. Kid shaking ice cubes, glass. Doug Lord himself over him, towering, gold chains, three-piece suit in summer, handlebar 'stash."

(DoLo) "I've seen you work hard. Good fighter in the ring. I want to give you a chance."

Sam's voice, dropped character, "All I could think of was my mom. She left her home country, had seven kids, one died, but she always made time to sit with me in mornings and have Cheerios. I sat for an hour that altar, crossing up, down, asking God what to do. Hurt my heart, thinking I might have to lie to her."

Symp, church, Mom. Do I feel anything? I scooted to styling exuberant— "Wow, baby I think that's a great opener. You really pulled me in."

I wanted to see, taste this script get made. I believed in my blood; Sam had talent and a great story. I guess we probably both could have done with a dose of humility: hunkered down to work on our creative, visions, projects. Money hunt was killing us both—I didn't see that then.

Sam jumped to the latest Little Lord Fauntler'-boy weasel-story.

Sam, "Jess promised me fifteen pounds, Bleu and Skinny as witness—"

Bleu was going by that night to meet up with "Cousin Mary." Sam had phoned up Jess, laid back to check on the fifteen pounds.

Sam shrugged, "You know what I'm gonna do though?"

Sam grabbed me tight. Up at the sky, rocked me light.

"Jess promised fifteen pounds, I mean he didn't come through yet, but he promised in front of everyone. He promised again today, in a few days' time. He has to; he has them witness his word. I promised I'd pay, I'll heist 'em off, Jess, as payback—flip 'em fast. That's ninety-grand cash. Keep. Wipe my hands clean of Jess for good. Invest. Partner up. Production. Growhouse, music, film, commercials. Babe, it's it almost your birthday and it's gonna be the best one yet…"

Then Sam showed me the gun.

PPK

Sam pulled this old Walther PPK/S handgun down from the kitchen closet.

"You ever killed anyone?" I eyed the thing nonchalantly. I felt strangely attracted to it, but wondered, *What does he plan to use that for?*

"Nope. Put a cap in some guy's ass one time," Sam.

He laughed; I posed a Charlies Angel, gangster lean.

"This is serious, babe. People in Florida learn to use guns, it's just about living," Sam said, turning the blond steel sexy confusing thing over, his grip.

"I usually stash it in a storage locker. Don't you ever say a word."

I, "Do I talk, babe? I'm like a mute in the world." I laughed at myself, so reclusive. He smiled.

"Jess doesn't come through with the fifteen pounds, I'm gonna have to get a crew, swipe his pad." Sam's plan.

Snapped open a black plastic box labeled GUNMAN KIT: brushes, swizzle sticks, cloths. I had never been so close to a gun before.

"Same gun Fleming gave 007 Bond. 380ACP D.A. 7rd stainless. Developed in Germany, 1931," Sam boasted.

I want to hold it. I'd always held a respect for guns. I thought...*Like a snake. Powerful.*

Something so dormant can cause such instantaneous change.

"But we're gonna have this around, baby. Means, you need know how to use it; in case you need to protect yourself or me."

Sam got to work teaching me to load, aim, shoot and clean Mr. PPK.

I'm always up for a new experience, street smarts.

When I was really little, my parents took me to a touchy-feely museum, in Philadelphia where we had lived for a bit before I was four years. Was the only museum I liked. I didn't know it then, but to me, life always seemed to center fundamentally around survival of the fittest, so I never wanted to just sit-stand stare at something. I wanted to know how all the parts work, and then figure out what works for me.

Sam held the metal. "That's the safety switch," he latched a small piece of metal under the slide.

Guns exist. I'm gonna live in this world, whatever world I live, wanna be solvent with tools required to protect myself. Anyone who wanted to gripe on that, be a real bore trapped in an emergency, I told me.

"Special feature this type of gun has. Lock it no matter what, so the gun never goes off by accident." Put his finger on my finger. Instructed me to switch safety: on, off...*could break or save my life.*

Sam went on, "Our country and it was started by a bunch of guys who used guns to take what they wanted. It's what Thanksgiving and our day of Independence are founded on." Sam was from a Cuban migrant family but felt strongly that the U.S.A. was his country, too.

I agreed, same thing's true anytime something sought is at stake.

"So, this is a steel blowback-operated semiautomatic pistol, with a fixed barrel," Sam technical, "To shoot, you pull backslide, pops a cartridge in the chamber. Hit the double-action trigger. Exposed hammer. A frame-mounted manual firing pin protrudes from the rear."

I watched him, didn't quite get it all. Something about a beavertail.

"Front grip panel, press a button; release this casing filled with the bullets. Magazine," he called it. Spilled them on the bed.

Sam placed the blond PPK in my hand. *This beautiful...Protection— without another fucking person to depend on,* was all I could think right then.

"K. Line up your sights," Sam.

"Look through the two metal things on top." Showed me proper handling, grip.

Bull's-eye. Ripe. I, "*Grrr...*"—aimed it straight, lining LED light on CD player between my eye line.

"Slow down, son!" Sam grabbed my wrist hard.

Ow. "How did I do? Imagine all the sexy film fatale gals I can play with firearms!"

"So hotshot," Sam smirked.

"Reassemble it now. Reload bullets. Cock it, latch safety. We'll store her empty."

I marveled

Sam-eye was dead cold: "This is serious. Most critical lesson: know *when* to use it. Lotta people abuse power. Greed is the number one killer. Separates chumps from survivors. Gotta figure keep safe, fend your own turf, but not get greedy."

That night I slept with the stainless blond Walther PPK—safety on, tucked under my pillow.

Triangular Dung

Things got complicated. Like that manky pile hot horse manure, stuffed with old rotting bubble gum and poached in Peppermint Patty's, left baking under three-pointed tumbleweed, gets stuck bottom your shoe—y'know, same crap you have to tear back your own shadow box fabric to find.

What I'm saying is:

Eric, tootled, stuck his head, "Peace, love, and pineapples!"

Sam kissed my forehead; "Sleep with the angels, baby, sleep with your kind. I love you." They split late night, who-know-where.

Rexing public. Over those next few March, April, May—three, four times a month. I hadn't realized that seeing Rex like this might make me rather dependent on him. I hadn't realized dating, Rex might infiltrate an army, or virus between Sam and my kind of love.

Funny turnaround, Sam and me ended up back at Wanda's old railroad. Two years after we'd met and fled that spot for hotels. Wanda: "I'll be relocating to La-La Land!" Sam convinced her that he and I were newlyweds, and needed family support. It was true, they were a month or so shy their first year married. He was real good, asking for help. I wanted nothin' doin'—*a loser who asks for help*, actually is how I saw it. It took several weeks of haggle-duking for Sam to convince old Wanda. Wanda demanded: "I can stay with you whenever I visit East."

Second year at Esper, I had begun acting in short films, putting a reel together, had just signed with my first agency. Started with Innovative Artists, bi-coastal talent agency. Exciting. Usually stayed in by usual Baudelaire, Helmut Newton fuck—all mood, working on music demo—but *who wants to hear that.* A certain Director Orange stepped into scene, decided he wanted me to write a script with him, a lead for me.

Me and Cindy—let's just say, if the two inside of me seemed confusing: they were.

Lucky Strike, well, old Rex and I had found a few more things in common...

Boogit

Another Frank was hovering over the table, pushing crumbs. Warmish vigor, April afternoon. We were lunching at Pen Bar high-rise, overlooking Manhattan's Fifth and Saint Patrick's Cathedral. A new find on Rex's part.

"You know there is a hotel in this building," Rex had belabored.

Fuck him. Peninsula Hotel; I made no response at all. *I've kept my end.*

Rex had appeared doldrums that sunny springtime afternoon on the cool, pavement, outside Chanel. "Lagerfeld premium just in!" Chanel sales representative had telephoned Rex—how personal the hoppy shop lady had become. Rex's creepy wild hazels evermore yellow rim bloodshot than usual. Something about the weather, he said.

Past few weeks, couple of days, I had gone quiet on Rex. *Silent Seduction Rules:* Disappear a bit, when you want to stall a man, and have him chase you. Really, I'd been trying to lay low off sauce, again; Was not convinced I could pull off public Rex hang in the bone desert. I phoned him up, payphone only, and said something about being mugged.

A man ought never to complain, how I abhorred an Eeyore man.

"Well," I sung, adoring gaily Rex's new blue jeans and lime-green-mallard checkered button-down appearance, "Are you looking smart?" Even sported a golfer tan: glove on one hand.

That day, we had walked with two pretty pink silk dresses. One powder Chanel Picasso frock crisscross backstraps, pleated midcalf; One magenta quilted, paint splatter, pleats. Plus, one signature Chanel exposed thread-edge blush crème weave waist jacket. One pair of white patent wedge platforms.

"Feeling eighteen!" Chap tried to brighten, as we walked down Fifth Avenue, four shiny, black Chanel Day-Glo shopping bags. My navy, heeled toes getting ripe in these newfound sunny outings. He, boasting: "Lost thirty pounds since we began dating!"

Dating? I grimaced, silently. *We must have different definitions for that word. It's your desperate bird syndrome this chick's boner deflator: a turnoff.*

"My divorce is almost final!" Rex beamed, rising tiptoe, he tried to grab my hand.

Like child batting a muted xylophone, I, "Music to my ears."

Man grabbed my arm so hard, I thought I'd get a red rash.

"I missed you. How could you ignore me like that?"

I uttered: "Of course, I missed you!" Loudly, I.

Trying to appear a lady, but, inhaled muddled lime, mint, rum sugar-rim up.

Rex's thumb rubbing skin my palm so hard, my eyes spit back daggers: *get off me, burger face.*

Can I have the fucking bottle of booze, instead of this measly stupid serving?

All I could think, eyeing little forty-five-degree angle metal gadget thingy, w*hat the heck is the proper name for that*; *Must concoct word next time I play Scrabble.*

Scrabble. Back in Jersey, me and Drew, Tanqueray eves, we had our own rule.

You can make up a word, that doesn't exist, spell it on board. If you define it with something your partner buys, or they don't challenge with dictionary (possibly forfeiting their turn if you are right) word stays on the board for points. And part of your secret language.

Like Drew's: "Boogit: The red cellophane wrapper tear-tie on gum, cigs, mints, etc.!" he said. *What the hell is the name for that thingy?* I couldn't argue.

"Of course, I have deep true feelings for you too, dear! You are simply the sweetest man ever! Makes me feel shy, often quiet!" I said, off his I don't know what but sounded like whining.

"I can't go on with no tangible way of reaching you!" Rex's usual verdant bulbs poured color urine yellow. *Like one of those Thailand stick insects I've seen Sam watch on Discovery Channel,* I couldn't help think. "Did you receive the flowers I sent?" demanded.

"My most stable address," I told. Cindy kissed Revan's cheek, "Weren't the yellows just beautiful!"

I had finally forked Rex a Fifth Avenue mailing address. Third-floor postal business for pickups; appeared residential from the street. Some Irish surname: I had chosen McCort. *Angela's Ashes,* and it had just won the Pulitzer a few years back, then. Thought maybe I could swizzle in a fib to Old Rex, some family tie to the McCort's would impress the old.

"I couldn't understand," Rex gripped my left, "why if someone had hurt you—didn't you call me immediately. I would have rushed to your side."

Dolloped hallmark, "Helping a dear are moments in life one treasures."

Darling, a girl like me doesn't call anyone for help she sucks it up and deals, I laughed, "Oh, I know you have your plate full, a wife and girls. Lucky for me, the thief only beat the side of my head, ripped my bag on the subway. But he grabbed my script, I lost all my margin notes, *Arms and the Man*. Bernard Shaw—I have a paper due early tomorrow." That part was true.

Man squeezed me, "I want to secure myself with you," Revan blurting spittle, "I have real feelings."

Guy doesn't even fucking know me.

Truth was, past few wobbly footed weeks, truth, I had found myself on a slippery floor. I had never tried to stop before. I mean, morning after, decide not to drink that day, but by five o'clock it seems ok to get back to. This wagon-thing—Seemed a rug swept up, left me a freaked-out clinging, fingered-kid inside. I was yearning to disappear: yet dying to be seen. *Who's going to save me from me*—Fantasizing, I even found myself thinking of Rex. *Maybe if I let him more into my life, he will care; talk slow, nice, treat me like delicate flower, princess; wrap warm blankets, protect me.*

Quick-side-swipe, I was struck by a sharp-chill-shudder, the nut of the whole goddamned cog: *It isn't even me Rex wants. It's her: Cindy. The Graceful. Oh, Mysterious. Confident...When he gets wind the dirty bag laundry girl I am at home, inside; the little trash girl who, soon as someone gets close I spontaneously fizzle and flip-flops, lose footing, begin grasping at quicksand, and then starts hissing evil—fiercely frightened. He would leave—surely the Rex would bolt. How embarrassing would that be, left by an old prune.* I was ordered by me to: *Stay in, hide that part from him, the world.*

Weird. He was obsessing Miss Cindy. I was becoming jealous of *Miss Cindy.* Dry to bone, I found me craving a magic key, *I want to be her 24/7. I'm loser girl. Surely if Cindy had steered the wheel of my life, we'd been a singing sexpot success by now; like Rita Hayworth, or some sizzle.*

Cindy. She was a part of me I had developed to take care of a different part of me: was becoming more difficult for me to unravel; *Rainbow Girl,* I called the young one in me that needed protecting. I also called her *Trash Girl.*

I chalked Rex's proclaimed feelings: *either Rex trying grasp some "thing" to fill his fucking void; or Rex throwing trick fishing line to gain footing in our silent who-gives-more, who-gets-more tug of war. I need plant some daffy distraction seed old man's spidery warped brain; keep him at bay, yet closely orbiting.*

Like I was a voyeur in my own game, I was watching, listening to Cindy—her quick-response abilities to mumbo-jumbo Rex, made me feel incredibly safe.

Rex-ing:

"You know, doll," Bug eye was grinning, "Marlon Brando performed *Arms and the Man*; his swan stage performance, 1953."

I smiled.

Rex cycled on, "Shaw was an avid socialist! A strong supporter of women's rights!"

"Yes," I blurted, something I'd read, "Shaw was even a teetotaler! And an Oscar winner!"

"A Nobel winner and one of the most performed playwrights in the English language!" His encyclopedic-jive-spout.

This got zing girl in me—a nerd when it came to books, especially plays—I felt like a whistling bee had killed the apple's worm. We two like bouncing good friends sharing boogie, a chat on Shaw's *Arms.*

"Marriage and war and the upkeep of appearances via proper social reputation." I piped as main themes. Cindy kicking me inside: *shut up you slut, sit straight turn him on, entertain him, don't enjoy him, he may get the upper hand.*

"Yes, dear," Rex, "and he was one of few in his time who'd written on Serbian War heroes," went on and into his conclusive point, "let alone this play's societal spoof on the kind of men who make honorary badges!"

Naturally, dork I, blurted some like the longest mono slab I'd ever delivered old Rex: "Well, I felt, at the start of *Arms,* each character, Raina, Saranoff, even Bluntschli was dedicated to following a societal norm. Nicola was the only one who actually cherished his work, regardless. But by the end of the play, each followed exactly what they truly wanted or believed in, or wanted—which led them to happiness. Seems precisely what Shaw meant is the truest act of courage!"

Rex liked that, bobbing his head wholeheartedly.

I loved sparring Rex with banter—a girl could eat *that* for dinner.

Hey, Rex found my thoughts intelligent! Twelve-year-old me, little Rainbow Girl, was happy. Really plainly, someone who took an interest in my interests, 'til—

Rex grabbed dab-nabbed me, most triumphant, "You made that face again!" Proud of his ability to recognize my traits.

"There's a way you pull in your jaw and squint your eyes," he said.

"Like it hurts to have your heart touched. Makes me think you've been aching there a long time."

Am I that transparent? Eyed my booze-on-the-low with contempt—*Rex catches a sniff your wishy-wash tremor in public: Game over. He'll get upper hand on you.*

I learned one thing growing up in all those Gentleman's bars—old cat, mouse between the sexes. *Silent Seduction Rules*: I leaned back, put my fingertips in my collarbones' lovely little indentations. Ran a fantasy within: This is a shortcut to quick spot mood changer. Make yourself shift feel, on command.

This is an acting technique. How an actor emotionally prepares. Decide what feeling you want to conjure. Fantasize, or trance into that: naked on hot sand beach, or winning Lotto, recall a memory—what kind emotional response you want to conjure. Your nervous system boots from your imagination or memory. The whole body thinks it's happened, bingo.

Revan tipped his hat, quoting Rick Blaine played by Bogart, *Casablanca:* "But then, dear, we'll always have Paris,"

I examined Rex's Rick Blaine slash Bogey mug; thin brow, furrowing inward, three creases shot up center, to form one long bridge across top.

Laid he: "Now, sugar, I've done the thinking for both of us. I have meetings *en Pear-ee* this weekend with a client, dear Cindy," Rex put down his drink, stiffened.

"I thought I might book two tickets. I assume you have never been."

I shook no, delighted.

He continued: "I always stay at George V, Four Seasons; imagine you will enjoy its view, the city's Eiffel Tower."

Sha-la-la—but if I woke up next to this man, I'd fall flat my face, crack up like one those big-teethed wooden chatterbox dolls. Besides, Cindy didn't have proper I.D. for travel. *Could probably get Sam to find a fake but not passport.*

…Brain wheels creaked…I started to pine for this thing I'd invented her mind: *'Vibrational Analyst Auto-Response Quick Changer.'* The device that would, "Calgon, take me away," to a better life.

Think: Woody Allen's flick, *Sleeper:* Orgasmatron. Futuristic gadget. No-touch sex. Hold the orb. Presto: instant full-body pleasure, long as you wish. Deletes all chances of love and germs.

My VAARQC tucks are tiny on your flesh. Scans your brain. Knows what you want. Scans the other person's skull. Computes what you need to say to get the other person to give it to you. Silently sends a synapse signal to your mind. Makes you say it all perfectly, word for word (with emotion).

Presto: *You get them to give you what you want.*

I still sat speechless. I raised "A toast! Perhaps when we two are close enough for romantic excursions; we shall be betrothed!"

I had no thought in the world of leaving Sam. Perhaps I ought to have, for Rex.

Just that morning, I had inquired while dressing, "Sam, why do you think Rex is dumping all this cash on me?" I often spoke like Scarlett O'Hara just for laughs.

"You're precious, baby," Sam played sitting bed zipping pants Chanel. "Guy's getting divorced. Probably needs to clean some account his wife's gonna dig into, figures why not have a good time for a while, midlife crisis. Take what you can, won't last forever. Get that fatman to take you to a hipper designer—"

"Let me take you out," Rex was.

"Let me give you a surprise, show my care for you."

"This weekend?"

I oohed. *Make up something about a mother and a baby shower? Nah.* Went for guts: "Really, I am an old-fashioned girl!" swooned I.

"Raised not to sleep with a man before marriage; and certainly not to tease. It would feel disturbing wrong, me travel as your companion if I didn't plan doing the jimmy with you!"

Rex large bald head flew open, wires spouting, spitting fire smoke, like that maid Rosie Robot mal-computes on *The Jetsons* when she gets confused. Almost choked his silver fork, my mention the M.

Rex pulled the "straighten-knot-of-his blue-green-gold paisley and tuck-it-into his-belt" move. Cleared throat, replied, "Oh, now you are being cute, dear. You really ought to know better than toy with a man's heart."

Good answer, Revan, I felt like clapping. *Survey says?* Oh, little guy on *Family Feud* game show who kisses all girls, barks out the player's answers, looks to scoreboard. *How many points ought Rex to yield?*

Cindy rose, to dash ladies' room, breast bounce "accidentally" gliding 'cross his bald head. Tossing, "Rex, honey, I can't wait for sparkle parade my new lips for you!"

Eyelashes, hers, batting a million; *who knows if Rex believes that. Cherry poppin' legs up by thirteen, slut*—"Really, a new agency I just signed with, bi-coastal! NYU Drama studies impressed them. I still plan to go on for a master's, sweetie, even if, I mean *when,* I book roles! I don't want to leave town just now," patted gently his hand. I told him about the New Yorkie Coppola look-alike wannabe great: Director Orange I called him. Came up on his set, asked if I wanted a tangerine candy. I said yes. He'd started calling, wanting to help me write a script with a lead in it for me. I blushed on.

Rex put down his sugar-rimmed cherry Drambuie chill, "That's a wonderful doll. Well, I'll have to spar with the chappy!" Rex had joked. Meaning the director.

Rex's stuffed shirt fuddle-forged a new diatribe, real haughty. "Mea culpa for not having spoken with more clarity! You must understand. I don't want you just for sex." He crunched my hand.

Oh, yawn. I sneered. *Where's that confounded wine.*

"I hadn't much sleep." That was true, too. I was beat. Felt I *had* been mugged.

Me and Sam, night before had broken an early dawn row. He'd worked the bar 'til 2:00 a.m. Rambled in daylight.

I'd been calling—No answer. Felt like a lame chic, worried about all that kinda shit. Didn't get why Sam couldn't just, *'Hey I'm out,'* text. Wasn't the first. Been happening a lot then lately.

Really, our big rift, me and Sam—was over me not talking. Sam been trying to talk to me. About our relationship. How to get closer. He wanted me to talk, too. Normally took three, four days pass before I figured out what the hell I felt. Had gotten worse since I'd been trying lay off sauce. Less I drank, more plagued inside, I didn't know what hell to say.

Thoughts of Sam's golden line: "Thinking and drinking, not a good combination!" *Surely Sam is wrong,* thought I, again: *It's thinking and not drinking, that's detrimental to my safety.*

Sam laid the rule, "If you're not gonna talk, I'm not coming home." That hurt my feelings.

6:00 a.m. that morning, Sam buzzed: knocked, yelled.

I had locked the deadbolt chain, lay. Silent.

After a while, he staired it to the roof, down the fire ladder.

I, watching. Window over bed. Sam actually bent back wrought iron safety bars—*with his hands?* Guess the glass was unlocked. He slipped through the small opening.

Who fuck does that? I was strangely satisfied by his valiance.

Sam wrapped his body around mine. Like a baby fawn, cried some garbled, "I'm so ashamed. I was just sitting, out to drinks with work buds, felt like a loser. I wished you'd just fallen to sleep."

Didn't want me to know—Sam went on, how he, "can't sit still anymore. It's all too much."

Then, Sam told me he'd gotten a therapist to talk to.

I didn't know what to say.

Rex was sitting in front of me chirping on. I got my head back in the lunch, "I have had ample time to reflect, Dear Cindy, after our Hudson dine."

What the fuck happened at Hudson to reflect on? I only recall the sum five grand. A dancer always: Works, walks, counts, forgets. Repeat. No joke.

"I had overlooked the reality of where we met," Revan.

Meaning a bar—condescension.

"I realized how I shared with you in candid, what had brought me to that place; however, overlooking that you must have encountered your own complex life circumstance, landing there."

I felt on a rollercoaster going down. "Stating so, it is my responsibility to understand, some things may have affected your abilities to trust. Respectfully I wouldn't pry, nor expect you talk about any of it with me, 'less you choose."

Shit-nab shamed, like a child who was forced to ride the special yellow short bus. Magical old faithful, Cindy thought: *I ought to charge this fucker more cash; my presence providing him opportunity feel good about himself, snoot down his honker at me. Thankfully he doesn't know I just turned the wicked twenty-six a week back. If he knew I was so old, he'd probably leave me for dust piles.*

"I just want you to know in your heart, dear Cynthia," Rex crowned, "my goal is to develop a mature relationship. I have large respect for your natural class, stature, and ambition. I am willing to commence as slowly as you need."

I almost peed out of my pores. *Why don't you just say you realized I am a totally fucked-up old chic, but still want to know me!* I always did have a problem hearing a compliment as honest.

Rex smiled jovially—his incisor tooth doing glinty-sinister. He smoothed one brown tuft hair over bald and went spelunking his cavernous mouth with a peppermint-flavored toothpick, appearing search for the right molar.

"Most men only think to take. A seasoned one tries to see from a woman's perspective."

Doesn't this guy ever have anywhere to be?

"Don't deny me the pleasure of spoiling you," the Revan replied.

My silent *Rules of Seduction* worked better than even Cindy was quite comfortable with.

Unbreakables

Diamond shopping. No shit. At Fortunoff amidst all jib-jab mind, I really did my best to join the charade—Rex kept repeating, "That is precisely why I want to do something special for you, show how deeply I care for your well-being," gleamed.

Rex and I ended up in a private room of Fifth Avenue's Fortunoff, taking Mint Verbena tea and ginger cookies in red leather armchairs. *If a guy I don't love is going to sit me down, buy a fucking rock, it better be at Tiffany's.* But the place had good diamonds. I have a natural eye, tell a cheap-o or a fakey in a dash.

Our Diamond Concierge, a cheesy string bean fella dressed narrow ankle pinstripe three-piece, oily curl edges his pencil mustache. "Please join me!" Hopped about, beckoning I sail with him, atop this magic carpet.

"Uncover the wonders of the four Cs!"

I felt this Stringbean's whiskers brushing fierce my right cheek he got so close. LED pin flashlights, microscopic lenses flying from his hidden waistcoat pockets: "Color, clarity, cut, and carat weight brilliance—all, yes!" His deep chuckles my ear. Light prism rainbows bounced, painting my arms, legs. His rickety finger bones covered in light freckles, pulled plump velvet cushions from locked glass drawer encasings;

Cornered by a failed actor turned diamond hawker, I assessed. I must have looked like a blinded 'coon on a highway.

Clutching one round multi-faceted diamond hunk of earth under bold halogen. His whisper, fiercely, "But divine cut brings fire to ice!"

Off to the racetrack, *like a good girl ought,* Cindy gave Rex, her churlish "ooh ahh…"

Old Rex sat sighing like old, happy Grandma blend inner tube losing air, "In all my life, never enjoyed the breathtaking beauty of a dame's first diamond experience."

Bean jumped hippity-skip, leading me down the garden path; His voice a high-pitched rha-rha like a Muppet, Fozzie Bear. His melodic memorized to a T hypnotic tutelage:

"The vast mystical history of unbreakable carbon atoms, arranged in the diamond lattice crystal structure," fancied.

Oh, foo fizzle spin-about. You know, I get off on scientific facts—

Bean mentioned, "Mohs' hardness scales."

I had taken up jewelry weaving with gemstones in high school, just before I ditched and hit the highway. Picking up a craft is good for survival. I'd borrowed a book, *Gemstones of the World* from Drew's Mom's coffee table, learned to identify different gems properties, for buying semiprecious off West Coast import market—diamonds are the hardest and hence used as blades to cut other stones, glass, and each other. I knew the basics chemistry: positive, negative charge, electrons, neutrons arranged a certain way to make each stone. but, no one had ever offered to buy, or give them to me.

"It's the rating system professionals use to rank stone's body strength, hardness, thus value." Listening to old Bean, I wanted to put on my charley horse geek glasses and ask him things I'd been wondering for years, like *where the hell did these things get charges that attract them to each other, in the first place*? Figured I would sound stupid if I asked: *Either you missed that year in school, they teach it in college, it's unanswerable and you should know that, or you're just stuck in acid tripping kinda brain, ought to join the real world—* Maybe it's like love. Inexplicable chemistry, bonded some familiar, fuck knows who why when but must be played through and changes everything your life.

"They sleep one hundred twenty miles in the earth for some like three billion years; thrust to surface by deep volcanic magma eruptions," Bean.

I was truly awed: I had never really put it all together. *Loads pressure, this huge rock trying crush you—one day you're walloped to the surface and seen. Shit, we go through makes us all the beautiful diamond later…the vibration of love. All the energy that goes into creating the molecules that hold this organic matter. All the energy vibrating my being.* I sat sipping Mint Verbena tea; like natural high.

Bean tickling cheeky, "Then pulled out of the Earth like a tooth in the socket of someone's mouth, for your girlish pleasure! Tee-hee-hee."

My grin dropped then. *Yeah, the mines are run by rich corporation-enslaving African miners; then dynamite hulled and sold through global Disney-fairy-tale advertisers that tell us, "A gal must measure her self-worth by ounces set in platinum, become chattels to man!"* Hitchhiking around out West, the feminists had drilled my skull. K-turn: *You think too much. Get with where the value is.* Flapping lashes at old Rex.

"Diamonds are valued by how closely they resemble a drop of spring water!" Bean touted.

"At the Gemological Institute of America (GIA) we use a color scale grading system. D the whitest, Z yellow. Boron in the carbon makes them blue, nitrogen yellow, lattice imperfections create brown, radiation turns the hue a greenish."

I started thinking about all the people who said I'd never amount to anything. Superintendent, Jersey High called me down to his office, after I'd been date raped by the lead in the school musical, and the town turned hating on me, said, "If you aren't careful, young lady, you are going to end up living in one of those refrigerator boxes on the streets one day. Is that what you want out of life?"

With Rex my mind said, *Damn, I'm good. Fuck you. I'm rich.*

"Oh, Rex, if I buy a red rock, I'd want it to be a real ruby. Blue, I'd want a real sapphire. Green, emerald!" I swooned.

Rex smile-drool. I liked having all of his attention; his quiver in my hand. I must be brilliant: *All the lines I have dished since date one with Rex. My insistent contrarian, "I will not talk marriage. I will not have sex; I don't have sex until I'm married."* Rated myself an untouchable marvel: *If I keep practicing this trade,* I could have satins, furs, successful men dangling from each finger.

"When I have my treasure chest of pure whites, Rex, I'll request the colors for Valentine's gifts. Just to expand my trove…" Added, I, touching his knee. *Fuck true love.*

S-Bean rallied, "The dark world of inclusions."

The GIA clarity scales, "Tidbits of minerals nearby trapped inside the slowly cooling pure carbon diamond causes the internal inclusions and surface blemishes." He magnified for me the utter mess inside the VS 1/2 or SI 1/2 (very slightly flawed and slightly included) and I 2/3 (Inclusions obvious).

I skylarked Rex. "Girls like me do not settle for any kind of defective varmint pimple lodging inside her diamond! Gosh if I wore that on my finger, surely I'd have constant headaches. Rather like the Princess and the Pea!"

"Internally flawless diamonds are extremely rare, dear! Most are Very Slightly or Slightly Included. Certainly, a VS 1 or VS 2 could be made yours. I would not ask a wonderful lady, with a particular eye to limit herself," retorted Rexie.

Crimson dive mortified moment of self-questioning: *If this guy actually has real feelings for me, what kind of shallow am I, taking him for a hayride?* My reply: *He is a sycophant. I don't owe him. I never told Rex I wanted to be with him—all I'd said was, 'yes.' I am doing Rex a service. Allowing him to purchase one dreamy afternoon fantasy-filled with hope that he won't just become an old, boring, fat, rich, sexless divorcee.*

I also wanted to teach the entitled fuck a lesson: *you can't buy people. Could I be bought?*

I had felt I was a Jezebel so long—Mom calling me before fifth grade, "you slut," and her breaking down, "I'm jealous"—while she kept her drunk in the house grabbing at me. She never sat with me, discussing my ever being wedded, or a mother, or even falling love.

I did have true love fantasies in my heart: My own frilly picture. My guy will travel the world, with his own hands he will dig from the earth or scan private gem trades—mine me a special emerald hunk, bring it back for us, raw. Have it set. We will make music together.

At Fortunoff, eyeing the lo-down with Rex, I knew, *Clearly, Rex is not that guy. This is my: Today I'll do this; tomorrow I will get it right.*

Beanman: "Marry her at once, Sir Revan! Most feasty gals in the imperplexity of their cunning cunts have their eyes set on exactly what they want before they even meet the man!"

Revan's eyes bulged true verdant.

Señor Stringbean buckled; excused himself as though he'd burped loudly, wiping corners his mouth.

I sat straight, wishing Verbena to champagne, silent. The scene flew fiercely.

Bean, sweating bullets to make the sale, strapped on his lavender striped ascot went to work obsessively illuminating, navigating, ogling each heavyweight three-dimensional of the finest values, "Cuts of marquise, pear, oval, emerald, hearts, cushions, triangles, round, bridal, Asscher, halo, canary fancy, radiant, princess." Settings: "Three-stone, pave, solitaire, side-stone, diamond band, antiqued, or traditional modern!"

Finale: Magical mystery tour fanfare, his arms waving up:

"Honey, you can pick what we have here, have it sized in thirty minutes, and flounce today with a new ring truly yours from Fortunoff! Or if nothing sticks you right, one of our approved jewelers will come in now, help you choose, build your own dream ring and within thirty days you will be galloping toward that happy-ending sunset life has waiting just for you. Lady's choice."

Rex began clapping "bravo," as though he'd just seen a new baroque pastiche.

S-Bean lost his marbles. I really did wonder if he were a Muppet of sort. Poor man flopped a chair, *wonk, soft, zonk*; deflated.

Revan lay his crusty skin hand on my bare sun-dressed Picasso print shoulder.

Me: I came full stop to my senses. My fairy tale wingtips disintegrated—Red alert brow zing-zang up. *This dude doesn't even know your name, he's considering laying down at least thirty grand. Where's the trick?*

Mind flipped like fish pulled from sea, examining various angles this surprise charade Rex had sprung. *Could this be some kind of a criminal setup? If I accept the ring and walk, am I held accountable based on my lies? I am already married.*

Must call Sam before green-lighting mission.

"Rex? I'm getting so flushed! I'll be right back." I, she, Cindy: dashed for the loo.

Ducked—*Privacy.* Stairwell. One bare bulb above my head, blinking buzzing fluorescent stuck flat.

"Hello?" Sam's gravel.

Psychic sixth sense, he had. Sam could disappear late night. Not answer. If I ever really needed Sam dire, no forewarning: he always picked up or showed up, always.

Heart racing. Scoop.

"No, he can't arrest you, baby, it's a gift. If you're already there, take it."

"I miss you." He missed me, too.

"I'll split the cash down the middle if we sell it. For now, I'll wear it. Tell everyone you bought it."

We said we loved each other.

I marched back. "Rex!" Sealed purchase.

"One pear-shaped diamond 3.94 carats G + VSI1 + in 4-point platinum side stone 2 round 1.5 carats brilliants."

Fitted. Shined. Walked with. No hassle.

That burgundy velvet, Bean office, a window overlooking New York's bustling Fifth Avenue in May, Rex took my hand. Slid cool platinum down my naked right fourth. Dropped his voice two octaves, deep in my eyes sincerely. (Imagine Mozart's "Allegro" from *A Little Night Music.*)

"Dear Cindy," Rex said.

"A friendship ring, no strings. Life is most pleasurable when a special young lady who ought to know her wonder, allows me to laden her with gifts of caliber."

Smokin' lingo Revan. I really didn't know if I was happy or sick.

Relative Dance

That's how Rex and Cindy ended up back at Hudson's.

Manager Felipe, a worried slight man from Northern Africa, appeared from the back office. Inclined to muttering talks with Revan on leaders Boukrouh, Ghozali, Party of Renewal; economic crisis as justification for power; reforms due to International Money Fund, World Bank. "We are inventors of our pasts and prisoners of our future," he said, popping chilled Dom, complimentary: circa 1985...

Rex bellowed, "Oh, *contraire*, kind sir, we are prisoners of our pasts and inventors of our futures! Miss Cindy, what do you think?"

I raised glass, *a prisoner to all and none?* I repeated his line and got the crowds approval.

Rex bellowed toasts, "May we never go dim in the hearth of our hearts! And May the good Lord bring us love, we never take for granted."

Frank dropped a lit layered vanilla red velvet. Cindy and Rex blew wishes. Fed each other forkfuls.

When Miss Singer ramped up her oldie version of "My Mother's Son-in-Law"—'course I knew every word. My connection to my creative left me feeling like something stuck between like a buffoon, traitor and simply breezy, high falutin'. Unbreakable on my finger felt good. Something Cindy felt born for—*living a life like Jackie O*...filled with glitter, intrigue.

Rex's throat stuffing delight, "Rich fluffy inner texture, scrumptious cream filling."

Pause: Stark usual reality-crossed coal in my skull: *Ho-hum—simply not compatible. How I hate a person recounting a meal play by play. I've always wished, imagined myself relaxing in a world of galactic orgasm. Like on a roller coaster before the next major drop hill—Stars, colors, bliss! Rex wasn't that.*

Rex was, talking, "I'm so blessed to have found true love again."

Insisting audaciously, he, "And now that you've shown me you love me, too, I can confess how I fell. Saw you are the kind of girl waiting for a man she can provide a wife. Warm cooking. Sleeping, a house filled with only people who share your same DNA structure, one rhythm…"

Later that evening, Rex laid news that he'd gone bought a five-room Park Slope apartment, down the street from his daughters. Invited Cindy to, "share her lady's touch, make it comfy."

Gag—none of this gave me any hot stuff between my legs. *No man should use the fucking word comfy.*

I was getting angry. I had no clue where Rex was getting off with this public celebration crap. I felt used. Far as knew, he'd made it clear back at the point of purchase: This was a friendship ring.

Cindy feigned, cool, "Rex darling, I have a horrid, allergy to strollers! I get real itchy when they're nearby!" Rex didn't laugh.

"Love Potion Number Nine," from the band, Four Clovers.

Frank dropped a pair of double snifter peach-pear nectar aperitifs. I slammed. Dunk, wallop, downed: *Alakazam flash gleaming high road Batman, no shit I swear on fucking Tombouctou.* Booze made it all go soft and lighten up.

I touched Rex, "I invite you to slip with me, inside a sliver, the one that exists only now, at any given moment and may never be recreated again."

It means: "Let's dance."

"Silent Rules of Seduction:" When a guy got handsy, desperate, harassing—I'd make it romantic. Works wonders, ladies. Instead of getting mad, get the guy to calm, simmer. We have that power. Guess, it brings soothing, which is all they really want. It's all anyone wants, to be held, soothed, told they are wonderful, touched, loved.

I leaned my head Rex's big man's shoulder, we stood and swayed like couples at the prom. Ultraslow. His pecker against my thigh. Actually, I had started to wonder whether the guy could get it up. He wasn't demanding sex for all he'd given—I couldn't figure.

Rex was silent, humming. Vibrating plane vulnerable, we were. Right there beside their table, Hudson. *Pianist's scamper up, down black, whites…something to this slowness…Like a crazy baby staring a mobile…watching swirling color, moving, sound. Calms us, everyone: to present.*

"Dancing with you contradicts Einstein's theory of special relativity, written in 1905," this Nobel scientist man used to say, visited Cindy a lot at Darlings, awhile—he *was* Nobel. He had given me his business card. —strange slimy teeth, sweaty palms, loose skin, zero fat. Wasn't much more to say on the guy's appearance. Polo cologne. I always walking away with his smell all over my hair. Pictures of my own dad came to mind. Dad bathed in Polo after he left Mom. His red Toyota blasting Phil Collins "Sussudio" air drumming against the steering wheel, reeking. Weird, remembering Dad mixed with stripping.

Nobel got to rapping Western music theory one night, Einstein's theory of special relativity: "Everything moves at the same rate, in relation to one another," Albert Einstein was quoted as having written. Normally applied to the speed of light. It proposed new concepts for space and time—interwoven into a single continuum known as space-time.

"The speed of light in a vacuum is independent of the motion of all observers," Einstein discovered. "Events that occur at the same time could occur at a different time for another." Makes us need to keep time, I figured.

I'm always a nerd for scientific theories. I get turned on by that shit.

"In certain higher gravitational fields," Nobel told me, "Sometimes time dilates to such intensity that rays of light actually bend. You, my dear, possess that kind of gravitational field, in human form!"

How I had giggled, in his bony ear. His real long, chicken-taut neck, covered little red goose ass rash: "You ought to bottle it—you'd be a millionaire." *Hey—nice to hear, 3:00 a.m. middle of a shit hole.*

Back to Carats at Hudson parade:

"We're slipping inside the spaces between the notes," I said to Rex ear dancing. "Everything around, in us, is vibration."

"See, in the West," I whispered on, "We tune instruments to concert A, an orchestra's on pitch at 440 Hertz. Our piano plays the exact same note for G-sharp and A-flat. A sliding note instrument, you hear a million delicate tonations between each full stop—we miss so much playing the scales in Western music. Eastern scales have quarter steps in their scales, and still," my yearning for more…

"But think of it," I let fly. "We are myriads of subdivisions of vibrational input, our senses our bodies take in; these notes, plus harmonics just a sliver, every millisecond. So much passion."

Both heads flew back laughing—Cindy and Rex. Holding each other up in that fake wedding celebration champagne lounge, swaying for dear life.

I actually forgot for a minute then, that I was a drunk liar Rainbow turned Trash Girl. *Did I deserve a better life? Am I growing like oysters and Frank? Starting to like everything Rex is exposing me to. Old Rex has a class I have a natural inclination toward. Is Rex a better life just because he offers cushion and money? Or should I stay in something like Sam, something familiar and maybe…What is the value of life?*

I didn't think I deserved much more than just day to day survival. A survivor trains themselves to feel nothing: trust no one; do anything to get by.

I had no idea what fulfillment meant, or what—some luxury I laughed off for some softee.

***

Miami Interlude: Cyberfuck of the Mind

Life. It's a no-nonsense, swanky mess that sometimes hurls a wallop of fly excrement in your face, ends up splattering dunk up your nostrils, and fuck, ya gotta deal. Shit's always happening way before you make sense of it. Things came to light in a way I could not ignore.

One-week prior Jet Blue-ing Miami.

Sun.

Sam and I decided we needed some sun.

Part II: Interlude Miami

Azure

"Babe, relax, let me rock you," Sam pushed my sunburned ass against the cotton bone sheet. Miami. South Beach. I wrapped my limbs tight around his, let my inside muscles go flesh, grabbed his hips; diamond head cock thrust deep into that pristine spot, and *Oh God;* he shivered liquid inside. *How the hell can sex be so maddeningly beautiful...life so fucked...*I came to from milky orgasm. Waves lapping outside. My head pounding.

Sam picked up his mobile. Dialed his sis, Barbie—DD, bleach blonde, Mercedes SLK500. Struck up some rapid raspy half-Spanish talk about "her." Which I soon figured was me.

Earlier that day, three of us had sat slathering cream among other topless tawny tanners perched on sand loungers, soaking rays under a blue sky by Jacuzzi pools, tapping painted toes to island sounds. Barbie and Sam had turned on me, "You have such a perfect ass, honey!"

Sam pointing to the Giselle-slim ass I had had my whole life. "All she has to do is get that edge off right here!" Detailing my glute curve, where ass meets upper thigh, with his finger, showing chatty Barbie.

I figured Sam just hated me—Plus, maybe his head was full of ass. *Silent Seduction Rules:* You can learn a lot about a person by the kind of porn they get off on—Sex flicks I'd found newly rented and stashed back at our apartment. All butts. Girls on fours, fucking anal, at least two guys. Not to mention other weird things I had seen. Like Sam's laptop. Don't miss this sentence: I'd picked up Sam's laptop to print some audition scripts, and a gay IM'er logged over, looking for a guy he described exactly as Sam. I engaged his IM and asked him to describe 'me.' Said they met the other night on E. 80 and Second Ave.

I was growing silently convinced that some joker had placed heavy sandbags in my limbs. I was lost for a cure.

South Beach hotel, I swung open the balcony doors. Scarlet sun gone dim, dusk moon up. Orange fabric swaying steadily on futon platform bed cabanas lining beachfront; turquoise silver rims, aqua sea. Rex rock my finger, dancing rainbows in the sun. Sam yakking Spanish in the bath.

Sam had just cum in me. I told him not to. Sam did whatever he wanted. We'd just celebrated our first year married. I wasn't sure why we were there. Sam had booked the room for a week.

We had dropped into Tiffany before we split, bought a new man band for Sam. I could tell he got uptight, people stopping us on the street admiring my 3.94 + 3 in restaurants, "Lucky girl!" they'd say, look at Sam. He'd just smile, took the praise. I kept telling myself, *Universe works in weird ways*— Somehow I felt Sam had bought it for me. Guess I wished it so. We both did.

Ocean's noisy churning blend wind whistle seemed to howl a repetitive ghost-like hymn, awakened some fragile unsettled yearning. I wanted a child with Sam. Did I? Perhaps Rex's family rap was making me consider what I, then, considered low-class thoughts: *'baby-making.'*

When I was thirteen, my dad had scoffed, "You'll probably be one of those teenage dropouts, pregnant by sixteen." He felt that women who made babies were of the weaker class, underachievers.

Sam and I never discussed it. Career to pursue, I told myself. Acting school almost over. *I am too messed-up to raise a child*—

Caribbean maid hoisting *climp-clomp* mop, bucket on wooden spiral stairs, how her braids swung; raspy lilting laugh in the breeze, managing a blab on her cell as she cleaned.

Rex—over cold shrimp, Goose pools before I split New York. I'd told him I had booked a part in a film and was on a "two-week shoot, Columbia film." It was true. I'd booked a sci-fi musical short film. A Bettie Paige look-alike nymph traipsing nature half-clad singing Porter standards—Rex loved that. So'd I. Actually, filming was set to begin in one week.

"You must return by June 21st," Rex instructed.

"I've arranged your singing date at Lucky Strike, the highly respected jazz venue in town, for that evening."

Rex then informed, "We'll have a special table of VIPs, special acquaintance contacts I've invited. I'd like to help you get your career off the bench."

I was shitting bricks. Too mortified to sing in public.

"Why not bring Mitch along to the gig?" Rex suggested. Rex had a good memory. I, as tipsy Cindy with Rex, had mentioned a brother, named Mitchell a few times, I had slip-mentioned his script, a few times, put him in LA.

I had invented Mitch in case I wanted to bring Sam into the picture, with me and Rex. I thought it may help me to have a family member along, to gain respect from Rex, and to help me and Sam with possible financial connections toward her musical career and his celluloid success.

Drop jaw, the reality though.

"I have a special interest in his script," Rex spelled.

"I would like to discuss partnering as a producer," Revan bellowed.

"This wouldn't be the first time in history a young starlet's rich gent friend got behind the wheel to deliver a supernova such as yourself to public eyes and ears!"

My best Mona Lisa.

Kicker was, Rex next threw down a fucking winning proposal: "I would like to secure you a cash loan. Perhaps a sum of twenty thousand dollars, my dear." He didn't have the dockets just yet.

"Negotiations with my accounting team. Freeing liquid," deliberated, he.

Shockers, me. Humor: We must have different definitions for the word liquid, but hey, a gal can't refuse the cold gs.

"I'd like to help you decide how to spend it, securing your future—first we need to discuss contracts. You will have to pay me back when you make enough as a recording artist, and actress, of course."

Why is he so gung ho to get behind my singing? He'd only heard me sing at the club, that naive happy-go-Cindy, singing Sade in his ear, or then at Hudson's, I'd sung some of "Cry like a Baby." Then singing standards in this short film.

Rex said, "My lawyer is drawing papers."

I—toasted. Drank. But—Rex still didn't know anything: my real name, history?!

I slipped a cute joke, "Rather, just meet in a hotel, we could romp any which way you please in exchange for the suitcase of cash, love!"

Rex had chuckled, "Keep in touch while you are away, is all I ask," Rex handed Cindy a working red Nokia, mobile.

Sam's idea—he had suggested I tell Rex to get me a phone on his family plan. Only use it for Rex calls. Solved constant Revan hounding me, digits.

How I hate to be kept on a leash. Cindy planted lips to his cheek, "Yes, doll, I'll phone you every day!"

Carrying that ugly piece of plastic phone on my person the whole time under hot sun Miami—perhaps as a silent getaway tool—felt to me like the smell of a wasted mouse stuck behind a kitchen wall. Can't dig it out, won't go away. But, I looked on Rex like my job, my employer—and a pretty good one was shaping up at that.

Cock

Pop champagne. Sam cam prancing out of the bathroom phone-chat, Barbie, prancing around naked; erect sculpture in hand. Spinning it like a favorite toy. Sam seemed to have a new fascination: Sam and his cock in the world. He'd been doing this a lot lately.

"Worship me May?"

I was fingering new Chanel. We'd stopped by the Bal Harbour shop that morning. Before jetting NY, I'd slipped a chat with my "personal Chanel sales-gal" on 57th and Fifth. Returned a few items Rex had chosen for me, I barely liked. Made the gal promise, secret, call down Miami shop and set up a credit-exchange. *He'd never notice.*

"You're going to love it, Cindy!" the gal had squealed.

"Chanel buyer selections will be fresh South Beach style. Much younger."

Sam grandly picked me a pair strappy silver heels, sparkly denim satin three-quarter pants, knit tunic for the exchange.

We had plans to dine with Barbie and her also husband named Sam, that evening.

"I'll tell them you took me on a Chanel spree this afternoon!" I la-la'd Sam.

"They'll be so impressed!" He, jolly, threw in a silk Chanel scarf, special for himself.

Really—Sam really didn't seem mind Rex's dime. I was starting to think he wanted a sugar paps as well. *Who wouldn't really?*

Getting hip to it all, this designer lifestyle; had never known or considered that runway selection would be different relevant to the region. What could be in store for me, in Chanel, Paris? Venice. Munich. *How can I get there, on Rex's dime, my rules, and keep Sam cool?*

I really did love Sam's particulars: diamond head; rim-lip at least a quarter-inch raised around its base, top of the shaft; so beautiful. Yet, I'd picked up a bit of a virus of the mind. I didn't want to say no to sex with Sam when he wanted, frankly—was afraid he'd go somewhere else. Nagging—*the laptop troll.*

9 For 9

Sam's laptop: me. Alone. Sam was tending bar. He'd picked up a barkeep thing at a Flatiron martini bar, good for small-time China (that's cocaine) dealing, and some cashed-up customer relations while he lagged on the Jess plan.

I just wanted the next day's audition script, as I said. Sam's gig was hooked up to the printer, *Wi-Fi*—My laptop wasn't configured yet, new Internet system I usually signed dial-up, plug-in through the phone jack. It was year 2000, stone ages. I signed on Sam's computer using an old shared AOL screen name Sam and I had started year or so back.

'I'd never IM'd. I could have kept it that way, but I'm a curious cat—and we all know what happened to that wondering fuckin' furball.

IM balloon popped. '*Wat r u up to?*' Sender's name: *'UES 70s Male.*

I typed back: *'Hi.'*

"Want to get together?" UES 70s Male said.

"Have we met?" I typed.

"Yes. Live around the block. Eight inches, thick rim." Sent a pic. Cock out. Goatee, blond.

"I don't remember. Nice pic. Describe me?" Expected this dude to describe Eric; I knew Eric had been playing with the laptop, I'd seen him over the house a few times in passing.

Nabbed Sam to T. *"Writer. Latin. Curved nose. Nine-inch cock."*

Added: *"Dreams of licking your cock again."*

Creepy. Felt like I had rodent scabies scratching under my skin. Totally forgot the audition. Ping-pong brain. I didn't have any real facts from this monkey horse's mouth—Sam was due to be back in an hour or three. I guess most wives trust their husbands and don't scoundrel. I decided I had to excavate.

Typed (pretending to be Sam): *"Refresh. I meet a lot of peeps. What did we do?"*

UES 70s Male pinged. *"Corner. East Eighty-Four and Third. Tuesday evening after 11:00. You had gold paint on your hands; said you'd been painting your new apartment."*

My head filled with steam. Sam doesn't work Tuesdays and I was out with Rex. We had been painting the shit railroad gold trim.

UES 70s MALE: "Went back to my place East Seventy-Ninth Street. "

'Slapping. Biting. Licked your asshole rim, Finger dipping—" gist. *Whoa—and oh fuck this is my life.* My mouth dry as gravel; heart crushed between like King Kong paws. My whirling blender mind stuck like stuffed with too much ice. Rapid fire questions expounded off one another fast, **1>** *You can't get on Sam about this. Who are you accusing Sam of anything? You worked and he was cool.* **Me>** *It's part of the job, letting them touch—it's money, extra tips. Sam doesn't tell you every time he gives a drink away at the bar.* **2>** *Maybe Sam just needs to go through this. I will wait quietly until he is ready to come to me.* **3>** *We all need to explore; you can never own anyone.* **4>** *Sam is a loser and you're too good for him.*

Kept hearing Sam: "You're the most prude stripper I've ever met!" he said it a lot. *I should loosen up.*

I remembered a conversation Sam and I had had around turn of the New Year. Sam wanted to try swinging with other couples.

I said I wanted to keep sex special. *Random sex with strangers just for fun?* Entertainment for money seemed more acceptable to me. *—when you cross that line, how do you come back. When is anything sacred again?*

But I had told Sam, "Sure. I'll try it." *Don't want to be chalked prude.*

He had put an ad on Craigslist, looking for a couple to play with.

A few pics some couples had sent him. *Old, ugly, fat*—I hadn't green-lit any.

—cyberfuck IM—I looked through Sam's laptop photos and found a bunch of solo naked cocks: torsos; eight-pack abs; rock quads.

I recalled; Sam had told me about Eric's IM lust storms back in Chelsea. I computed: *Eric must be trolling get laid on Sam's computer.*

Apparently, Craigslist and a pile different screen names get any gay guy, any corner Manhattan, laid 24/7 free—"To relax," Sam had described it, "when he's on break from his law studies. Eric dashes out to some random apartment, laughing over his shoulder, 'A real man never uses his hands!' He'd be back in thirty-minutes refreshed—usually head, could be anything." Sam thought it was kinda funny. I was wide-eyed to the newly popular cybersex hook-up culture.

Thing was, with Eric: I hadn't seen Sam wired on cocaine since the first couple of months we met. Now, with Eric was the new usual. Careened last time he was over the apartment, "Sammy, we're gonna get our grow-houses in Miami finally! Seeds and clippings," Eric.

See, if I'm not moving too fast for you, it's like this. Sam had sunk into a quick heroin relapse that first six months we were together. I had found his dope stash in the bathroom at one of the sublets, Stuy. I snorted it all up myself. I had no interest in being a junky; was *prove a point to him.*

"You do it I do it," I said hotly. Sliding down the bathroom wall, dancing naked to Tricky's album *Maxinquaye,* British trip-hop. Nodding.

Freaked old Sammy out: "You can't become a junky, babe!" He went to detox and hadn't touch that or coke since.

I thought all that was behind us. Sam always claimed, "White pony sure way get old horse prancing back in." (That means heroin if you don't know). Now the Eric, IM trolls?

Suddenly this shmoozeball locust scene makes looney tunes Rex seem Easter Sunday cakewalk.

Cats-chasing-tails, I started writing my journal, 'Maybe Eric is Sam's salve for Rex; Rex my salve for Sam's dope; Dope was Sam's for my stripping; tick-tock; When does it end—It's a necessary evil, when your heart is hurting—to finding a way not to ease the stinger's pain. What if Rex becomes my salve again now for Eric? Was my stripping for Mom's Polish boyfriend; Dope for Sam's Uncle tying him up? Will I leave Sam for Rex? Scary.

Time pounded my head. I wanted answers.

I got an AOL, a 24-hour service person on the phone.

"Well," her Texan fingernails scraped my bones, "I have a list of every single screen name and date enrolled, but can't provide detailed log times or anything. I can e-mail you some now, and send a certified mail copy, for your records."

I was aghast reading four pages: "Big 9 for 9. Big 9 for 10. 9 of Steel," one after the next, on and on. Kept telling myself, *it's all Eric.*

Sam has always shone braggart from day one meeting, "Babe, look at my big nine-inch cock!" Said he'd measured it.

Hey—certain things, you just say, "yes, honey." *Hell—his stick works for me.*

I will keep shut, I told myself—but within ten minutes of Sam opening the bedroom home from work; I opened my flood-trap. Told Sam the whole story, every single detail. My flushed cheeks strangely plastered in a big smile. Acting happy when devastated, like I had perfected in kidhood.

"Are you crazy?" Sam didn't seem half-phased. He dropped his work clothes. Climbed in bed.

"Babe, if I were gay, I'd hide it a lot better than that."

Hm, true.

"Those were Eric's pics; you saw him playing on my computer the other night."

Yes.

"Probably all, Eric," Sam said.

"He knew I was at work. Probably saw me (you) online, started fucking with me. Knew it might be you—toyed with your head on purpose."

"Why would Eric fuck with my head?"

"'Cause he's an asshole. Let me tell you, babe, if you think I'm gay, surely you've been reading too many Tennessee Williams plays."

Could be true.

The marriage thing was hard—

Rules of Marriage

Sleepless starry nights, whirling marbleized in my mind were cinematic films: Sepia-toned, images of gay men—Sam the star.

Ten Rules for Marriage, Little White Chapel, Vegas gave to us. "Don't go to bed mad, apologize first, pick your battles…" Me and Sam used to read it together after a fight. It would help. Suddenly to me that seemed: *tawdry crap for toddlers.*

Like cold chills gurgling through electric shocks, I wanted to ask those Ten Rules: *How much space is too much space to give your spouse? When is that space called denial? When does it become that endless chasm of unspoken shit you can't ever come back across?*

I asked Sam, in daylight, "What should I do?"

"You're delusional," he said: "Focus on acting. You pay problem attention, stronger it gets, babe."

Bottom line: *Sam may be putting your health at risk. You need to know if he's lying so you can protect yourself.*

Sam had a therapist, he had told me a few months back. I looked through his desk and found her card. Shrink—the suffix on her cognomen—ski. I never on my life—the ring of those Polish names always: *shudder.* I called the ski shrink anyway—*answers.*

Doc Ski, Ph.D. requested, "Tell Sam you called," she said.

She'd do the same. She wanted to see us together.

Doc Ski

Sam in dust lavender Kenneth Cole, I in Ann Taylor plum twirl, shirt to match. 2:00 p.m. Special sure to abstain from the sauce before this big meeting put my sarcastic ambiguous haughty copping at its peak high.

Strolling Upper East Side Manhattan's depressing act of bland: high-rises, doctor offices, Irish bars, chain shops, thinking, *Wasting my goddamned midday, visiting a clinical shithole to find out if my husband is sexing men*: *WTF?*

On the usual, when I was in pain, I played false regale theatrics, like playing Miss Austen's Elizabeth Bennet from *Pride and Prejudice,* snarking at Sam for his choice in doc 'ski.'

A door swung. "Hello," Ms. Ski, Ph.D. nodded. Fifty-something—salty black clipped curls, glasses colored red. Woolen knee-length navy suit skirt, navy square toe-heel three inches. Nude yet very thick almost tights. The kind only still thin enough to be classified as non-sheen pantyhose. Cheap gold anchor buttons lined her single-breasted jacket.

—*I smell mothballs.* Ski perched an oversize-library quilted leather. Heavy blue ballpoint clicked on white ruled tab.

Doc Ski's stockings—I wanted to ask her, 'Are you covering varicose veins? Then why not pants? Wishing be stylish, yet shy from silky sheen real stockings that show a bit of skin beneath, because you fear appearing sexy in the business setting? Then try black?'

I believed: A truly powerful woman will bring forth intellect by embodying her full sexual being.

I couldn't help deduct—this bird may lack the smart-sharp wit necessary to wrangle inside the psyche patterns of Sam (and me).

Ski cut to it. Her high-horse throttle: Dishing juice she claimed Sam had squeezed her way about me—details of my childhood, history prior to me and Sam's meeting, even our recent spats. HE final statement: "Your husband asked me to bring forward the present issues. You spending time with this other, older gentleman."

Sam nodded. *Fucking likely Sam harnessed one of his tricks for distracting subject. He is the queen bee of this. She isn't fly to his games?* Fuck it was me against them.

Chanel. The club. How I met Rex. Why he buys me things. Ski wanted to know it all—the ring stayed out, no mention. I was surprised—but, Doc Ski harped on my Chanel in particular. Seemed to get her goat.

If we shopped Gap, would you feel better, babe? I wanted to ask.

"Think of me like Sharon Stone in the movie *The Muse*," I explained, "We give the man my time. No sex. He's going through a divorce, I help give inspiration. He gifts money—he has a thing for Chanel. I don't argue. I've been honest with Sam from the start. Share with him whatever I get."

"You are asking Sam to compete in an arena he isn't fit for financially," Ski said.

"Maybe I ought to have used *The Gift of the Magi* example instead of *The Muse*." I grimaced.

Story: two people who sell their most prized possessions to get the other person what they desire, out of true love. Ski and Sam gave her sneer-lip-with-straight-eyes combo.

"My concern is about being subject to disease if Sam isn't honest about random infidelities with men," I said.

Sam, blarney tantrum, "She's crazy! Gets things in her head! Can't let go! Drives me fucking nuts!"

In boiled legalese, like Ski was Judge Judy, I handed over the four-page Xerox certified copy AOL documents I'd acquired via mail.

"This appears to me like it was some kind of an Internet prank," Ski stated. "I do have a concern that your husband uses sessions like confession. Dumping; reenacting the same behavior weekly. But I assure you, your husband is not sleeping with men. Ought to be the least of your worries."

Sam beamed her way, "Yeah honey! She always tells me that—about the confessional thing."

I looked at Ski looking at Sam. Figured she meant he was sleeping with broads. *Who gives a shit? So goddamned exhausted.* Hadn't slept in days…No answers. *I'm going to have to live with this…can't hear anything, sounds fuzzy.*

Suddenly: I decided right there: Sam's been telling Ski exact details of what he'd been up to: only switching the gender from men to women.

My mind flash: Ski is unhappy, her lame husband sits in front of world news channels at night, dry discussions over four-course meals—all Ski can think of is Sam. Week after week Sam visits. Tells her stories. He and a blonde in a back alley, a redhead with an ass like a basketball on the floor, in club bathrooms, nineteen-year-old rock-hard body in the back of a cab. HE says

149

women, but they are all real men. Ski is so engulfed in her anxiety, using all her energy to mask wanting Sam—vetoes her ability to look at Sam's stuff, to read him…*I knew her stockings were fishy traits, unresolved sex stuff*

Twizzler twist: Ski buys without question, his stories as fact; Sam gets to believe his own stories. Even wakes up mornings (when I believe we are most in touch with our truth and foibles and lies and like) he still feels okay.

"Sam, well I don't think he has been honest with you," I told Ski.

She glowered, "Are you aware that you live your life setting up circumstance which gives you an excuse to get out?" She added, "Sabotaging your marriage."

"She's my little runaway!" Sam's tousled my hair.

Ski wanted to speak with me alone. Sam left.

Her scrutinizing, pen in hand, "Your creative life is causing a roadblock with your intimacies."

I could not peel my eyes from the dirty, cheap, Venetian blind blocking back alley view. Sam been saying lately then, he wanted "a more normal life, filled with 'couple' things"—watch TV, shopping, eating. I called it, *unfocused mainstream lollygagging, distractions that suffocate life force.*

"I never thought of myself as artistic." To me, artistic meant you create something of value. I was just a charlatan. Mom had told me my whole life— 'You don't have an artist's mind. Aidan is the true artist in the family.'

"I have like a monkey my back," I told Doc Ski. "I'm not a real artist. I just burn off emotional grit, vicious self-questioning. Creative helps."

Ski wanted to know when I had started being so creative.

"Guess poems as a kid, songs, color. Nothing I created worth speaking."

Silence. I *have* always appreciated a chick who understands quiet.

"I don't understand. Sam had a fucked-up kidhood, too." *With his uncle touching him and all*, I didn't say. Didn't know how much he'd revealed. "Sam says he's an artist, but—he's just treating me like a wifey. Wants drag me to Bed Bath & Beyond, Kenneth Cole. Then he wants to do drinks with other couples, people he'd met at the bar, to discuss their Hamptons houses," I told her, "He seems to be giving into adjusted society persons, boring."

Ski told me, "Sam had a stable family. Values to draw from." I was in horror—Sam been raised with unshakeable suburban Catholic values. He still has it in him. *Softee Wannabe?*

Ski illuminated further, "Sam is using his script, the story, as a way to get closer to his family. He thinks he's not interesting, unless he becomes a big shot. Yet he admits to me—he yearns for that family man life more than anything, and wants it with you—but you will not allow."

Air, once a purple-lavender, turned gray through the edges of those classless blinds. Shiver: *He's a poser. We met in Sam-rebel phase. Deep down he's a normie, softee wannabe…*

Like an old ship's drone—Ski: "What do you feel alone that you can't when you're with Sam, or others, I presume?"

"Getting rid of everything. I feel most powerful, free, weak at once. Like tiny and big. Can't explain…I don't understand myself. I hate fucking words they confuse me."

I didn't know much about myself; wasn't sex abuse, or what it does to a kid, or any of that in my opinion. It was Sam. He was the fuck up—these were my boring marriage gripes.

Wham. Ski ended session right then. "You might consider therapy yourself." Handed some lady doc's card. "Good luck to you."

I wanted to scribble Ski's face with the blue ballpoint.

Chooch

"I'm not dealing with you fucked up," Sam tossed.

Miami hotel—*Cocaine is up.* He was cutting a few lines the stone slab, "Coke at low doses will keep you good and social. A rolled bill."

Now Sam was getting down on my drunken daisy. Yeah, I fell over. I pissed on my own clothes. My tongue forked black venom. Like often as you cooking eggs in the a.m., maybe. Fill in those blanks. Sam was sick of it.

The first time we'd gone to meet his parents, just after we got married. Fort Meyers, I'd gotten sloshed and thrown a fit because his Mom and friends were talking Spanish. I wanted to feel like I finally had a mom, and she wasn't paying love to me like I wanted. Sam said she was just giving me space, he had trained her not to ask questions. Then his Mom had been so sweet to me, when she realized I wanted love like that. I almost couldn't take that either. Love, no love, yes, love. I was confused. Drunk for me was not hot.

Miami, Sam took me, his wife of one year, all over. He spilled coke in me everywhere we went. I was on display…

"My girl's in a movie! Isn't she beautiful?" Sam raved.

"A real sci-fi musical—Bettie Paige look-alike yep—black bangs, and all!" For the part.

Sam's dad even had my 8 × 10 acting headshot silver-framed in the family gallery. One of me and Sam year the before, in Fort Meyers, smiling on the beach.

"Yep, she's a 1940s pinup dash Barbarella-dressed nymph; sand dunes, spaceships, all while singing a Gershwin tune, 'But Not for Me,' and Johnny Mercer's 'I Thought About You.'" Sam was so proud.

I felt real stupid, getting everyone's attention like that. My Mom would have given me a dirty glare and told me I was being a slut.

But hell—I even sang out my throaty siren, "They're singing songs of love, but not for me…" at the dinner table for all: *Holy Toledo. Actually didn't ribbet!*

"What a voice!" Sam's uncles, aunts, mom, sisters, they all swooned, jumped up clapping, "you're going to go far, young lady!"

Whole place so full, joyful celebration. I kept on flying chatty center! Posing pictures with his family; making cocktail chat with this sister, that. People started dancing. Family friends grabbed me, taught me salsa, rhumba. *I guess that's what family is supposed to feel like? Or is it cocaine?* Become your favorite superhero instantly, bursting talent, muscles extraordinaire every orifice.

"It's so nice to see you light and breezy!" Barbie twisted my way. Everyone was real impressed with my Chanel garb, our Mustang out front, rented on Rex dime, the glitz diamond ring we said Sam had bought me...

"Oh, Sammy," his Mom welled up. Green-eyed, blond Cuban; . her light yellow lace dress. Sexy and leggy in her '70s. "You're a man with such a wonderful taste. I'm so happy to see you in love."

"Sam was right!" I called out to Sam's beautiful mother.

"You do look like Lauren Bacall!"

Mom-in-law pet my head.

"I knew when I found the right girl, I'd stick for life!" Sam.

'Course everyone made fun of me 'coz I didn't much like food. People get real freaked on that. But no one tried to get to know personally, take me aside, sit me down. Everyone said they were so happy with our marriage.

Barbie shoved her princess cut diamond forward piped, "I have almost the exact same ring from my Sam! But, this cut is worth more in retail value," giggled.

Whoa, she's like Shenzi, that dominant savage female hyena in The Lion King trio. I should have had these insider practicalities when I picked this damned ring out, case I gotta flip it later for cash—mental note.

Sam was proposing champagne toasts, "She made connections with a New York independent film director! He's worked with all the guys on *Sopranos* and she met him on set of his new film!"

Director Orange. I had introduced them. Director Orange said Sam a loser, going to hold me back professionally—Sam hadn't heard that.

"She has a singing gig, too! All her own songs! And we're meeting with New York producers when we get back to get a cash flow forward, start production on my film! I'm gonna make you all real proud!" Sam was puffing up. He meant, Rex.

Bragging about getting a loan from Rex—this unnamed producer? I suddenly saw smoke billowing out of Sam's ears, nose, ass, armpits in the middle his parents' living room.

"I'm going to get my script made and tell the story of our family!"

Sam's dad was shimmering glee. Gave me a Cuban cigar. Sam asked him to help with his script story. Bits stories of Cuba…We sat on the back patio porch.

"The Bay of Pigs." Sam's dad stamped his foot so hard in the dirt. His eyes were crazy. Something about, the B-26s being late.

"John Kennedy couldn't tell time!"

"Six American planes shot down by the Cubans, and the invasion was crushed."

Dad just sat down stewing, staring at the pond of water outback. Mom held his hand. I didn't know the whole story.

"We already had two babies," She.

"I'd already gotten to Miami safely by boat. But the day of the invasion…"

Dad: "Nineteen sixty-one the United States secretly teamed with Cuban exiles in Miami to strike; Cuba had teamed Soviets, gotten wind of secret attack…"

Mom: "…swamps; bad weather stopped ground force, insufficient ammo. Thing was, soon as US camaraderie got revealed—President Kennedy pulled out on the second planned airstrike."

Sam: "Couple of days later, guess Jack Kennedy felt like a coon. The Cuban air force had taken over. So he authorized an 'air-umbrella' at dawn— six unmarked American fighter planes to help defend the brigade's B-26 aircraft flying."

Sent Sam's dad fuming, "But the B-26s arrived an hour late!" That's what Sam's dad was on about. "The United States hadn't calculated: Nicaragua and Cuba, different time zones, teams hadn't synced." Sam's dad's arms went flying up, he was sputtering, and fled into the cool AC of his man-cave study: I saw a La-Z-Boy recliner, fifty-two-inch screen. Bookcases of thousands of VHS tapes, Hollywood blockbusters.

"That's more like my dad," Sam laughed, pointing.

"That room is where he sat most of my life."

Sam's Mom gently, "Your father got locked up in Cuba for over a year. Bobby Kennedy traded baby food and pharmaceuticals with Castro to get them freed. We've been in Miami ever since." She looked at me.

They lost so much. I was.

"Bobby Kennedy sold out the Mafia!" Sam laughed aloud.

I had heard Sam say that a million times. Story his dad always told him as a kid: CIA-Mafia teamed together. Money was transferred by a CIA official to White House, to overthrow Castro. Only it gave mobster Fiorini leverage to blackmail the CIA; Bobby K didn't own up—pulled out. Sam said.

"Their father, the original Kennedy, got all his start-up money bootlegging and stocks!" That story seemed to make Sam feel better, like he had a shot—highly regarded folk get their start in illegal dealings and gambling.

I watched Mom's eyes tear, she touched Sam's hands.

"I miss you," she. So far away. Asked about our marriage. How the first year had been.

"First year is the hardest," she smiled. She'd been married almost fifty.

"No secrets to it, though." Mom smiled.

"You just don't break up no matter what; learn to works things out over time."

I couldn't believe his Mom was so warm toward me, after my meltdown. She said how she'd loved watching us together in Fort Meyers…"On the beach, walking all day together, playing, talking, laughing."

How peaceful fun it was then, with nothing…Loving each other natural; watching fireworks, holding hands. Hot sand, skin the beach, barbecue, sleep at night. Every day at 4:00 p.m. the sky spits a few minutes' of tropical rain. Sam and I would go swimming, like baby seals sexing in the water…Everyone said we'd get hit by lightning, but we didn't care.

In Fort Meyers, he had collected rocks and shells for me on the beach, and said, "This stuff is cute, but it's not enough, someday I'll get you the expensive stuff you deserve!" I had giggled, the rocks glittered nice. They were just beach rocks, and they were more beautiful than anything to me, then.

Made me remember, how we'd just trusted each other; the quality of our love. Yet, was that enough? Is ambition a loaded gun? If I, we —went simple wife, girl—I might *be* boring; *get* bored, too. I wondered if Sam thought that—about him.

Chicks

There was something else on my mind that whole time. I couldn't get her smell off my hands.

After that first night, dining with Barbie. Clubbing, dawn. Hot tub. Two girls came to light off the beach, outside the hotel. Sam was good at talking to girls. I watched him. Spanish. *How does he see it?* Two girls. One longer leg. They were moving, bobbing. *All I see are shapes, murmur talking.* Morphing, my mind making movies, *filming prisms...water rippling behind skin.*

One came back to their room. Sam did it. We had never done, I hadn't. He'd wanted, so long. This time she did.

Sam laid us back, finger in both. I turned her face to the side. *She is real pretty. Lips so soft when I kiss her.* I never felt that before on my own lips. Couples at the clubs over years came in a lot, liked Cindy, took her upstairs. But that's nothing. *A doll for entertainment.* I never felt a thing.

This girl, one with the shorter legs. *I like our breasts' touch.* Her waist really pretty, little, she was. Brown, light brown. Silver belly ring. *Maybe Brazilian.* I pulled down her ruffled pale panties. Little round bony ankles; pink, sparkly toes. High little arch feet. Smelled though. *I can't really devour, lady-kind smells. Sweaty too.* Coke on nipples, Sam put.

I kissed her eyes. Caress. *I did it like I like to do it with my own fingers.* Stroke her. Clitoris. Silky cleft, fine hair. She parted her thighs. Steered my fingers. Holding her wrist—she did. Shoving me in her. She, gasping.

I wondered what it would be like to have one, a penis. I couldn't imagine using tongue on a girl. She did that on me. She did. *Grabbing my little pearl between her lips, teeth. Underside to top, and back down like a sloping mountain.* She teased. Squeezed my thighs around her head. *I shake into her tongue, She smiles, my eyes; she smirks.*

After, we froze a moment in time together; unwashed, nor dirty. Hips, small back. Elbow. Sam forced my thighs apart with his knees. Raised her hips from the bed. Rammed pillow under her buttocks. Pressed her button.

Touched looked like film, imagined myself in Sam's role. He looking at me...she, me...I felt like floating...above the room, watching down. Like Sam and the dolphins when he died. They, rhythm…all three holding. She, his lover. Sam, imagined herself in Sam's cock…*Sweet, nature, bathing warm.* Me, him; me, her…the girl…*free lying off cliff…water-pool dive-bomb…*his or her own lover. Sex that had taken place between me and Sam…Couldn't bring ourselves together…she is me…I am he…She is *ourselves…bring us together. The silent anonymous girl…the affection we feel for each other…can I fuck…?*

She wanted Sam. Plunge.

"Rules are—she's boss," he said—pointing to me.

I had to okay it. I felt unsure. He didn't, do.

He did go drop her off. I stayed. I didn't know why, I didn't go. They were gone maybe awhile. I wanted to say, or you'd think I'd say, I was real pissed off, or had big imaginations: him *in* her in the car. 'Course I did. Sam and I never talked about it. Maybe I wanted him to, but didn't want to see it. Maybe I just wanted float on my own in the room alone…*water-pool dive-bomb…*

I did…have a fairy-tale dream that night, dozing. Something about being close to that girl; like little girls innocent, two girls playing. Felt something I hadn't felt since I didn't remember. *Sweet, nature, bathing warm light, womb…*

Whistling from dark. "Angel, my angel. I wouldn't be here if it weren't for you."

He sang—he always said I had saved him. His, "wife for life," Sam always told me that. It was dark; but for the moon shadow through the glass.

Sam had pills that night—Xanax bars, pins. No big deal, help you get to sleep.

Part III: New York

Sister

Wanda arrived. A visit.

I got no clue why she was in New York.

"Gold, pink, black," she said sticking out her tongue the freshly painted walls, minute she dropped her bags to floor. "Blech." We'd ruined her New York domicile.

"Fine," she said, squint huffed—to my,

"How are you?" *Same sniffle thing Mom does.* Rolled her buggers.

Could just be some perpetual common cold, I always tried to think.

"Baby's own five-song set!" Sam was bubbling all over that railroad.

I was in the cramped bathroom, painting my idiot lids. They just aren't as sculpted and sloping as I would have liked…Cobalt blue. A new Mac color. *'Deep'* it's called. Ass-length black hair, from the Betty Paige shoot. I had an idea I wanted to look like a haunting Jessica Rabbit singing my gothic sensual tale.

Yes, the long-awaited Lucky Strike gig was that night.

"Ten o'clock!" Sam pranced, pulling chocolate velvet Gautier jacket over jeans.

"Everyone I know in A&R is coming! Makin' baby a big star!" He even called my mom on the phone. Like he'd arranged the show.

I turned from the glass, lips red blood; hair curled to one long ringlet down my breast, peeking beneath oceanic cobalt sequined silk vintage negligee.

I had stayed up all night a few days before, hand-sewn this dress, for the gig. Ironing, scissoring gingerly. I'd picked up sewing while hitching pavement as a way to get by at the Dead shows, selling babydoll dresses. This creation: Chain metal straps swung down shoulders, meet scoop low gather small my back. Triangle dart, twirl skirt fall. Metal strappy heels revealed painted the Essie brand color *'Wicked'* toes.

I really did want Wanda to come. NY theatre stagehand, now LA TV script supervisor. I was feeling some kinda proud: building my life, acting, married.

I wanted to share my filming experience with Wanda, the Bettie Paige flick. Imagined discussing the young director's Cocteau, Welles-style filmmaking; I wanted to describe Southern Jersey sandpit cement-site locations simulating apocalyptic doom…costumes: red-and-white polka dots shorts to lace garters. Shot setup: greenfield in full-length leopard gown on thirty-foot tracking dolly wooden platform rolling forward, background blue sky. With the camera staid, focus moving toward me, same speed, tightening, how cool it made a tunnel effect!

Wanda didn't ask a thing. Not even. Delusional I felt. I didn't fill Wanda in on my bad body double, Cindy, yet; figured she'd come to the gig—and Rex would be there. I told myself, *Wanda'd be cool with my webby world; and tell her, "A nice gentleman helping me financially with my career. Booked this show."*

Wanda knew I used to strip; she acted like cool with that—back when I had rented that room from her. Wanda also told me once or twice, she thought me a horrendous embarrassment.

One time she cornered me, "Were you sexually abused?"

Her therapist had told her most girls that "behave like" me, were.

"No way! I'm just very free!" I had touted, bigger than life.

I keep secrets to protect myself from ridicule. Last thing I wanted, was Wanda's cold nose in my stupid pussing gash. If ya don't know what it's like to be touched funny as a kid, here's it: *You have to be very careful who you let in, they can make it worse; most people think they care but deep down they think you are responsible, slut.* That's what I thought of myself. Somehow, I knew better than to invite other people to tell me, too.

"Bring your friends, too!" Sam bubbled to Wanda.

"No can't make it to the show," Wanda pulled on her checkered flannel over black cotton tank, flats.

"Come to the party later!" Sam had all these new clients, connections through the Flatiron Martini job. '80s hit-flick and rock producers. Dealer for the stars, Sam was all over that role.

"Yea!" I chimed, "A swank Tribeca loft, a pool on the roof! I can introduce you to Abel Ferrara, new movie with Chris Walken…Met him a few weeks ago at Tavern on The Green with this indie film director I can introduce you to him and—"

I suddenly loved tossing names at Wanda. Felt like Really Rosie *('you better believe me I'm a great big deal!')*

"We won't get there 'til midnight! All come!"

Wanda sighed.

Who the hell am I kidding? I knew. Wanda's UES Irish beer-bar Ivy-League politic-debating socially opinionated five-bitches college girlfriends—now gone law school or become gossipy theatre crew—all hated me. Wanda had known them since Jersey. She'd toted me to a dinner party once, my early years—in town for a few days from 'Frisco.

I sort of knew better than to discuss politics with people I didn't know.

Their: Who's running office, mayoral debates chat—I chose: no comment.

TV came up: I simply knew nothing—*if a person sits quiet, listen too long, and too many topics go by…*"you're a stupid irresponsible citizen, ought to read the rags and get opinions."

Hum. So—they got socking the usual on unemployment statistics, tax cuts, corporate greed, "yada wah-wah-wah bad Republicans."

They were all voting Green Party—which to me a lovely ideal, but when Democrats split, lose power, Big Guys get in. So best be a team. I kept mouth shut.

I did finally foray my little red wagon out for a mini spin when they started complaining about unemployment. They needed the government to make more jobs for people, and give more unemployment checks. I have never been a fan of people who work freelance, and then take unemployment between gigs. I jumped in on the debating table with, "It's an entrepreneur's market! Especially when the economy is low. People ought to stop complaining and get creative, start a business! That's what makes jobs, currency flow. Not just working for corporations or taking government money."

Their talk fizzled. Like a steam train rolled their picketers-line.

Uh, oh, I computed, Wanda's told them all I am a stripper. Case you don't know: Do a job like that, tell a normie, they go tell all their friends. You're suddenly a nonhuman exploit droid, marked for life.

It's a fucking job people get over it. *I pay taxes, too,* I wanted to say.

Sam and I stepped into a town car. Wanda took the subway.

Lucky Strike

Naked, am I? I'd just finished singing tune number four.

I stood under a single spotlight in front of a crushed burgundy, velvet curtain. Frantic zigzag up my spine. Shaking at the mic. Me and a piano player. The oscillating fan above brushed cool prickles on my exposed arms, lower back. *Did I dress today? Did it evaporate? Did I drop my own gown to the floor?*—

I eyed what looked like the Picasso painting, *Paris Nightlife*—Crowd sitting, clapping, carousing. Rex's pro contacts stood, leaning on bar—a brief shake hello before hitting stage. Two dozen red ones, plump droplets water clinging to petals. Fresh Courvoisier XO 750 mg, three snifters sat on that RESERVED front marble round, satin-cushioned booth. Two men talking. Rex to Sam. *Rex is talking to Sam, starring as my brother Mitch. What the fuck am I doing?*

The Young and the Restless. I had spent half of third-grade year home from school, watching relapsing in several bouts of strep throat. Have I grown up to shamelessly emulate those frothy characters?

"Why can't I just sing for nature? Why need people?" I'd asked Sam back at the railroad after the ice-storm-sister chat. Shredding my whispery song style.

"God doesn't like wasted talent. It's a sin. You have talent. You want a career. You have to perform." Sam's pep talk. A powder pony jolt to get me on that Lucky Strike stage.

Sam shaking Rex's hand: "Big gift for my little sister. You mean well?" (On the ring).

"Buying time, chum," Rex kissed my fourth. Chuckled.

"Good things are worth a wait. Think I'm a knucklehead?"

"Not at all," Sam cajoled.

"I'm the dummy in the film biz! Buy time, get what we believe in, right? Ha-ha." Sam's gravel.

I'm on stage. Pianist cue: A-min. He was looking at me. My oak eyes, him. Em, G, D7…Melody arpeggiated plunking like steel strings, a music box.

164

Handwritten charts, I had stayed up all night for a few days reading books on simple charting for piano—hadn't skipped a measure. I looked down. Silk clung to my skin. The notes of the song, come to me in those early morning hours, when most of my creative juice sprouted, now echoed into the night for the first time—to touch people.

I looked at the bustle: *a beautiful oil, painted by hard thin brush.* Then, like hot water spontaneously springs, magma jolts through an iceberg, my heart moved. I felt the drip drops, the steamy heat of my own tears. My cheek. Maybe I had torn, then, through an old blue shadow, and I was moving. The white light shone down from above; all of the people bled to in another. Yellow watery marks melding, liquid in glasses moving, expansive lines: red, blue, indigo, green-lime. Suddenly, I was in the night, clip-clopping down the cobblestone street, alone. I was sputtering that, my song, clammy in the moonlight. I was on the street, muscling, wandering, pulling on coattails, naked, wandering. It was there, in that space that I uttered sound, wondering, wandering. Like that sound from a little child. A little child's voice uttering, shaking, from me. There, I was on a precipice about to try something new. I was fresh lily-white with tune. As my child's voice sprang, needed to speak. I wasn't thinking about Rex anymore. Wasn't thinking about Rex or how he'd hear it, or how they all saw me, or if I was good. I stepped inside that fucking thing I'd imagined doing my whole life; a finite space, on stage, in time, in vibration of sound, and emoting something; lived in it, breathed it. Nothing else was there. No concerns—my work, marriage, what is right or wrong or bad or good. I just was, and even sort of safe from it all. *I want to hold that feeling long I can, please.*

"The streets are cold and I don't even know your name

Oh, won't you please just take my hand I'm so ashamed

I'm all alone, Mister, I hope you understand

It won't take long but I could use a little change

These are my little girl's eyes for you

These are my little girl's eyes for you…," I sang.

I don't know why I picked that song. You know an upbeat pop song would have been more well-received. I think I was using my song to try to say something I was feeling, maybe to get over or through something, to feel better by exposing the pussing wound inside. To me, it's what art, creation, expression is for.

Descending stage, I was. Clap—Smattering and hooting. Murmurs moved passed me, "Haunting," "Eclectic…" sounded blaring, like a muted blur from behind Plexiglass. Wiping blue tear. My once matte lay-sheet of onlookers

165

transformed into 3-D; I carved a tunnel through the mash of color and moving shape. My hands extended from arms as I passed tables.

Bluntly: Back to three snifters. I would have been wired, an itching time bomb approaching Rex and Sam, at the same table. I was overpowered.

Behind us, off my pinball glance, I heard, "We'll make you a headliner if the crowd serves right!" owner, Lucky Strike, one of Rex's cronies bellowing into the mic on the stage. Rolling forward back his toes, heel; pulling waist, his pinstripe pleated suit pants. *The Post* peeking inside jacket pocket. I eyed the pillbox slat stage. That terrifying land I had just meandered was just a dirty piece of particle board tacked together with a couple of colored lights on. *Hell's wrong with me.*

Tuned into Lucky still barking at the crowd: "Five gals, five-song sets. Most applause gets a regular booking at our club!"

Some round ass, short-haired, little suede skirt, cotton tank, long dangle gold earrings warming up her hollow body acoustic on stage. I felt stuck aghast, a ghost, surreal. Numb. *Hot flashes under flesh.* I wanted to slap Rex. Ticked.

Courvoisier. Swallowed one straight goulash to the blood.

"Your music is lovely, dear. You looked beautiful," Rex, the old sallow blarney did not move a muscle. Dry hands folded on marble oval. Controlled to the point of the dead—*perhaps he is,* I silently.

I had wondered if Rex were on a heavy dose of serotonin enhancers, Lexapro. Those 'scripts are slightly traceable; scent: toxic mothballs. When I was hitching the Left coast, gal who'd picked me up took me to family dinner with her father: his zombie eyes, the scent. I had looked in their medicine cabinet, piles of anti-d's: made a mental note. Over years I'd picked up the exact same in clubs: glazed eyes, scent. In that environment, if you talk to someone long enough, they usually reveal their story, psychological fucked-upness. My Rex theory, unproven.

Gotta stay competitive. I grabbed Rex's arm, "Thank you so…all you've done for me." Flocking sweet charm, squeezing glee.

"We wanted to see how the crowd responded before booking you a bigger show, dear," Rex patted my hand.

Checked Sam sitting playing with the rim of his cognac. "Give my sister a show all hers, I promise you—I'll pack the joint and get the press hounding!"

Rex's heavy-hitting pro cronies gathered. I saw stray eyebrow hairs. Kind you just want to slip the bloke a pair silver manicurist scissors, send him off to the boys' room.

"You've really got something here…!" "Amazing…!" "Did you write those?" Grasped hard my diamond-adorned left hand, wagging it up, down.

My nipple must be sticking out of my top—I never believed a nice comment.

Foiled again. Two and two: Rex had neglected to tell me, this gig he'd hyped as all mine "with headliners" was actually some kind of competitive female singer-songwriter musical revue night.

My head flung in a circle—applause. The pop singer-songwriter-storytelling college and guitar in a café-style. *She's better than me. Well—not my cup of gin. I'd never listen to that. But she's more commercially viable. Why was I born unsalable?*

"I know myriads of high-profile clients, label owners, producers galore"—Rex's oldest chum, introduced as an entertainment lawyer. Extended his paisley from olive three buttons, bowing over wingtip shoes.

"Just tell me who you want to meet! My dear, such a pleasure to make your starlet acquaintance!"

Felt under his gaze, *I am chicken on the rotisserie, slowly dripping oil*—like he was seeing me in whatever porn scenario he'd been obsessing lately. I wondered where Rex had told him we'd met.

Double jolted rigor mortis, *It's alive*—Rex suddenly dubiously hep, "Yes, she is quite the gorgeous peach, and a stunning talent!" *Raving goofy blah-blah.*

Applause spun my head further. I hated to admit jealousy—even an ounce. *Weak. Needy.* Cindy didn't get jealous. Cindy always won. Trash girl—a dumb girl who's going to get ravaged, left on the side the road to bleed. Afraid: I was *her.* Two triple four square six cubed times nine exploded, *Dangle my darn-dang dreams; then take them away.* Men and midlife crisis Rex sizing if I'm on level for his: "buying time." I'll just keep my music sacred, for the life force, forget people. Where's Cindy? I felt stranded, trash girl.

Wanted chain myself Rex's wooden calf cry, "Pygmalion! Spend your money, transform me, fix it—tell me how to be different than me, make the masses love me!"

Three men turned back to round marble. I played smiling, happy as clam, bobbing in glee. Lucky owner poured more booze. Olive lawyer grinned Cheshire.

Intimacy with something I really actually cared about always brought on such a hurricane.

Rex turned to talking about my cash. Three men hovered, dove quickly shared aside. Pulled Sam join.

"Mitch, my boy, I plan to grant Cindy start-up funds. Perhaps you'll be the business exec on this with me."

My earshot strain picking, "loan docs, legal contracts," on Rex recent divorce proceedings. Sam was nodding. Entertainment cronies seemed handling the case. "Sums of considerable amounts."

I still hadn't agreed to sign contracts: "I have to trust you more before taking a loan of that consideration." Hadn't figured how to swing it—admitting to Rex my real name? He'd probably walk.

Guy, Daffy Duck suspenders—saddled up, chimed himself a Dresdner Kleinwort portfolio manager, grinning, grabbed my left elbow. I felt fourteen—copping pot in Washington Square Park. One dealer grabbed my left arm, other squeezed my right elbow, offering a lower price—

"My youngest plays guitar!" His phone, pics, pointing. Daffy's adoring, silly cross-eyed—how I'd always imagined a proud father looks. I'd never seen one.

"This is the Snow White birthday party my wife and I threw for his fifth last week!"

I big smiled: *Don't want to hear about this stupid wifey shit.*

"Why Snow White for a boy?" heard myself no filter.

"Oh! We wanted to teach him to play the prince…you know."

My ear peeled to man-gab:

"A promissory note for Cindy to sign—" Heard lawyer pose. *Why's Rex so into this loan?*

Remembering: Sam. Coral Gables grouper stand, Miami. I'd filled Sam in on Rex's recent cash loan plan. I was never much good at knowing when, how to break news.

Sam had swerved off long dirt drive, I was gulping warm salt breeze.

"His wife's gonna grab half!" Sam roared laugh.

"Maybe the guy's got a private stash she hasn't frozen yet, figures liquidate, and spend it havin' a fuckin' good time!"

Divorce American Style—that's a flick title also, Dick Van Dyke, Debbie Reynolds; married couple, stops fucking. My own parents' divorce, I'd heard about that my whole childhood.

"I got screwed on the deal," Mom complained. Used dad's mediator rather than her own lawyer.

My *Paris Nightlife* crowd turned roaring for the pop-chick on stage. Lucky Strike owner bear-hugged her.

Rex wanted to hear about Sam's script.

"So, give us the story," Rex implored Mitch—about his script.

"We old dogs want the jimmering perks of your entertainment world."

Sam did his usual, pulling the lapels on his chocolate velvet Gautier, "Cuban Godfather," guffawed, "Urban world is marketable right now." Told the tired Burt Young story.

Suddenly, I was sick of hearing about Sam's script. I hate creative pulse that comes to no fruition. Like an unsatisfying fuck.

Leaned in, hushed, "See, listen, big guys, you'll make your greenback spades, that's not a problem. But, I've had interest crop up past twenty-four hours. Major producers want exclusivity. Requested I resign pitching meetings."

That's not true you fucking hornet head. Supposed to get Rex to love the script, want invest, give us money.

Sam pulled the king of the table position. His arm around Rex's shoulders. I pulled an undertow shudder breath.

"Rex here—wants to marry my sister. That would make you close to family, mate. Meaning first dibs on this project. For now, I have to stamp this: PRIVATE TALK ONLY. Until all's in writing."

Rex nodded. "No harm men, strictly business."

Three men split for the bar. *Sam kicked the other guys off.* Sam spun snifter. I fell jamorous. *Sam's fucking genius.* (Oh, it's a word I made up. Definition: *Jealous of someone's ability, but when you see them do the thing—you love them even more.*) Sam had spied Rex's cronies were really there to shake me down—see if I am a worthy investment for the rogue divorcee's frolics. Our mission: Suss out how much we could get from Rex.

Sam, drew Rex's eyes: "If this movie gets made, Rex, you could be the man, have some power in the decisions. There's a starring role here for your fiancé, my sister. Bring your and her dreams to life! Thing is, I gotta tell ya—I've got a copy with Bob and Harvey right now and if that works out well, y'know—"

I was beginning to want to climb over the table, jump on Sam's fuck bone—Sure, one-on-one I could wool a sheep for cash, smoke in mirrors swindle—when it came to my art, so the value of me, I couldn't eek a syllable. That simple ability—which seemed to me the only way to make it in this hell world—I was damned a handicap. I just wanted to present, have them love it, tell me they'll sell it—so I can go back to round-the-clock-write-more.

Sam cooked spotlight. Fast-paced showy chew chat.

Blue my silk tits on Rex's white crisp-turned squeezes, giggles on the fat man. Now, you'd think with Sam there I been holding back on cuddles—Opposite. Sam there—*my keeper, my stable rock force behind the whole charade*—felt I was doing it for *us*. Buttering Rex seemed important.

A bitch how my mind came up with all those goddamned suspicions.

There—Sam was pitching scenes I'd had never even heard before. "Stina," Sam said. "She's the part for my sister, your lovely muse," Sam pointed. "Gus wins Junior Golden Gloves. He and Stina in love..." and "...acting in prison! His childhood dream! Inmates doing improv scenes instead of fighting!"

Rex was drooling. I was, too, of course, my self-obsessed hate talk, *Why is Sam with me? Fascinating...skill. Could get a much better girl.*

Sam soared, "Lady Parole Office Corrections Unit—in-house arrest. Stina's waiting for him. Oh, she's now a beautiful painter, has a studio in their house, sings in nightclubs, too—like Cindy!" He points to me.

Rex will join forces with Sam, both kick me to curb. Sam will help Rex sow his oats hot women—better actresses than me. Move on richer, leave me dust. Why the hell did I bring Sam? Blah blah-ing—

Sam's hacking. Rex is chortling holding my ring finger.

Sam threw final bait: "Stina and Gus stay together...Parole Officer good word, released. He gets on Amtrak to East Village, New York, to make it acting. Stina stays in Miami. They plan to make a life together, once he's successful. Only he gets addicted to heroin. He never sees Stina again; her whispers, inspiration stay with him. Guides him getting better. Ends: Gus alone, older, living in a little studio with horn-rimmed glasses. Typing his story."

I busted clapping. Rex followed. I silently thought the ending needed work: *Who the hell's the girl Stina he left in Miami—Sam was still waiting for her to come to him? Never told me this part.*

Lost in plans, I totally forgot my singing stage competition. A clearing had come to mind. Ever since the Bettie Paige film, this vision had become evermore lucid: *A lead in a feature written just for me. Best yet my husband's film, like Cassavetes and Gena Rowlands. Only I get to sing my songs. Like Rita Hayworth in* Gilda *or* Miss Sadie; *Marilyn in* Bus Stop, *or* River of No Return.

Out of left, Rex gripping hard my diamond finger. *Blood rushing, Ow.*

"Interesting Cuban history, I didn't know you are Cuban, dear Cindy?"

"It's not in factual, Rex!" I blathered. "It's art! Not life!"

Revan whispered in my ear: "Do you think this is a good vehicle for you, dear?" Patted my hand.

"Well, Mitch. I'm a man who went to Harvard Law. I certainly am from a different world. Cindy, aren't you as well? I mean you are in very good schooling, nice family. I see you in more commercially viable pieces. A leading star, not a druggy movie."

Revan pulled that toothy-glinty-Jack-Nicholson grin. Put his arm around my shoulder. Sam grimaced; temporary high balls cut.

Shit, huh? My pinpoint perspective turned. Like one of those triangle-origami-fortune-teller things you make in grade school. Hold it in your thumb and index, both hands. Pick a number: open, close, 'til stop. Unfold, read, like:

'You're going to meet a rich man,' or 'Play the lottery,' 'Be a movie star!'

Sam, depleted in the creamy stars of his own eyes. He really had hoped that rich bloke might solve his own life's pretzel nugget twist, take a real interest his flick.

I turned, maybe Mitch story not a hot plan; don't lose Rex.

Quickly altered motive—turned. We all three did.

"You'll let me know how it goes with the Weinstein brothers, young Mitch," Rex nodded.

"For now, I'd like to put all my liquid toward creating your sister's debut album, and being her knight in shining armor. Betrothed." Drawled long 'o.'

Rex winked my way, proudly noting his insider joke: batting Cindy lingo: betrothed, from months before.

Sam adjusted cards, "Of course! Tell me about your wedding plans then! Monte Carlo, a yacht…"

"Rex dear," Cindy petted, "you promised you weren't going to get into this wedding chat when I accepted your generous gift…" Meaning the ring.

I don't want Sam thinking I actually am planning to marry the drone. I was planning to stay loyal to Sam.

Rex acquiesced, boldly. "Yes. I have learned to understand one thing in life. A woman of quality and confidence needs to test a man. She will push him at first to see how much he is willing to provide and just how much he can take—if he's strong enough to protect."

I gasped. *Stunning.* Rare a man understands that a woman needs to flip every so oft; tell him how much she hates him. Turned me on, *Ho hum. If only the older wise men sexed as hot as the still-sensitive ego-flip-if-you flap young ones.*

Then: "Corazon, my dears?" A strange Elvin humpback skipped spritely. Ruby red-thin circus lips, grinning in grand. Splaying a man-size glove hand behind a blown glass heart-shaped bottle. Apparently Lucky sent over a liquor sales gimmick.

Rex lifted his brows, "What is, do pray tell?"

"It's a new tequila, dear. Means *heart* in Spanish," Cindy told Rex. *Point for me on Spanish—*

"So good it can be sipped like cognac!" Wicked-gibbous giggled.

"Impressive, Dear," Rex squeezed Cindy waist *ow* tight. "There is very little I have not yet seen in this urban town."

I batted lashes. "I plan to turn you on to all sorts of new things you don't even know about yet, Honey!"

Sam nodded.

"Bottoms up!" Cackle burbled. Poured this top-shelf tequila over Courvoisier puddles, our snifters. *Bit of liquor crime.*

Wink. Clinked—though, does make a good drink. Three times, repeated.

"Viaje mañana a París!" Rex winked, baiting *español* comeback. (Translated: I'm leaving tomorrow for Paris.)

"Nueva York te extraño. Igual que yo." I had picked a bit, sloppy in Miami. (Translated, I thought: New York will miss you. As will I.)

Rex, "Back-to-back meetings scheduled for this Parisian excursion. Early flight," was all I heard. Rex on the leave.

"Mitch, my card, keep in touch." They shook.

Sam stared, 'DRESDNER KLEINWORT, REX REVAN, DIRECTOR OF FOREIGN EXCHANGE'—title.

"Miss Cindy, my voice," Rex bowed.

I touched Rex's jowl. "Good-bye, my dear."

Leaned in close. He kissed my shiny ring.

I almost let him go, but—*will I ever see Rex again? Is he going to leave me? Will he ever come back? Where are his cronies? I don't have their cards. Don't see them at the bar. They are supposed to change my life. Rex is. That was the deal. How am I going to get the twenty grand? I can't sign a promissory note.*

Place was emptying.

I placed my lips smack on Revan's.

I never had before. Never wanted to. Didn't have to—fuck explaining.

That night I opened my mouth and launched one big wet one, with tongue, pat on the man's skinny salmon lips. *His breath like a candied apple been rotten sitting out too long.* Swirling tongue; *ew, it slimed.—Well. Tongue gumbo it cost. I suppose, to secure my place in Rex's life.*

Maybe I had venom, Sam. Didn't want to gamble losing Rex on account, *him.* Maybe I wanted to kiss the old guy, see how it felt. Fuck knows. I smooched Rex a few foolhardy minutes. Him grabbing the small of my exposed back. His tongue darting wormy mingling, shoving mine. All I was hoping was that he'd come back to me from Europe, wanting more.

Don't we all do that: Afraid the person will leave, bend to what we think they want, to make them stay.

I don't think I would have kissed Rex if Sam wasn't there. I felt it a game. A safe game. Back then, I thought it…*all a safe game.*

Rhythms

Back in black, we were. My hair up twist, silk blue gown back to flowing—
Arm in arm, Sam; *us*. Glided gallant, strutting up spiral marble case through
white wrought iron gates to balcony floor. Pool, crystal shimmer; people like
glass ornaments, turning reflective in aqua.

The party had a bunch from Julian Schnabel's circle. He had just made
another movie that year, *Before Night Falls*. Javier Bardem played a Cuban
poet Reinaldo Arenas, openly gay and publishing negative social ideas during
Castro's reign. Leaves Cuba in Mariel boatlift and dies in Manhattan. Johnny
Depp played a drag queen. Bardem had won the best actor at the National
Board of Review Awards at Tavern on the Green in December of 2000.

Heard myself blindly, whisper Sam's ear, "Baby, I can't wait until this is
all behind us. When we have our own Tribeca loft, and your film made!"

We'd just beelined the party's nearest porcelain, I'd dropped bare knees to
chilled black slate. Blue silk bunched palms, sweaty locks dripping aerosol
taste between lips, tongue—acid tequila, cognac.

"Hold my hair?"

Wasn't frequent I lurched—Maybe it was the singing. Rex on my lips.

Sam sat on the edge of a claw-foot, whistling. He was dishing ammo on a
marble counter: hundred-dollar Baggies coke. Hoped pull in a few thousand,
this party.

"You people who understand your music vibe, babe. You just don't give
up. Never give up," he said. Sam squeezed white pony his thumb joint, me,
"Get yourself cleaned up." Tucking packies his velvet waist pocket.

I was on a…"people liked my songs, or no? I can't tell. But Rex, he had
some people there; promised a full regalia next…"

Sam gently pressed tissue 'neath my blue tears.

"You kissed that fat fuck. You shouldn't have kissed that fuck. You
sleeping with him?" Sam.

"I kissed him barely. No, never. I was just appeasing, y'know, I'm gonna
get his twenty grand. For us." I threw a joke, wanted Sam feeling better.
"Besides, baby how can I hook my thing on anyone who says Spiderman is

their favorite superhero? He lives in a closet at his mother's and wears underwear!"

Sam didn't flinch—"That guy doesn't know anyone. You're wasting your time. Most you get is that ring. Few months, get it insured. I'll set a heist in our apartment. Robbery. Claim the money. I'll give you thirty more days or so to play him out. That's your best."

I had promised Sam, "We'll hawk it, split the reap." But that night I was, *I'll give you? Get your own score, scoundrel setting rules for me.* Though, staging a robbery on the rock perked me. *Pretty smart.*

"Time for another drink!" I whistled.

I remember how then I was becoming attuned to the rhythms of being a drunk. A drunk can hit the floor their knees, below zero. Sick wears off. Hit go: re-up. Start a whole new drunk. A drunk doesn't know where they'll end, but it holds promise: It will always seem completely different from the last. Secret is, usually, it's the exact same place. A drunk never remembers that when they start.

Funny, right now that reminds me of T. S. Eliot's "Four Quartets 4: Little Gidding:"

"We shall not cease from exploration; and the end of all our exploring will be to arrive where we started; And know the place for the first time."

Except, Eliot's thing is about the pure willingness to fresh eyes and presence.

I ordered Chilean red to start.

Posies

This is where that night got hazy. I'll tell it to you fragments. That's all it takes really, most the time—little jabby moments that get under your skin, form a grim yellow pus-filled bloody head of a cyst, until it pops, oozes, and…

Sam knew everyone—and if he didn't, he was introduced. *Dealer for the stars.*

"You should have been there, man. My girl sang!" Sam hobnobbing, jostling. People pulling Sam. "Yeah, just had a great meeting!" Heard Sam saying.

"Producer interested in my script man; it's gonna be a big one." Phones out, bags, hundreds in the pockets, his chocolate Gautier.

Producer guy slapped Sam's pec, "Ahh, let me know, you're the walking icon, can't wait to see it!"

I believed in his talent; he did mine. What more do I really need?

"You better come down, man, her next show—make money off my girl's voice while she's small enough to still talk to you loser!" Heard Sam saying, as he scuttled off to an aside.

I was left standing with a flute bubbly, passing tray. Blue silk skirt brushing naked thighs, cool rooftop breeze. Squinting my eyes…I often did this in large crowds, pressure to social and didn't want deal. Platters silver, waves, mirror light in pool, *like icicles squiggly.* Trance mix drum-bass electro-Ibiza spin. Circles humans bathing…became fuzzy and then to ridiculous birds humming. Hallucinating. Watching people, something like, with tufts hair head, white-faced, red-cheeked, sparkles and holding hands, leaning back slow motion.

High-pitched screeching: *"Ring around the rosie, pockets full of posies, ashes, ashes, we all fall down,"* baby song…and each double she took, they were shrieking louder, ringing ears—but they weren't: Back to normal focus. I wished they were—*a little more absurd; schmoozing, real-time life is all these fucking people were doing. Nothing outside of the lines. Life takes itself so seriously; how the hell do you get out…*ponderings of a drunk—

I went to back to my usual flip-forth: *Do I wish to become a part of it? What would happen if I live my life forever just as I am, some weird quiet girl whose songs no one understands, dances exotic, flipping sugar daddies, marriage, celebrity, drug dealer…who cares, anyway…could I accept myself?* Sure. anyone there or anywhere, would say, "The person you are isn't good enough, you have to become something better"—maybe I don't want change.

"Is Cindy your stage name for singing?" He asked.

I, *exposed? Shamed.* Familiar boyish voice. That Director Orange chappy. Coppola ho-hum look-alike.

"I heard your set at Lucky Strike."

He offered me a tangerine cream candy. The unwinding wrapper cracked loud.

Thank God he didn't say hi at gig; linked me Rex, dancer girl. My big nightmare: being found out. Ruin contacts, chances. An actress must be linen white for the media.

He must have skipped early though—Sam—those two had turned a silent checkmate.

Earlier that year, Director O had taken me blazing stretch limo, red spaghetti straps, tea skirt like Martha Graham dancer, to National Board of Review Awards at Tavern on the Green, Central Park. Introduced me as the next "It Girl," to Al Pacino—supporting Ellen Burstyn's Career Achievement Award. Aronofsky's *Requiem for a Dream*, special recognition. Ennio Morricone, Career Achievement. Christopher Walken. *True Romance*, an all-time faves flick.

"I saw you sing on Broadway, James Joyce's 'The Dead,'" I'd said to Walken. Kissed his cheek. "Your voice had haunted me so," and it was true, I'd seen and loved the play.

"Would you sing for me right now?"

Chris blushed.

Orange gotten angry flushed angry, split. Dir. O had his eyes on me, something about his Mom wanting him with another pizza-bagel (Jewish Italian.) So, I played sweet, maybe-one-day to his fumbling 1950s Brooklyn, never-been-kissed kind-of-way.

Dir. O lavished, "You looked pretty on stage. Now, I'm even more sure of your talent! Did you write those songs?" Orange shake, holding the cranberry iced vodka concoction melting in his hand.

Yes, I batted lids, cobalt.

"We are only days from getting money to make that film. I'm going to be the one to discover you! Make you the star you are!"

I must have some please-save-me-desperate look, my coke high told me. *My whole life I've*—wandering, hitching, posing face to Man's "I'll save you star" hero stint. It always ended up the same: *They want Sex.*

Sam always said Dir. O was using me—wasting my time. Dir. O said Sam was going to ruin my career, try to saddle me with kids. Treat me like a hen. It's what all men do—-to keep a woman. I had ignored picking up the last few phone chats, Director O, discussing writing scenes for this film. Thought he'd started slipping away.

"Is it OK, if we meet for a drink this week? To talk about that?" O.

Like a ghost-shadow breeze in the dark creak of night, I felt Sam whisk me off on his arm.

I was beginning to wonder if Circles would be a better stage name. Seemed to be what I was best at going around in.

Trophy

I can't say exactly what happened next. A whole bunch of what got up my nose.

We were at the party in the backroom. There was Eric chortling on, something about,

"If there is something you want but can't have, show contempt for it. The less interest you reveal the more superior you seem."

My bare legs from silk blue over a micro-tufted midnight club chair facing slate slash Formica table, beautifully sprinkled with snow. Two bottles Goose icing.

There was Calvin and his gobs of cologne—bartender Sam's martini Flatiron District bar and Jess's spooky doppelganger, except business hair, fancy pockets, Euro flair. Calvin's current fame, a national spot in a Sleepy's commercial.

My mind was swimming to murky suspicious: *I didn't know Cal knew Eric.* Sam was cutting lines. Convo pinging five-way. Eric's arm hung around a young Puerto Rican, tats-up pride flags, a Sumerian warrior holding a bloody skull. I didn't know what exactly they were talking—*pontificating Machiavellian power games interesting enough, oh,* figured out. *Is this the crew Sam's with while I'm out Rexing?*

"Yep. Kick him, he'll forgive you," barked PR.

"Flatter him, he may or may not see through you. But ignore him and he'll hate you!" Calvin.

"Contempt is a dish that is better served cold and without affectation." Paul, Israeli pierced up down, goatee.

"Idries Shah, *Caravan of Dreams*, 1968"—Eric called quote. Referenced some Professor Kaufman. He slapped Paul Israeli. Fordham brothers.

Sam jumped, "You fucking law school junkies! I could ace that shit, too— I'm just smarter than spend all that dough on some degree!" Sam often said how successful he'd be at law, if he could "just settle in on getting the degree." My Mom always piped on about his super brain also.

Clipped straw passed.

What's wrong with me? I was still skapooey from Earth's surface after the whole night's events. It usually took me three days to assimilate the fact that I even needed to assimilate. Most of the time I just kept getting high until something blew up.

Sam put his arm around me, said, "Listen, baby, this is funny."

"Shush, let me tell it!" Israeli said to Eric.

"Finally I said, darling. Where's your wife?"

"He did a double, 'Am I that obvious?' An *X* on my head?" Quoted Calvin.

Eric, "Turns out he's married twenty-five years with three boys one girl in college, and proudly bragged of great wife in Jersey at their 'other' house!"

"Let me report, he gave really great..." PR. Blush smiles.

Eric turned to me and Sam, "Married ones always do. Hungry for it."

Jabbed me and said, "Better get it together, honey, us boys will take all your men."

"That'll never happen!" Sam boomed.

"Cheers on that, son." Israeli, Heineken in air.

Paul, "I can see all the blackbirds in the land, still, I live!"

Someone called it: "*Caligula.* 1979, Malcolm McDowell, Peter O'Toole, Helen Mirren."

I'd seen it. Sam showed it to me. Kid Caligula lives with his syphilis-ridden Roman emperor great-uncle, who makes him watch rough sex shows—pedophilia, boffing various freaks nature. Summoned to kill the uncle by some underground, Caligula becomes emperor. First very revered; then twists mangled. The sister he wants to marry won't—so he rapes a bride and groom in a jealous rage. Marries his courtesan, marries their daughter, fucks everything in free-love-ism sight until diseased—Caligula overthrows Senate. He forces all women to become prostitutes.

I looked at Sam; Eric's arm around him, "Cheers—" Looked at my blue, shoes, face. Goose shots to my blood. I bolted? I blacked out.

Flash

I woke sprawled starfish. I didn't know what for. Came to. Ceiling. Cracked plaster. There was a big African-American lady officer standing over me—I didn't feel a thing. Metal, handcuffs her belt buckle shift shuffling. Radio my ear. My eye half shut.

"I never have seen anything like it," Lady was shaking her head, talking to herself.

"Bites," she kept saying.

"Three bites—Bloody."

Flash—Ouch. Polaroid picture.

What—a uniform? I caught view of the film coming to image, laying on the mattress beside me. A pile of them—white, plastic hand-size frame, ink developing. Purple welts on a skinny calf. A photo of one massive eggplant-blue bruise on what looked like flesh, thigh. A nasty bloody black eye. A strawberry forehead.

Whoa—hot, spinning wallop *hard to think,* like a speeding cement box dropped on my skeletal, pounding. Real-time—*it's me.*

My mind went sucking back, like matter in a blackhole, like Gumby, that green cartoon character that stretches miles, my mind went peddling back. Straining to regather pixel fragments of a blackout. *Sam's face, lashed to fury, foaming mouth.* Heard him belligerent. "Why'd you kiss that fat trick…"

"I was in it, felt it."

"Where?"

"Gay. You're gay. Gay," I remembered taunting Sam.

In real-time, I heard Sam in the next room: "That crazy bitch! I didn't do anything!" Sam's voice hollering.

I heard men. Cops barking. Sounded they were trying hustle him out the apartment. Sam kicking maybe the desk or the doorjamb.

"I was asleep on the couch; she started beating on me. I was asleep on the couch; she started…" He was yelling over, like an echo in the barracks of a World War II shelter.

I can't see. I heard sirens. I heard sister, Wanda. Red shame: *I'm some Southern white trash TV.* Forgotten Wanda was staying there. *Was she here when I got home or when walked in?* My backlog residue came up fuzz.

"Some vacation to New York, huh?" one cop voice.

"Oh, ya know, just one crazy family!" Heard Wanda flirting, giggling like a hyena.

Funny how people respond to authority.

Back in Jersey, on some Thanksgiving, Mom had served two gallons Julio Gallo to us three kids and her drunk boyfriend. Aidan was found drunk, puking in the creek at the elementary school across the step path. Wanda batted lashes at the cops. When I was fifteen in the Jersey precincts, Mom used to outright bat eyelash swing, hip, flirt.

Hot salt fell from my eyes that morning after. Shaking uncontrollably hurts when you're all bruised up.

Lady cop's eyes, like a dominant momma deer.

"You understand this is third-degree assault," she said. Your husband is going away for a long time. "I'll make sure of it. We have a clinic you can go to. The city will issue you a restraining order; protect you if he is released."

Lady cop told me what had happened. I had dialed 911. Reported that my husband had beat me up. When the cops arrived, I had identified Sam as my husband.

All I could clearly remember was that morning, Wanda's face when she came into the bedroom. Sam gone.

"Always drama in this family," she scoffed.

I tried to stand. I saw Sam's blue iBook lay smashed to bits all over the hardwood. My blue silk dress was torn. Place busted up.

"Pack a bag. The police will get you a shelter, they said."

I didn't want to go to a shelter. I didn't want to go anywhere right then. I wanted silence. Sunlight streaming, touched my broken skin through the window over our brand-new king bed. Sam's buddy had an open truck sale. This must have been wee morning hours. Wanda went to sleep, or left. Air, silent.

My mind started piecing back together, *what?* I heard a hollow—like the tunnels in Central park I used to wander through, homeless in New York, back when I was hitching around, singing Billie Holiday alone; New York for visit—

I remembered holding Sam's laptop, "You're doing secret shit with it..."

"You're doing secret shit with him..."

"You're a liar. Own up to who you are! Sneaking around using that thing for hook-ups instead of your script. I worked to buy it for you!"

181

His laptop. Sam's hands gripped it tight. I saw him throw it hard to the floor, demolished into pieces.

Maybe I pushed him with words, my body; I couldn't conjure how it started. I remembered the moment he turned on me. Knuckle to my skull. Obstreperous blaring in my ear. I was fighting, kicking back; I remembered that whatever I did to him, he did back to me. More force, with a kick, a blow, a belt. His hot mouth, teeth sinking my neck, my tri-cep, my thigh, glute. Thrashing back, I was. I did remember finally giving in. Afraid. I remembered lying across the bed—terrified of what fighting back might bring. So, I went soft. Gave in. Waited for him to be done. Hush. *Delirious.* Sam's feet kicking legs my legs. His eyes seeing red.

I remember feeling like a seal being clubbed…praying, *Just give the guy a baseball bat and call it a day.* Rolling back and forth with every blow, I was. Waiting for him to lose his steam and be done with me.

I didn't remember calling the cops. I do remember that I didn't want to go out on the street alone, again.

I lay there, wondering if this meant my self-esteem was getting higher. Or I was waiting to die.

***

I woke up again from black. There was Mom standing over me brazen, beady-eyed as usual, waving a ripped page of mini metal ring-keeper paper. *Am I hallucinating?*

I felt the pink glitter glaze heat, a warm spring noon…my mind jogged to find some better place in the Cave of Trophonius…"I was walking through the park one day, in the merry month of May, I was taken by surprise by a pair of golden eyes." I often sang this song when frightened, had since I was a girl.

I felt like a terribly inconvenient fuck up, *mom.*

"Honey, I was in Manhattan already," Mom responded to my apology for being a burden.

"Wanda and I planned to meet at Aidan's for lunch. I only get to see her when she comes back East now. I wish she'd live closer."

French doors, I fantasized. Wrapped under covers. Throbbing and booming and groaning, colossal. Like a steaming old wood engine. Aidan— hearing his name. We had had a falling out, hadn't talked in a while. *Such romance; sheer white curtains hanging over. Hell, you got two entrances, two outs.* I had heard people say, "One door closes, the next one opens, but it sucks being stuck in the hallway!" *French doors,* at that instant, *there's always a way out.*

182

Aidan and his college girlfriend. French doors. Pretty prewar building on the Hudson. I didn't move. I could feel most concretely, a purple bruise under my eye. The rest just seemed a dream. Apparently, Wanda had informed Mom of what I shamefully considered the lame dramatics of my low-class soap opera life.

Damage control: "I'm fine, Mom. Looks worse than it is. Nice of Wanda to be concerned. I am always fine, you know that. Just my period. Moody, ya know? Sorry to disturb you." Mom never proved helpful; only judgmental. Get her out.

Wanda was in the next room packing her suitcases.

"Well, instead of enjoying Wanda, I spent this morning going through *Yellow Pages*," Mom ticked her tongue, stern.

"Call one of these groups, they'll help you," she shoved her ripped spiral paper in my face. Pencil scrawled with several phone numbers: Domestic Abuse Treatment Centers in New York.

"I don't know anything about this stuff, honey," Mom was saying, "Nothing like this ever happened to me. I'm not the right person to talk to. Women, who've been battered, sit in groups and talk about it or something." This was the same thing she'd done and said when I was date-raped in high school.

Really, I wanted to chop the thing who called herself Mom's head off. *How fucking hard is it for you to sit and hold my hand, help me?* I felt like a rotten slice of mango.

Then Mom had Aidan on the phone. "Aidan wants to speak with you."

Aidan, yelling: "You are a fuck-up lowlife. Getting yourself involved with people like Sam."

I guess they don't teach love in expensive universities, I thought. Aidan sounded scared. I could barely move.

Mom's tight-lipped, crazy grimace, shared: "Sam is evil."

Yeah, last week you were hopping all over him like a dog on a hydrant, traitor.

Then, I guess Mom like kind of "Twelve Stepped" me, as they call. Mom pulled a nifty pocket-size hardcover, blue with gold printed face: *Twenty-Four Hours A Day*, Hazelden. Daily meditations.

"I found it in a thrift shop. I had it in my pocketbook, meant to mail it to you."

"Thanks," I.

"You do realize in you're in an abusive relationship, don't you?" Wanda asked, leaving.

Funny, words stung. Didn't know what I was *supposed* to do about it. *I have to leave him?*

All I said, aloud, "Yeah that'll be awesome," a wave of my hand, the air.

They all three left me alone with an aching that wouldn't go away.

I leafed through the little blue book. Felt kind of uplifting, words, prayers on alcoholism, desperation, some kind of return to a vitality, connection to source, sort of a pointers for getting well; I had never read any of that before. Been to a meeting with a drunk boyfriend in high school before hitting the highways, but just saw a bunch of coffee and people talking real grim-faced. This was about fear, faith, peace, mistakes, failures, heart, inner love, truth. *Neat. Kind of calming*. Felt kind of judged though. Coming from Mom in this 'you're fucked-up and I have to go now,' way.

I mean, what do you do? Maybe Mom's right: there's nothing you can do or say. Give a few numbers so they get help. Who the hell knows? It seems to me that people need a transmission of some feeling of love, but…I was left alone. Maybe that was a way I could get in touch with my own will to live, beyond needing someone else's love. Maybe the book was love. Who the fuck knows.

Alone

The next seventy hours were like this:

I was in an out consciousness. Came to: Radio Shack incessant blaring my ear. Lady D.A. My file.

Rapping sonar: gruesome photos, "Never seen anything like this." Intimate Partner Violence, and Domestic Abuse Laws.

"Did you get to the hospital?" she.

No. Flat.

"You'll be defended, we'll put him away for a long time. This is third degree, easily," she was energetic.

"I need you to come down to the courthouse early morning on Tuesday to sign papers. You have people taking care of you?"

It was Monday afternoon. I wanted to help all the women of the world who have cases like this. I wanted to set an example and put all the bad men away.

"I'll be there." I hung up.

I really wanted to disappear.

See, when I was sixteen, I had been through this. Jersey shit. Date raped. I wanted to put that guy away. "I will make sure he will never do that to again to another girl, especially now that he is off to college." I was willing to be the example. I had said it myself and others.

Problem was: People think they care—but it's all too messed up. The grey spots, the blackouts, the no photos, the no hospitalizations. So, you (I) take that justice through political action. Though, you find out, it's not always the best thing for your heart and healing to go to the law. I got written about in the Jersey town newspaper. I got gossiped about. I wasn't cast in choir madrigals, even though I had been training for them since freshman year, because the teacher said he couldn't put me on stage with parents in the audience knowing I was 'that girl'.

Jersey cops had held me for hours at the precinct, dug me for answer; millions of personal questions. Took my whole life energy to try to get myself to sit through all that. Just to press charges. All I wanted was to get the hell out of there, go somewhere where I could heal my mounds, forget it, move on.

Wasn't worth it, anyway, I knew, with a lawsuit, *I'd never hurt him like he hurt me.* Something in the local paper, didn't say my name—I was a minor, but still the phone calls. Girl students who'd I never talked to before, digging gossip. I was so stupid, thinking if I told them, I'd be safer, I'd be protecting them. Like it was my plight to defend them, too. The perpetrator's family spread their own gossip.

Soon I was turned the, "Town slut. The devious drunk chic, who was trying to get boys arrested." Bottom line end was: Cops told me that I didn't have a case, because I didn't go to the hospital right away. "Which meant it couldn't have been that bad." I suppose passing out in a boy's room because you trust him, and waking up with his dick inside you isn't that bad.

I don't know if you've ever been beaten up like that, or raped, touched sex by an adult as a kid. Most people, want the girl, person to have been proactive as soon as it happened. If we aren't, they judge us and call us liars. Really, I didn't know what to say about that. I didn't know why I didn't go to the hospital. Didn't know where it was? Didn't want my mom to find out? Didn't want anyone to know? Wanted to climb under a rock? I couldn't answer that question to the Lady D.A. that day either.

I will say, admittedly somewhere inside and ashamed to say, all those times that abuse, assault, rape, and violence have happened to me, all I wanted to do: *pass out, forget.* I have never found it helpful to tell people, especially the police. It only gets worse. I'm sure I'm not *supposed* to say that.

***

I hadn't moved from the bed. *You're whining weak, nothing's broken,* the voice was saying. Hot knotted spine, femur, wrists, skull, cheekbones. Couldn't feel much else. I'd seen TV shows, heard stories women been beaten up repeatedly way worse. *It's my fault. I'm drunk.* I kept wanting to be a superhero: *It's my responsibility to show up. Help the women of the world be defended.*

"Hello?" Sam called, "Babe, you gotta help me get the hell out of this place."

He could have at least apologized.

"Phone that D.A., tell her…"

Sam had come up with a story he wanted me to say, to get him let off. "You hit yourself. Lost your mind. You *didn't* call the police. Say someone in the building must have. You don't know how, why, anything."

"That's not true," I said.

Thinking of the Lady D.A.

Sam: "That's the only way they'll let me out. You have to. You don't know how bad it smells in here and I can't go to the bathroom. I miss you. I'm sorry. I don't know why you are so jealous. I love you, you have to understand. You should see the bruises I have. The guys here think I got attacked by a dog. They can't believe I'm in here and not you. Tell the D.A. you don't want to press charges. They're rough on guys. They won't touch you. If she argues, tell her you are crazy, memory failing. You are certain, I was sleeping on the couch and you came after me. Tell them to let me out."

"I'll call her," I whispered. I wasn't sure if I would. Just didn't feel like listening to him. He said he'd call again soon—to make sure. 'Bye-'bye.

Nothing—especially not the weight of justice—seemed important.

Poof: Blank

I was laying on the bed holding the Walther PPK. Magazine loaded. Safety: switch on. Pushed metal; against hot aching skin. *Coolness soothe me, touch me, kill me.* Less lonely. My mind wants to set free from worry, and these memories never go away:

I am struggling: Come back! Screaming: I can't make a sound! Sitting: cuffed…Laughter: children, the other room, taunting. Mom's Polish drunk: pulling me from the kitchen. He threw me on the bed: I was lightning bolt tingly warm, my sex, moving, pushing, rolling warm steel, dirty fingers. Something so wrong, guilty…so bad if I told. I should not be. I am letting. I am doing. I was screaming. In my head, screaming at me:

You are dead, inconvenient, trash—I can't stand your stench.—Poof: blank. Ignore. Ignore! I couldn't. More. Hitching solo, a car, creepy driver; scary, stay—and again, the clubs, nameless faces: touching, grabbing, pushing. Rex public: Hudson's looking, wolfishly. Watching Sam huddle close with Eric.

I lay on the bed. PPK in hand gone limp. Children seemed to gather, all singing, *"Cats and dogs went out to play. This is what they say—'never cause another day.' Don't delay."* Curled, darkened, flamed; tunneled, spiraled upward visions…Mother, red top, knifing, kicking Polish out. *Stupid girl,* I was hearing his voice again clear as bells: *Stupid girl. Grow up.* Melting char, turned heat shimmering above a long expansive road. Room, to lightness: floating.

My father: proud busting feather chest, pushing me high on a swing, into blue, above the playground. Sun-feet and swings, gymnastic bars, green and brown; *Pushing me.* Us two, me and Dad, two laughing as one, together. And—I whispered between dry cracked lips, on the bed, me and Sam shared, "Where are you?"

I want my daddy, the voice beneath had never gone away in me, still, to this day: *I want my daddy.*

Arnica

D.A. threw a shit fit on me when I told her I wasn't moving forward with pressing charges.

I got that a Lady was trying to defend me. I wished I was a stronger, self-esteem woman. Stand up, pack, walk, go to social services, domestic shelters for battered wives.

D.A. declared she'd move forward, press charges on Sam without me.

I told her I wouldn't cooperate. Hung up.

Sam and twelve red flowers, naked; stroking my knotted hair: "You are my soul. Closer than anyone's ever been. I know I've met my wife, love of my life…"

Is this the Universe, teaching me how to love? Why don't I feel anything? When we'd met, I had felt I'd been given a gift, love—and then I felt I had stomped on it: Rex, my whole way of being in the world.

Sam wanted babies. He stroked my hair. "Baby, you look rough. Your mind went to a dark place. Let me help you!" Got some ice.

He looked pretty beat, too; he did have a nasty bite on him, no joke. Had a hunk hair missing, the cerebellum part his head.

"You did that," he said flatly.

—after beating dead horse an hour—

Sam's angle: "You feel bad about Rex. Projection. Makes you think I'm sleeping with other people."

Turntables by hoisting psychoscan theories? Sam didn't even acknowledge that he'd done this to my body.

Look at what you did to me! Rip his head. Then, *He's right.* In the head: *it's my fault.* Makes it so you don't end up alone—*easier to think it's my fault than have to be mad at him*—he's all I had.

"I am sorry," I told Sam.

"We just need to turn our mind off awhile."

I promised, "I'll never see Rex again." I meant it: Rex appeared suddenly clearly: a distracting waste.

Sam had gotten Jess on horn already—they had a plan to meet. "He owes me. We'll make a fresh start, me and you, baby," Sam hugged me.

I did have a thought: listening to Trent Reznor singing: "Goddamned, I am so tired of pretending, pushing and resenting, when all I am doing is trying to hide, keep it inside, fill it with lies, open my eyes, maybe I wish I could try" song "Where is Everybody?"

My mind told me: *no way I'll stay by Sam.* Flipped image, my Italian Grandma Grace's *Enquirer*: "Beaten movie star glams huge black shades." *Maybe I'm training for the starlet life.* Took myself out to the pharmacy, musing, "All a girl needs is Arnica: turns black eyes, blue legs, to yellow, flesh; melts mini-watermelons in a week's time."

I'd be dead without humor.

Sparkled to a final rope-clinging fantasy, way to get through the day:

Sam gets ninety grands from Jesse. I steal it from Sam, like Wendy Kroy in The Last Seduction. Linda Fiorentino's husband score's a heist, but then he beats her around. She swipes the cash—and bolts town. She changes her identity, on the run.

I did not know then that I was pregnant.

This Was Like That

Lavender-gray pre-eve—Fourth of July.

Sam sauntered 'round Jess' old Thirteenth Street abode. Loaded Walther tucked in his three-collared leather button-down. Jess wasn't expecting this visit.

Why he picked that night—why we weren't on river's dock watching electric ripples glow—I do not know.

I was inside that broken railroad, "Nocturne, op. 9, no. 2," cranked up, Chopin. Windows wide open, boomers out panes glass. My heart beating fast. Broken. Lost ego. Beaten to humility. Facing the inner chaos. Broken to new light? I do know a new crack in my mind appeared and new thoughts shone through. Maybe it's having the shit kicked out of you by the one you think you love—was only one week after me vs. Sam knock-down brawl. I was without buoy: *'trying to give up that which makes you feel safe, to change'* kinda thing. I felt two things at once: disintegrated, lost, floating some abyss; I felt powerful, free, magnetic, strong. Maybe I could taste the cash Sam was going after, and it got my blood up.

I was gliding on the hardwood floor in that broke-down railroad flat, decorating the place with white candles, red roses. I'd pulled my old velvet priestess gown, train four feet behind, from the wall. I had found it in a free box when camping out in West Marin. My poet friend Miller died. Swallowed his tongue. We all, town, stood atop Mount Tamalpais, 360-degree view of land and sea, holding hands. How I kept hearing, "Fah who for-aze, Dah who dor-aze," like in the *How the Grinch Stole Christmas*.

This was like that. Like I was setting a ritual, a prayer. I was letting my fantasies. I rarely let myself fantasize. I don't know what, why, then. I was imagining. Sam would get the money. *Stick to the plan: no more Rexing,* I told me. I could find some solace in spirit. I could live in love, create singing, "I've had two weeks of silence, the knocking's seemed to cease, the hours of distant drumming…" my song lyrics. I was singing at top voice.

Gliding, "Everywhere I turn now, reflections in the trees…" my song, I was. I'd made a deli trip after Barnes & Noble, planning to build a mock replica of my night dream in our living room. I thought of it as a video set, for my song "Hush."

I'd had a recurring dream, night before, second or third that week. The dream started in high school, when I met Drew, least far as I can remember. I am in an old, wooden house with spiral stairs, turret windows, something gothic. Many rooms. One long staircase going to an attic filled with private rooms, decorated with gilt gold and velvet settees. Rugs; Dark wood. I am often staying in one of the rooms, but can't tell anyone, or am not allowed upstairs and am longing to get there. An old woman, the same old woman, a presence of wisdom, calm, love always sat in one of the rooms. Always the same old woman, same house. She always sat in the same room, at the front up the enchanted staircase, rocking in her wooden chair. I felt was watching over me. I was always in a different room. I was always aware there were other rooms. I couldn't always get to them. I often felt completely safe, or wanting to get somewhere but couldn't find it.

I'd woken up feeling like something haunted, old life in my bone marrow been awakened. Like someone had died; I had a longing, or something had been forgotten. Like when you're on a train and it stops but it hasn't shifted back yet, so you're jolted forward, waiting. I'm not alluding to the baby thing. I guess this child was a good five weeks my body, then. I had no conscious thought. Hadn't noticed blood gone missing; never knew what date, when. My breasts usually just swelled up, I knew then, and blood just happened, and went.

Earlier that day, I'd found myself in Barnes & Noble, leafing Jung, literary essays, read: "Watch closely your night, daytime fantasies, dreams: They are signposts to your soul's unconscious desires,"—this dream felt that. I felt suddenly, again, that maybe there was something else. I don't know. I was aware that I'd been in touch with this stuff before, but I'd lost a feeling with it—meditation, manifestation—since I'd come off living on the road, gone urban. I was thinking, more like shaming myself, and wanting to flapjack into a new mindset, that I had taken a wrong turn somewhere, trying to manifest my dreams through money and manipulation. I'd lost a convergence—I wanted suddenly to be in touch with some kind of other existence, again.

As a kid with Wanda, Cousin, Tabby, we'd all read a book, called *Astral Projections* together. We'd found it in an old cave out in the Enchanted Forest, across Anna Road on the boheme campus. This cave where a college student told us someone had hung himself. Rope still there on a hook, dangling morbidly. We'd read aloud, from the book: "Blend your spirit with atmosphere. Imagine sending your body to visit someone else in their home, anywhere the world, alive or dead." We'd lay down and try to send out energy into somewhere else. Chilling, shakes. We'd each witnessed figures passing before us, dead, or transitioned as we liked to call it. To somewhere else, we didn't know but wanted to feel.

After that, when I was nine, I'd taken to practicing "Seeing" by myself. Sit outside alone, moonlight, by a window. I'd hum one note, my third eye spinning, open. I'd send my spirit to the middle of the ocean; hearing the wind whisper, floating, imagine sinking deep into the water. I'd see images; listen for truth; ask for guidance. I'd write what I saw in my journal. Sometimes, these visions came true.

This night I was planning, conjuring vision. Creating a ritual, a blessing. Our plan was coming together. I was on fire—and vapid all at once. The more I decorated and dressed, the more I was in some vague haze, unclear and totally lucid. Kind of close to the way I felt when I got on my gear and hit the floor for dancing, work. Thrill of the kill. That's what I mean. I was of two minds. Was I in a spiritual trance or was I buzzing because I was finally going to get a big score?

I'd ironed my hair, pin-stick straight to the waist, glossy sheen. Painted thick my bruised eye-rims, indigo. Raccoon-lined my gazers, stuck curled eyelashes to brow. Pulled my favorite garters, Italian lace, onyx satin push-bra. Slipped stiletto platforms, gray snakeskin.

I could see my dream so clearly, I felt it was a calling, but the dream was contingent on Sam bringing home the bag. *Sam and I will buy a gothic, wooden house with a spiral stair, some far out rural place where we can create. Have a family, make a safe, warm place for both of us. Write, act, record, sing, shoot film, edit. My first music video will be filmed in that house.*

Same time, I kept thinking: *Sam was right. Let Rex go and take the ring.* Been one week since the Lucky Strike gig. My red Nokia pumped few times a day. Glancing Rex Parisian texts: *'Eiffel Tower! Thinking of you!' 'Jacuzzi-adorned hotel suite!'* I could barely figure memory, gray'd out, *who hell is this guy? Why does he feel so close to me?* Like some gnat-like shadow stuffed in some island part of my mind, buzzing frantically disruptions wishing 'cross the light in the landscape my reality. I felt confused at the thought he had even existed, and hadn't a single reply. *Why don't I just unplug the thing?*

I had sent him one text. He'd brought up the loan again, at some point there in the week's haze, I'd batted coy reply: "Embarrassing news, my bank account's on hold from overdue school loans. Direct deposit or credit card my name, will be frozen immediately. Cash only." Maybe trying to get rid of Rex, maybe setting him up—

Sam was probably wrapping Jess a big bear bro hug right around that instant. Jess wanted Sam out after that first hello hug—I know this. Just trust me. I wasn't in the room either, but take my word for it.

Say Again?

They get pretty serious about the Independence celebration shebang in New York. Folks burn rockets all over that city all night.

When Sam walked in, was asking, fixing pillows like he'd just gotten home from his 1950s office job, I a Stepford Wife.

"Come sit, sweetheart," I.

He was smoking a red one, I was sipping room temp Johnnie.

"How did it go darling?" I.

Pyrotechnical needle snakes: clumps red, white, blue trailing smoke; flaming tops hissing, sailed over the high moon, East River.

"Yes, I got the money." He kissed my head, stripping leather gloves.

Black marble his saucers shone moonlit streaks white. I wanted Sam to tell me I looked pretty, twirl me, firelight in silk; Say, 'I'm gonna take us off some exotic island, make love in the warm sand!'

Something's awry. "High on something?" I asked him.

"Little vampire den? Only face yourself in the dark now?" Sam jested, hoisting Walther from his pant. Laid the metal snake on our coffee table.

Last thing I want is to start a fight with Sam, duh. Seriously, duh. I sussed quiet.

Sam, sketched—pacing.

"I'm looking out the window because I am thinking we may need to stay at a hotel. After what just went down. It's called protection."

"Oh," I said.

"God, I'm stupid. You're rightly, sure."

Don't piss him off.

Like a phlebotomist drawing blood, I felt. *Diseased blood.* Next two, three times sixty minutes—Sam paced the window detailing this, that—dishing zip-rolo, deflecting the story. I sticking sensitive procedure, rolling gingerly placed questions. My sexy rubbing his shoulders, his feet. My gliding my ass across his lap. Fixing him drink. Striving to bring forth a lick of what the hell happened and where was the money

Shit, bro, could have been on a plane, landed Tahiti by now. 'Stead I'm trapped in the confines of your, scared to surrender, I wanted to blurt. I could never keep my index off a flashing detonator.

Finally, Sam shook his head. Settled a sit and screamed, "Ahhhhh! I got the money, you money-hungry bitch. But I don't have it. I scared the shit out of him. It's fine!"

194

Like his spirit flashed out of the flesh of his body, Sam deflated. Like a limp white sheet tied at wrist, ankles, neck. Flapping the breeze—then he repeated what felt like about thirty times:

"I couldn't stand to look at him. You shoulda seen, black under his eyeballs, indigo, you shoulda seen it."

Kaboom out the window. Sam, almost tears, cut the sham.

"You shoulda seen the black charcoal under his eyes," Sam repeated.

"The indigo veins his lids; I mean I thought he might keel over seizure right there, what then. I walked to the sink," Sam.

"Kept the gun on Jess whole time," Sam began to unfurl, "Jesse was a white ghost."

My gruesomely horrified face shriveled at each wallop. This time, I computed what he meant.

Sam told me all this:

Sam walked into Thirteenth Street, something like, "Hey, my friend, I've missed you, man."

Little Fauntleroy hopped a scrambled shaky jibber. Flame Adidas shorts, nipples nude, making way around his usual coke foil trays, crack pipe. Clicking on, off lamps, pressing play some deep trance Master Ohm meditation music. Twitching usual right lip, fingers through greasy gold locks: "Yea, I thought the shit was gonna hit the fan for a little bit there, my brother. I been sittin' ti-ight."

Jess parked in lotus under his Buddha, like he always did, and pulled this plastic electric cravat. Pitched a scarlet sitting pillow on the seed infested Asian carpet for Sam.

Sam crouched like a hunter next to the bobbing blond girl on brunette girl, porn, the flat screen on mute. Gauging: *How far will I have to take this guy I used to call my friend to get his fair drawer, and walk?*

Sam most definitely eagle-eyed every single hair on Jess's arm standing, as the Joni Mitchell looking Jess poured two saucers of some kind of jasmine tea. He rattled one over to Sam. (You hear it now? I do)

Basic same foreplay these two had been pawning for months.

"You think you can hook me up. What happened to the Cali in-loads we set up together, bro? I thought we had a good thing goin'." Sam.

Jess, stuttered, "Yeah man, me too, bro. Been dry, real bad. Anyone you know who can come through for us? All our guys been calling, asking. They have been trying to hook through you, too, no?"

Only this night: Sam cut the usual pussyfooting this time and flat out called Jess's bluff for the very first time: "See, funny thing is now, I think you are trying to fuck me."

"I told you, man, I made the calls. I been tryin'," Jess whimpered.

"Don't fuckin' act innocent. Least you can be honest, bro," Sam on.

"No man, I told you, man, I made the calls. I been tryin' to get us wet. East Coast high, guys over left been busted. Weather's bad—one thing after two, man." Fauntleroy dragged his red wagon.

"I wouldn't lie to you. Guys are all hungry. No one cut you out. Later if it all comes through, I promise you I will get you straight on what I been promising. If I were rolling, you'd be rolling, bro. Believe me."

Picked his tea-jimmy hopeful, offering: "Cheers, man"—tried to clink Sam.

"No fuck that. I thought I taught you. Told you not to pull the wool over on me, on anyone on your side. But shit you say fuck that. So I say fuck you. See the thing is I need that dough right now, dude."

Flash: Sam suddenly pulled the hidden PPK from his pocket. Stood up, over the Jess.

Jess turned purple. "Whoa, what are you thinking, bro?" Cowered his hands over his head, whining: "You don't have to hurt me, man."

"Think you can hook me up now right? Like right now, buddy?" Sam spit on Jess.

Jess: "I'm in a tight spot just like you, bro."

Sam went cold-cock of the trigger, and pressed that metal gun muzzle hard into Judge's-son-Jesse's right ear-hole. Jess's left ear went over and the shaking Long Island boy, son of a judge, went cheek to floor. Legs still in lotus, knee up in the air sideways.

Sam, went shrill, diatribe: "But, bro, thing you ain't in a tight spot. You don't know tight spots! 'Cause I brought you to the sun, and any other tight spot you might be in is some pussy and I seriously doubt that with your cracked-out ass, unless you are paying for it. See, thing is, bro, you're trying to fuck me and I don't fuck skinny white boys like you, I only try to help them. Now, obviously, you don't know who you're trying to fuck because I'm the one who made you and that—well, that kinda makes me, dear brother man, wonder if this whole thing ain't *my* fault. Shit, man. One could say—maybe I didn't teach you right. *Right?* See ways I see it—I taught you never to steal and never to lie. I taught you carefully not to pull the wool over on me. But shit I say fuck that. See, funny thing is now, I see you are trying to fuck me. But what you don't see, my man is you are really only fucking yourself. Right, buddy? The simple act of masturbatin'! Right, bro? Hm…Is the spirit of the Buddha inside you now, my bro? Or are you high with the rush of fear—'Cause that my dear, is the only spirit I know. The fear of death that keeps me fighting. The spirit called: survival. Yea, that's the one that keeps my heart from

196

stopping. Ha-ha! And so my backhand brother, Jesse, the thing is either you can get on with your business like you been trying to hook with Bleu and whoever else boys got my back over you—or you can cooperate. Or we will all come after you. Y'hear me or is this gun too big for your ear?"

"No man, I can hear you," Jess sobbed, "I didn't know you knew them, real?"

Sam pulled hammer spur rear-ward 'til it locked, fully cocked.

"Oh, wow. Now you know how I hate liars. Didn't we discuss that already?"

"What do you want man?" Jess frantic, "Whatever I got is yours, bro!"

Well, Jess splurged gold all right. Yellow line pee right through his sweat shorts. Spit running downside his jaw.

Bombers still fizzing pink and fishtails outside sky.

Sam laughed, growled, "Well, I think what I got in mind is to slice you up in pieces, sell you off like the weed I can't get. But I won't 'cause my girl wouldn't be too happy. I'll settle for straight cash. Any unfair action can be made good with the exchange of the dollar. Isn't that? And because I've been mistreated by you and you're pretty eager to make it right—and you've got the dollar and I've got the problem—give me ninety grand cash right now, forget the fifteen pounds, you motherfucker and maybe I'll let you rest easy at night."

Jess, "I don't have that kind of dough."

Sam, "Well, that's too bad. How are we gonna fix my problem? I could have your firstborn? Nah, I don't think I want that nappy sight. Heh. Any ideas?"

Jesse reasoned, "Listen, man. I've got dough in a safety deposit box down the block. The bank. We can walk down there and I'll give you what you want?"

Sam stuck Walther's nose square Jess's Joni Mitchell cheekbone.

"The bank, huh? Oooh. Turning into a regular old citizen ain't you? Man, I taught you well. So let's go!"

Jesse whined, "Well, the thing is they're closed right now and I can't get in. Fourth. Tomorrow is, we can then."

Sam taunting, "You must think I'm a mook."

Jess preened, "No, I swear to God, man. I don't have the cash here. I thought I was being watched so I stashed everything."

Sam, "Oh, fuck, you for real? You really wanna fuck with me that bad?"

Jesse stammered, "No, man, for real. I'll give it to you but you gotta wait till tomorrow. But I promise you, bro. Listen, man, I will not fuck you. Trust me, bro. I promise you. Tomorrow, man. Please. Just trust me on this."

Sam spat in his face, twice, "You gotta be kidding."

Jesse postured, "No, man, no joke. I'll hook you up. You've been a pal to me, man, you the best and the baddest, bro. You know it."

Sam shook his head.

Me: I hate whiffing a dead elephant.

Sam to Jess: "You fuckin' promise? 'Cause I will blast your ass and sit back in prison again if you fuck me on this deal, bro."

Jess's parrot: "I promise, bro. P-R-O-M..."

Sam backed off Jess with the gun. Propped the shaking Lotus Fauntleroy back on his ass. Kept Walther's cold nose pointed on him. Kept his hand on the dink's shoulder.

Sam said, "You gots cut that shit out, man."

Sam picked up Jess's spilled bong; coke in the stem. Walked to the sink. Kept gun on him the whole time. Refilled his bong. Packed a hit for the quaking Jess.

"I hadda do this to ya, bro," Sam apologized.

"Ya left me no choice. Way you been doin' business behind my back. Whole thing could have been avoided if you'd been square."

"I hear ya, bro. I understand," Jess, shaking.

Sam handed him a lighter, said to Jess, "I mean if you weren't such a cocksucker, none of this would ever have happened."

Jesse held Sam's gaze, "I totally agree."

Sam to Jess, "But I do feel for ya. I'm sure you need a fix after that scare from me." Handed Jesse the bong.

Sam lowered Walther.

Jesse lit the fire, "You are the greatest." Mouth to bong. A kid bathing bubbles.

Sam sat cross-legged in front of Jess. Let out a sigh, relief, told him, "Whoo. You know I've been under a lot of pressure with my girl and all. Money's been bad," he said.

Jesse, "Ya, I feel ya. Want?" Jess passed Sam the bong.

Sam wiped sweat his brow, slipped PPK, waist his jeans. Sam even told me this, "Yea, what the hell. For old times' sake." Two friends gettin' high like old times. Sam and Jess, across from each other Indian style, passing bong.

Jesse shook his head, packed a hit, said, "Good for you, man."

Sam even apologized, "Yea, it's tough, I always felt for you like a brother man. Sorry, it's come to this. It's a bad business, man, that."

Jesse agreed, "Here smoke this up, man."

Sam, "I guess it's just the way things go, man."

"Me? I was flat on the floor in my priestess gown, listening by the end. My own blood flat, like a has-been powerful stallion whose cock dropped."

"So," Sam finally said to me, a bit of twinkle his eye, looking like he felt a whole lot lighter, "Jess promised he'll give me the money tomorrow when the safety deposit box, or the bank, is open. That's how we left it."

We? Now you guys are 'we?' Sam is lying. I was paralyzed. *He has the money, stashed it somewhere, plans abscond with the dough—Leave me to die alone, this shitty railroad.*

Sam, "Babe, I really think he feels terrible, he got the point, he'll come through."

How the hell would I even know if he was lying?

"Tomorrow?" I sparrowed. Hand on his shoulder smiling. Last thing I wanted to do was pick a fight with Sam—I'll say that again. Grabbed Johnnie. *Drink. Kick it down-tempo soft drawl.*

"Why didn't you rope him up? Why didn't you just tie the fuck to a chair, wait until morning?" I, like mommy bedtime symp-talk.

"He had somewhere to go," Sam shrugged.

"Sooo, You went to Jesse's house, held a gun to his head, demanded your money, he didn't have it and you agreed to meet him tomorrow for a scheduled trip to the bank?"

I swooned, kissing his head, "Baby. Are you the humane society? He's not going to be there! I wouldn't even believe this if I saw it in a movie, baby! I'd say, 'no way a guy like this guy, would do that.'"

"Stop it. You're fuckin' me up!" Sam, head his hands.

"And then you got high together after that?!" laughed me.

"Once you are in there, you wait. Tape him, rifle his shit, escort the chump to the bank whenever the fuck it opens, you asshole!"

Is he lying?

"It was a national holiday!" Sam whinnied.

"He'll be there! I told him I'd kill him! He's scared shitless! You should have seen!"

Red spiral kundalini heat; rage with a lid feels like choking. I swear, I wanted to rip off my top, beat my tits, wild. Want to rip off Sam's face. *I could have taken Jess down better, you pansy-assed softee wannabe pussyfooting-imbecile.*

Last thing I wanted to do was pick a fight with Sam—

The crux, leftover fish fry bottom of the steam pot: last thing I wanted was having to accept the thing I feared most. Horrified. *Am I stronger, more street tough, than my man? Is he a freakin' softee?*

I lost it—I hate weak. Weakness in any person. Arms up disgust, blaring tears: "You are a man, Sam. A strong one. You can go out, take the streets, take over, just take it, dominate whatever. I can't! I will never know walking the earth with a man's strength, your physical stature. I have wanted to be you. I have been envious. I have to depend on you. You're a Mickey Mouse fuckin' gangster! That's all you are!"

I couldn't shake it. This incessant feeling. The lingering I'd woken up with, from my dream the night before, like something had been stolen from me and I wanted it back. Something gone. Only this was real. Cold, hard. I could touch it. I couldn't reach it: Money. Money was the thing I thought I wanted, right then. I wanted what I felt was mine.

I didn't know then that money was just a symbol for something else.

I left Sam in the ruined landscape of my dreams. Climbed into kitchen, on the cool sink, I sat. *Alone,* with Johnnie.

John Wayne

I was glug, glug the Johnnie. Hidden landscape my mind, I was back on the green lawn, behind our old split level in Tivoli. After the boheme campus before Jersey. Mom had us in some split duplex. She was with the drunk downstairs, I was upstairs with Aidan, but he was with dad. The drunk was everywhere. The rickety steps outside to get to the kitchen. Mom worked two jobs. I was in junior high. I was running for Miss Teen New York.

I learned how to drink from watching old Polish drink, in our kitchen or backyard when he didn't think anyone was watching. I started learning to sneak in some neighbor's house steal a bottle liquor, sometimes even money. I learned then that keeping secrets made me feel special, strong. Paint my real bright innocent smile. My cover for Trash Girl.

I'd gallop into the trees. Hack up a good spit. Just like him. Firm grip the label, head tilt back, glug it back fifteen, thirty seconds. Length hurl back depends on vapors. Let 'em out your nose. If you must, gasp out your mouth. But that's for pussies. Then sit. Soak in. Again. Up. Glug. Down. Gasp. Soak. Up. Again.

On the sink, Sam started snoring next door. My mind bubbling old footage hadn't watched before. Long hidden from my day mind. How he used to squint his eyes, like the sun was bright, but this guy, the drunk Polish, Victor was his name. He did it just inside, squinted up, at the dinner table or something.

So, I did it too, private. I'd wallop my loogie on the ground, see what kind colors: yellow or green or brown were in it, from liquor. Cock my own hip left side; swagger. Stomp dirt. Talk one side my mouth, some commanding garble. Scratch my pits. My chin, pretend like I had an itchy scruff beard like he did. Just like him, I felt proud.

Never showed a soul. I didn't take this to the beauty pageant. My way of strong, I guess. Stopped hanging with my best girlfriend Alissa 'round then.

Victor. I guess I'm getting more comfortable saying his name. He wanted to be John Wayne, he said. People say I'm supposed to talk about this. Say lots of us experienced this kinda secret our whole life, good to talk it. Wish I could hear you talk too, right now. I mean, it's no fun this kind of secret stuff. Telling people never made it better either.

That's the money. Money made it better, felt numbing. Like in the bathroom stall at Hudson with old Rex; every time some guy slid his finger up my yank at some club; every time I felt I was going to get left stranded by Sam—the money. Made it better. Money meant, no matter who fucked with me: I knew I could survive.

"Macho," Mom once jeered at me. "Walking like a man," she heckled. "You look so stupid."

I was fifteen. I'd accidentally swagger'd one Jersey day walking kitchen to the bedroom in the two-room ranch she got. Mom said she wanted a fresh start—to get away from him, not because of what he did to me. Mom never knew—or acted like she didn't. She was looking for a new husband and kid. New York City—

I didn't answer.

Mom was asking if I was gay. Drew was locked up then—his friends, guys in their twenties were watching me most. Taking me out like a little sister, like the Natalie Portman in *The Professional*. I was straight, to my own detriment probably, but—putting guy-like tough airs, making men my role models, made the world seem safer.

If I'm losing you on this, I hear you. I was lost myself. Here, I'm telling you something I probably shouldn't even tell anyone at all, ever.

Sometimes a drunk blacks out. Sometimes a drunk recalls every single detail, like a detective's mind. Every little glint light hits the wall as you move; every subtle nuance a word spoken. I remember clear as day that night with Sam.

Kick Back

That night, I was like a snake with tits. Slithered into the living room. Drunk as what. Sam was curled up in the chair, snoozing. Sucking his thumb. Snapfire dragons out the open window. I wanted what was mine—if Sam had the cash stashed and was lying, I was going to find it.

Walther PPK was sitting that table, out in the open. I put my hand on it. Grasped its handle. My arm went up in the air. I wanted to scare him. Pointed Walther right at him.

Fucked came up in a split second—as it does. Sam went awake: was one eye open—grabbed my forearm, wrist. Like how you are supposed to grab a snake's throat when it's lunging at you. Pushed me back, threw my whole shaking body down flat.

Pow. Screeching ping. *Whap.* Gun kicking back?

I fell ass in a pool of fuck hot wax mush, embers kindle. I heard broken roses, glass. Splattering everywhere. Pitch dark. All I saw were clouds, inexplicable. Dust.

My face went papier-mâchè, "Sam?"

Silence, no answer.

I stood. Sam was laid out. Kicked back completely, arched back over chair, staring blank up. I saw wet all over his chest.

I squashed a scream. *Shut up,* I screamed at myself. Trembling: I want to touch. Check his pulse. I saw colors: *shrapnel, fusion stone, nitroglycerin, TNT? I can't think.* Sounded like a helicopter flying over. *Put the gun down.* My heart raced probably 180 bpm. *It's fireworks outside,* I thought. They'd gotten closer. They were probably about every fifteen seconds or so.

Scramble. Too shocked to stay standing. Six whirling fit-survival thoughts launched:

You don't wanna be fingered for a crime. How fuck I handle prints. Should I put the gun by him, say he did it. Call, say it was self-defense. D.A. is still on my side. I wanted to shoot him. I didn't mean to. I'd like to say I had shot him. No, he's not dead. There are no bullet holes, the walls, the chair.

Sitting amongst ramshackle, I heard herself talking out loud, like answering an agent: "He made me do it. He was going to kill me. He took the gun in his hands, yes. That's it. Put it in mine, grabbed my arm."

"You are sick," I heard.

I screamed.

Stark eyes. I lunged at him. He pounced on me.

I know it's dramatic; it *was* dramatic.

I wanted Sam to hug me.

Sam grabbed the gun. Stood over me, staring down at me. I froze full stop.

"Babe," he had the gun on me. "I was fucking with you."

Sam grabbed a stack of cash from the drawer under the mirror, his keys. Walked out.

It's a cool rush thinking for a minute you killed the person you love—and then not having to live with the force of its being true.

"I love you," was all I could. I sunk and cried.

***

Sam never told me the straight story.

One day, he said, "They were blanks, babe! I heard those rockets blow outside and thought 'let me fuck with her, she thinks she's so badass, see how she feels if I'm dead.'"

Sometimes, he laughed, "It wasn't loaded."

Apparently, Walther wasn't loaded when Sam went to Jesse's either.

I looked meticulously for a while after he'd split. No holes in the walls or chair. No blood. No neighbors ever said a word.

I went on, relieved. Sam went back on my pedestal reserved for *him, strength. Least I know the guy can still kick my ass.*

***

"It's not safe," I told him, as hours wore on.

Sam was dying to get back to Jesse's. "Run in on Jess…get paid," Sam really seemed convinced Jess was gonna take him to the bank and make it right.

"Probably has guys or even cops planted all over there now. Or he's booked to his parents," I shook my head.

We didn't want to chance Sam get arrested, or knocked off.

Sam called Jess a million times. Line disconnected.

We sent someone to ring Jess's place: No answer.

Sam and I just lay there on the floor, the couch, the bed. For days.

I got to thinking, in my silent psychostab: maybe Sam, deep down, actually cares about Jess. I asked him once; he didn't really say much. Maybe American blond blue-eyed from a rich family—Sam really wanted to be like Jess. Like it's what made him want to get close to Jess, help him; same time to try to crush him and go soft on him, all at once. Could be just Sam got meekish. If he'd done the rope Jess up thing, he might get arrested, with Walther and all. Could be, seeing old Fauntleroy, peeing his pants, Sam just felt plain bad. Actually, that got me chocolate kiss sweet on Sam again.

I started remembering that kid Drew had set up, Jersey. Drew had pulled a dirty trick trying to get himself absolved from the first charges. I wanted nothin' doin' when he mentioned some set-up—I happened to be at the kid's house, playing poker drinking vodka, the day the fake UPS package arrived, from Drew. Intercepted by the cops. I sat there, watched Uniforms cuff the wide-eyed surprised recently turned eighteen-year-old softee. I watched then drag ass out. I was fifteen and cuffed to a kitchen chair. I have never once forgotten the look on that kid's face.

Makes it all different. When you're actually there. Seeing the kid's face.

Who knew I coulda fallen for such a softee, I thought.

Sam had lost our chance at a load.

I did pick myself up, eventually.

Rex.

Ho-Hum-Twiddle

The afternoon Rex and Cindy ended up happy birthday suits in the Penthouse, Pen Hotel, Cindy thought for sure Rex planned this to appear an accident.

I had taken some time to try to play like a Jennifer Aniston type again. Like be sweet, and do everything like that society would approve of. Ignored Rex texts. Got serious about Innovative agents, put on the button-downs and smiled my way into TV and film auditions. Kept a full-time bartending gig at the W Hotel, one of Manhattan's hottest. I didn't mind hard work, had slung construction as a 'grunt' one spring season out in West Marin at eighteen years for ten bucks an hour.

"Proud of you," Sam would scruff my head. "Making nobles your life, baby." He'd mention his movie, boy smiles—*never going to happen.* I'd roll my eyes.

Rex's twenty-G loan looking good. Red Nokia buzzing, mute. I might have let the battery go dead. Promised Sam, I hadn't picked up or replied. I watched: one toe out.

Waited. Trixie my mind. Either I saw too much, or I saw so clearly that I couldn't cow-tow to sheep-dom. Mainstream society was tough for me to get with.

I detested the thought that I might live the rest of my fucking humiliating existence, 'a fan.' A puppet. Voyeur.

Sam was working that Flatiron martini bar, yakking mediocrity. "Drama in the staff, this guy's a jerk, that customer this;" ga-ga over whatever famous face graced the joint. Excited about that week's *Sopranos.* HBO, April 2000. Sam was acting an idea that he was Tony. Sam was just a guy who watched TV from what I could tell. *Sopranos,* great show, sure—but what I wanted to live, raw. Seemed the whole of New York was going softee. Barbie was phoning up from Miami, raving about *Sex and the City! Fucking shit show, ruining NY,* was what I thought about that show.

Sam, asked me, "Are you a Carrie, Samantha, Charlotte, or Miranda?"

"I possess aspects of each chick on that show and then some, on any given day. All women do, I believe," I.

"It's a put-down to claim I am only one of *them*."

I—the word itself. I was beginning to wonder if I knew what that word meant. Broke? I knew what that meant. Was I a petulant child who didn't want to grow up?

"Just relax, keep auditioning, something will pop!" Sam's go-team shit confident sounded like a greasy two-week-old egg roll sitting on a dumpster in the hot sun, Cali. I knew, I had lived off dumpster food when I was homeless at ages 16-19.

I could go on: W Hotel bar owner trying to lick taco of each hiree he dressed in 1960 stewardess mini-dress outfits, I told him "bug off, suburban jack-ass," counting wet singles 4:00 a.m. four, five nights a week, split four ways—overstaffed 'cause he doesn't want Wall Street fucks waiting one second for a drink. House making high rings off labor, booze markup on bottom-shelf liquor.

Like a rat in a microscopic study; a horse trapped stable. Trying get stupid fucking roles I didn't even really want: housewives; student, fuck-able teacher. Every sniveling casting director, droned: "Play the lines, don't craft a character." Hating waking, *I want to be free.* Somewhere I felt: *I am powerful. God's sakes, something fucking meaningful.* Was growing up about becoming whatever gels and sells in society?

It seemed to be Sam's answer to happiness, often said he and me were, "thrill-seekers that need domesticating." He'd pulled that killer thought from Doc Ski. I just couldn't do it. Was growing up about becoming more of me? I didn't want to become what family and friends want, keep to their subjects, fit into society, by adhering to its moral means domestication rules. I wanted to express myself, I wanted to find my own place in the sun, my own way.

I decided in the hours of the days that passed, that all I wanted to do was sing my songs, even if they didn't sell, and write myself a lead in a movie, and play the part.

Fuddy Director Orange kept calling. (Actual fun fact: Mom had stopped calling so often after I had lost the fight with Sam.)

Director O: "Been up all night writing new pages! I'm going to make you the world's next Sophia Loren," he'd leave messages. I'd started picking up the phone. Act sweet, flirty for his salivating, to try to get a part secured.

He called it "our script." Romantic comedy—Jen Aniston type. Struggled trying to wrap my head around that vibe. I sat for drinks listening to Director. His famous friends, legacy careers, he was going "catapult" *my* career. *One part is all I need,* I, bated breath. *If this is my debut lead, no one will suspect the real me.*

Sam suggested I see a shrink.

Pekinese

Session Four. This lady-shrink's lanky, young, sixteen-year-old son answered the door of their prewar two-floor family home high-rise. She'd dashed to move her car, spot. Doorman let me up, elevator. Error on his part. Shrink-lady fluffed on to me 'bout that later.

Alone, I sat in her overstuffed green chair, there, counting dogs: Polka-spots barking wall painting, peki-cocka-doobie matching purple bowtie for doorstops; embroidered long-beaked tail wagging woof pillow. Tissue box with pink nose bull-thing, forlorn tongue. Flop tail pointy ear-sheered chocolate, bookends. Howling husky curtains. Gray-faced longhair sculptures. Shrink lady came in, pert square vanilla dress suit, white-faced freaked. She was panting. I saw her tongue hanging out with drool.

Real kinda out of touch with the world, I observed and then was immediately accosted by her white curl hopping snappy. Dogs are like pigeons to me—overpopulated dirty creatures of the world. I didn't ga-ga pet ooh ah, the shrink chick sniffled. Made me reminisce silent the old familiar sniffle: Mom and Wandy.

Spent my entire two-hundred-dollar, fifty-minute hour stuck on her son.

"How do you feel about having met my son?" Shrink-lady asked, soon as her roundness found pillow chair. Then, my first answer wasn't good enough.

"Seemed a nice kid," I told her, nonchalant. Really hadn't thought much of him. I wanted to talk about what the hell that was blocking me from success.

"But what does it make you feel," ash-blonde fluff cloud deliberated, "to see a boy at sixteen in a stable home at a normal rate of growth for his age with parental love?"

"I felt nothing other than happy I didn't have to sit in the lobby downstairs," I told her. I was getting a feeling Shrink was afraid I'd flirted with her son. So, I dug deeper within, genuine, "Actually, it made me trust you more, realize you're more normal than you project in these sessions—like you have kids, a family and all." I meant it. I just wanted to be understood for me and my way too.

"When you had so little at his age? What does that make you feel?" She pressed.

"To me, Dr.," I said, "everyone's got problems. It's the people who think they're better than someone else because they have 'something.' We all have something. We just have to find it."

My opinion, then, whiskey and a rack of pool balls served better therapy than this. All these queers the world, I'm supposed to be nobbing and jobbing with if I want to prove my worth, just seem out-of-touch pansies.

Guess she was the straw got me over to Rex.

Zipless/ Monkey

Amazing what the yearning of one man's cock can create in the lives of so many, I thought. Picked up the red Nokia. Chanel Girl red mouth, strident.

Tits hurt, swollen hell. Full-blown 38C, natural. PMS, any day. Afraid to pee on a pink stick. I hadn't been in touch with Rex in over a month. *Tits like this make good money,* I kept telling me. Missed men seeing me naked.

I was listening to Vanessa Daou talking "Zipless Fuck" electro-jazz, excerpts *Fear of Flying*: "No one cuckolds a husband, humiliates a wife. No one trying to prove or get; Just pure energy…"

I needed to feel understood.

"You're the wildest and unpredictable person I know," Rex sounded grinning through Nokia.

Hallelujah, I swooned silent. *Maltese Falcon* repartee. I felt like the precipice tipping point just before the orgasm. "Well, I hope they haven't hung you precious by that sweet neck, where you been?" swung dipping.

"Yes, angel, I'm going to send for you," Rex gamed.

"Always knew it was you!" Gushed, lady. "Won't let you from my sights again!"

Breaking old Spade-Wonderly spit, I sold: "this gal's been stuck traipsing slopes sand across that Jersey cement factory," harping final scenes Bettie Page.

"Phone a hassle to mind and…"

Rex lapped details I sprinkled, "little polka-dot bikini costume" they'd dressed me and to my breathless: "Missed you more than you know."

"Well, I can do better than any celluloid reel, cupcake. I've got a case of liquid! Are you ready?" Rex bellowed.

"Of course, I'll sign that legal note, dear," I promised, lightly. *Who is this man?* A quasi-worldly sav-. After so many weeks of me gone cold, Rex, still hankering to cash me?

Rex surprised me with apologizing for having been gone so long. Firm and still holding strong, his end of the deal, he assured.

"Next flight out, our wedding trip doll. My Scots Irish birthright, we'll bow our vows!" The Raven.

Hmm, Rex is even rhyming again. Oh, well, old, he probably hasn't been laid in a while, is betting tricks on old me?

"Wild and unpredictable, huh?" Cindy kissy-kissed the phone.

I'll show you, I thought.

I'd have rather worn a dress. It was fucking hot late July. I knew Rex would want me suited, and consider it a sacrificial-relationshippy 'I was willing to suffer the heat for his happiness,' *barf* that would make Rex feel more valued.

Slipped Chanel navy suit, hat. Lunch: Pen Bar. Orange Hermès shopping bag in hand—I had bought a gift for *him.*

Oh, how greeny-hazels, even more, haggard yellow bags beneath from travel, lit like a child!

Complimenting his linen weave herringbone three button.

Clocking first: one cheap torn Samsonite green vinyl brief on the floor alongside Rex's Coach attaché. Looked just like the one my dad used when he had tried to quit the University life and sell Prudential Insurance—I'd never seen Rex possess anything of such poor quality.

"Colors paint the sky like a Rothko!" I sang melodic.

Rex admired the glinting diamond, my fourth.

I was famished for pampering. Taste of Clicquot, Jumbo Alaskan, stacks Benji's; *if this is real, I'm truly fucking cool.*

"Peek your gift!" Cindy handed his Hermès.

Rex's birthday had passed. Gemini, if that means anything. Twins: two faces.

I'd never bought Rex a gift. *Silent Seduction Rules,* learned in the clubs: ladies don't buy men gifts. Men don't need more ego massaging. Convenient for a gal-me who was—I get the gift wrong, daddy walks. Months earlier, I could have left Rex in a beat. I was in a danger zone: slipping into caring about keeping Rex around. Rex over the months had often flipped his tie labels, remarked, "Amor." I'd never been to a Hermès shop.

Sitting there at the table, watching Rex's pudgy fingers ripping tape, pulling ribbon, gosh, *I hope he doesn't hate it*—my sweating ears under Borsalino.

I had him-hawed an hour, hawked by eye-fluttering and prim sales boy and gals—picking through stodgy argyles, pinks, kelly greens, *argh.* Honestly, three hundred bucks on his neck seems stiff—oh, does that make me cheap?

Laughing to myself, *Hermès fits name…Means Gods of merchants and thieves. I didn't have much cash*—but he's given so much.

Monkeys. I stood, frozen. Navy silk necktie: Wild little sienna-rim cream monkey monster faces scream-stared up at me. Rows and rows of the varmints, stacked on top of each other, marching, clutching tightly one another's tails. *Cute. Aren't monkeys considered good luck somewhere?* Recalled reading about a monkey-god in some culture.

Rex would know an answer like that! With a thrill, I imagined Rex would open laugh heartily, his glinty tooth, once-questionable, now maybe-even (could-be-slightly?) sexy. He'd whip the monkey tie around his neck; hours us, drinking, eating; Revan spilling historical facts—un-blank my silly queries about wily beasts, sighing, "How I enjoy a man of walking encyclopedic smarts."

Alcoholic Rule: We often scowl on what we do have; yearn for it when it's gone; kill it when it comes back.

Skelter reality at Pen Bar: Rex's eyes gravely on me, his face wooden, like chilled grim-prickle. He stared—I stared back. His eyes darted back, forth, back: *Monkeys, me. Me, monkeys. Monkeys, me. Me, monkeys. Me, monkeys, me. Me. Monkeys, monkeys, monkeys, me.*

Trash Girl burning helter: *He knows it's not this year's latest design, I'm too stupid.*

Rex's thin brow furrowed inward, three creases shot up center, to form one long bridge across top. Bogey most mug to T. Laid, he: "You don't have to trust me, Cindy, so long as you persuade me to trust you. But don't worry about that now," flatly. Slipped silk, ribbon.

I did not know what to make of that, another Bogey-clone moment. Geez, I imagined Rex sex, pulling these little theatrical tricks. Does the Rex have surprises? Magical feather touch, so hard, big I could forget all the rest of him…

I wasn't thinking right clear—ought been concerned, Rex's strange behavior.

"All I can say is twenty thousand dollars is a lot of money, Cindy."

Rex's manicured fingers scratched a hairless chin. Pulled the fresh print promissory note, legal document. Passed it my way.

Cindy blushed, smiling. Scanning quickly: signature, social, address—

I pulled back tenderly, the only *Falcon* I recalled instantly: "You know I would never place myself in this position if I didn't trust you completely."

Seduction Rules: Someone does for you, act like you're doing *them* spritely favor.

My plan: He'll suggest we use the hotel, a lady certainly would never offer sex; but I can hint. I'll relax him, charming, dozy-droopy-loving spoonfuls of whatever makes him pass out—and split with the case.

The beat went on.

Cindy thanked Rex. Folded, slipped note in my white Chanel handbag. "I appreciate your understanding, and willing," I extend a shake.

"Before we intertwine," suggested, "let us spend a soft think. I'd like to approach a notary together, perhaps in the morning. Secure a safety deposit— and both have a key. God mercy, anything should happen to me, you'll be my keeper."

"A gal who reads my mind!" Rex hard shook, bald glowing.

"On a most festive, perhaps you will consent to a shared evening, upstairs. I've brought special gifts home from Europe, in light of our upcoming union. I would like to dress you!"

Cattin' Prowler me said, *Bingo! Surely Rex wants to sex me. Guy says he wants to marry me, must wanna sample the goods first!* And oh, my Cindy hard-nosed face and staunch, imagined juicy ways I might entertain this fat man's fancies. While Little Rainbow Girl felt scared, *what is to happen next.* Little index wrapped tight around Revan's pinky, as we jetted an electric cubicle high through the New York City sky.

Tartan

Thrust it on this man you barely know and will never truly yearn, old familiar echo commanded.

Chanel suit stripped to floor. I was dancing, slow. Only my eye was touching Rex. Other eye hadn't left that green Samsonite case laying on the chair on the other side of the bed: stacked dollars. My overgrown tits stuffed in one padded demi-Tartan bra.

"It's the closest thing I have ever owned to a kilt!" Rex's nasal drone voice sounded like the echo of what I imagined a squawking Eeyore getting choked in the middle of some lake out in Mexico might.

Rex was laid out the white bleached linens like a beached whale pulling gingerly at his new scarlet-midnight tartan silk brief. The elastic band dug that fleshy inner tube. Brown argyle socks strapped beneath the sagging knees. Trumped in beauty by the penthouse, gift à la Pen Hotel concierge: gleaming un-drunk Veueve, dozen fresh yellow ones, a still-lit-flame vanilla-strawberry layer Birthday cake.

A gold, oval chair held me erect. Ridgies my fingers traced painted, carved faces that engraved its arms, back; ornate, cool, smooth raised corners. Like how a quarter feels, running top Washington's nose, forehead, mouth, cheek on twenty-five-piece—my tips ran lineaments. Trembling, my pussy lips, petal spread, like the Stradivarius's inner curves burn, tremolo while tender files bow; silk string lost in wet—sex engorged vibration, guided me forth, unbridled.

"I have always imagined," balked he, suckling like baby pig his finger-stick icing and-back-to-lips, nibbling, "for my second wedding, returning to my ancestor's land. Walking the flowered path in Revan tartan tradition, hand in hand with my lady."

I flipped my head over, trying swivel hip. My ass set plunk, plush velvet pink, straddling pillow, pressing where soft fur surrounds. *Chanel three-inch pump negative for stripping, hum.* Puffed my red pout: *look sexy,* inner pimp commanded. I missed my shoes: Slip leather spikes elongate the calf-to thigh-to-butt. Hot for squat and arch.

Now: Several Minutes Earlier: Rex had shut that bolted mahogany door. Dropped sincere on one knee; kissed my glinty diamond ring. He opened the green Samsonite case a peep so I could see but not see, snapped it shut and confessed, "I have kept a secret from you."

Aw Mister, life wouldn't be so interesting if we didn't keep a few privates, I gazing his verdant expressers. Forgot then how haunted I'd been, Sam's lies. Rex, I watched peeling down bone suit jacket, unbuttoning his ten mother pearls, his top-half, semi-bounce bubble-bump flesh-thing called body, and flourishing vocal-nose-dead-goose-honk sorries: "I missed a few days phoning while overseas."

Quiet please, Cindy: Rex nude equals vulnerable. Green case blaze: my name.

He, inspired by my "presence in his life," had done something, "only ever dreamt of—: My dear, I finally took off from my desk and visited what's left of the Ulster region of Ireland! Where my old Revan clan Scotsman lineage migrated, many moons ago!"

Ho Hum lineage entitlement…

And add: oh, how he'd "boasted to the Revans!" Shown Cindy's photo, bragged of, "her beauty! My family was strikingly enamored, as I am, of your young budding beautiful actress; and they are *so* happy that I, their Rex, has found true love!"

Cindy glided gaily about the two-room suite, cooing brightly, "Oh, Rex, I was so upset those few lonely weeks you blanked. I worried about you, if I lost you. Thank you for offering to help me understand!"

I, freely bouncing on the bed, jumping, springing, tra-la-ing, "Oh, Rex, all the wonderful romance that can occur in a luxurious setting as this!"

Rex 'whooped' and 'hurrahed.' Then, "Be serious, dear Cindy. I need to know." Then pulled me to sit down. "Do you have some special wish for your first wedding?"—"Our wedding," he corrected himself, chuckling, strangely.

Swamped for what to say, my eyes like those big wooden circle rings on the fleur-de-lis curtains. *I have no idea. I don't hang with people who get that kind of married.* I never thought I'd be pure enough to deserve, or cash enough to throw—had chalked weddings: trite.

"I don't care at all, my love!" I found myself dancing with the floor-to-ceiling curtain.

"I just want to be a princess in a big castle, gazing over rolling hills!" Open, close, giggle; open, close, and dosing cheap cutie-glee thrill over the towering sights; glowing lights of Fifth Avenue, Manhattan. They do make a cool sound when you draw swag.

"Well, isn't that perfect, doll!" Rex chimed in. "My family, one look at your astounding beauty, turned, suggested we hold ceremonies at their old family castle!"

It did suddenly occur, *Where did Rex score my photograph?* I wasn't at all comfortable, him with my picture. I tried to ignore that.

"Irish prayers, plaid tartan," Rex went on sepulchral illustrating, the ritual of an Irish wedding ceremony: "Your matching gown sash, because, of course, you aren't a virgin and they are strict about these things!"

I slowed, not at all sure exactly *what* he meant by that—

"The union pipes songs," Rex verbosely, "Bagpipes my dear!"

Doodlesack, boner deflator. Fucking poor excuse for musical instruments.

My curtain game, reverted to flushed cheeks forced fake smile saccharine rebound, "Oh gosh, a thrill! Do you have a recording? I would love to see/hear!"

Any 'maybe-I-could-marry-Rex delusions' I had momentarily fabricated soured to visions of kicking legs in skirts to terrible four/four. I could never marry a man whose voice sounds like a bagpipe. *I want my own money so I can do whatever I want.* I was sure as rain, right as day, clear as mud on that.

I spun-twisted wire-retaining-metal-ring on orange label Veuve Clicquot, swiveled back to shrewd, "Let's celebrate!"

Rex pecked my head, "Shh, Sweet Cindy. I made a promise. I always keep my promises." Forked over that green Samsonite, gallantly, "Something borrowed…"

I probably squirted juice into my white lace panties beneath Chanel wool I was still wearing.

Kilt

Where the hell is WD-40 when you need it?

Squeaking the jaws of this long-awaited and bewitching, green briefcase was like setting off on a journey through ancient jewels, to peer the bowels of Moby Dick.

Rex was acting like weird dude, pressing his nipples against the Chanel fabric on my back, his thick rust chin perched on my shoulder, like a wet-nosed dog panting. I clocked the frame of his magenta lips; a gleaming strip of saliva his sloping 'cupid's bow,' the vertical vermillion groove, where the labium superius oris meets the face flesh.

One: "First, my dear Cindy. Something new." Rex's fat arms reached around my frame, two manicured indexers lifted neatly, from the cardboard box tied by a plaid ribbon inside of jaws, "A gift." His lips curled an almost leer.

Box's calico italics read *Victor Scot*, no joke. "They are kiltmakers," Rex handed it to me. "Untie."

I smiled, probably so the glands undersides of my tongue popped. Flashing like the Northern Lights atop Kilimanjaro in August, stuffed neatly in the orifice of Mr. Green, beneath that fucking box—one glowing bunch of mint.

You'd think girlfriend of a drug dealer would, but no. I had never seen. Hundreds. Bank noted. Wrapped. Stacked: *My twenty G's total cooking.* I was betting farm.

"The exact crest tartan fabric of my beloved Scots-Irish family, Revan clan!" Rex repeated proudly for the millionth.

My own hands had blindly unraveled the sheets of air-blue tissue and I was holding his slash hers: matching midnight-scarlet-white-square cross silk Revan tartan. The tiniest string panty I had ever, one demicup brassiere. His boxers.

Rex chortled. Folded in my left hand one of the bundled thousand-dollar stacks from within. *So that I know dash is real,* I thought.

Oh, if ya don't: *Dash* means a small portion of something. It's Brit slang for tip, gratuities. It's short for "Dumb Ass Shit Head," or moron. I use it for straight cold cash, ducats, dollars: dash.

I watched Revan closely...*Oh, green love of mine*...He shut that briefcase. Clamped its silver seatbelt-like buckles. He set the case opposite side of the bed from us, on the chair.

Rex Revan, that man I met almost a year and two in Darling's and had taken a chance on. Here we were with a mighty roar. "Pop that champas, girl, your turn to blow some candles!"

In one split second, all glories were his. Rex dropped his featherbone linen trousers. I realized that I had never understood the term *chicken legs*, really. Red, ruddy, wrinkled thighs like a lacrosse stick (if it were covered in some kind of rubber padding); kind kids use in elementary school gymnasium. Watermelon knees; dehydrated, sagging, skinny calves.

Revan pulled his new set of tartan boxers up, very quickly. So I didn't view his willy, I supposed.

Down laid he, on the bed. Tartan man directed me to follow suit.

Copy: That's how I ended up dancing on that fucking gold lamé chair, where we all started this scene. That's how I got to hum-umbling (that is humming and mumbling at the same time) some strung together stream of conscious, like I often do, as you know. The words this day were, "In the sun, one day soon I might find a place in the sun, all my own..."

Rex was twiddling fancy across the room on his own private island.

For now, here goes...

I unhooked the tartan bra—for the eighteen-thousandth-millionth time my life: Only this time: '*Wump*': Winced. Mammaries filled heavy to limit, like flesh might burst and gush-throttle-forth—if even so much as pricked by pin. Nipples swollen hard like apples, red but.

"My, I haven't seen these jugs since back at that club! So big they are! Much more than I remember! I ought given you a larger size! Oh, sugar, give me a nibble." Rex grabbed my forearm.

Why the fuck do they hurt so bad? I want champagne, waah...

The tartan man pulled me to the mattress. Teeth nibbling my raw play pillows. Sweaty palms grabbed my sucklers hard, squeezing them tight together. Rex drivel-drool-dribble salivant like slimy dog, furrowed his face my swollen cleavage, *ow*.

I was used to it. Guys thinking they are doing something ultra-sexy to my body, really feels gross—but you just let them get their thing on because instructing them often makes them lose their gusto and all I wanted was it to be over. *The man likes your mammos giant, good girl,* pimp commando in me: porn Cindy, "Ooh, ahh!" smiles.

Part of me wanted to fuck him, just to test run it: *See if I can make myself do it.* I could survive anything: *Focus on something, always helps: eye on bling.* Reached my fingers underside of his jelly buttocks. I counted methodically *1, 2, 3, 4*—and forced down my eyebrows, to keep from shuddering. *I am covered by a sagging muck of coarse curly soggy sweat—* salt-pepper-gray twirly fibers on Rex's like little girl titties against my cheek. *Stupid girl, act professionally. You can let Rex-slime roll off your skin in a few days. Trick of dancer's trade: What do you care; you'll be jack with cash.*

I hugged him closer. Pulled his shoulders, *fur-like ape, pressing*: Rex scissored me. Pecker inside his shorts, I could feel its minute head, pointer finger resemblance peeking against my inner thigh. My stomach churned, knots, like a baby squirrel was crawling inside my intestines, and scratching from within, wanting out. Rex pushed to get a hump on, trying yank my tartan silks aside, *get my hole?* He didn't even try to slip my panties down; guy just wanted in my center *now right there! Rushing horses like buckets clanging, metal-steel charging cross 'scapes embattlement trenches, the goal, the onslaught crushing and driving on.* I pulled his panties down—boxers, I know, you call them on men. Panties I call them in my head often, to keep a running giggle.

My hand around lumpy stretch-marked buttocks squeezing, scuttled. Triangle matted hair groin, his little veined cock, wanting push on: Rex drooling, sticking darting his tongue, in and out of my ear. *I'm tough. Can handle*—Body rock, juggling guy; he groaned, "Baby."—A perspiring secretion. White and liquid. Smelled of sunflower seeds, maybe pumpkin— Rex was finally drenched with love sweats, wet through his own panties.

I looked down. My silks were still in place. His white pool messy liquid spilled all over his shorts, his belly, the triangle tuft mound leading to his cock.

The one extralong black pubic hair covered with jelly, lacquers my mind image for life.

Clear as bell, Rex yelled in ear; grabbed me hard, my wrists. "I ought to have you locked up."

I laughed gaily out—*maybe he has some fetish, some kind sex chat.* I often laugh when horrified.

"Oh, humdrum. I'm happy to be here!" I'm hard for answers on how the hell you reboot after Raven's recoil.

"Oh good!" Rex shot back. His saucer's overblown, staring into me like little limes spurting zing.

Stay, get him drunk and goofy. I eyed Veuve, bedside. *Race the fuck out.* Quick-land: *Petting.*

"Let's get back to loving."

I laid on Rex some Dr. Ruth I don't know what, thought Rex may shine to that kinda gooey whisper, "Good sex comes from a couple being with whatever emotional life is happening, speaking truth, not walking out—that's what keeps people growing together."

"You're good, very, very good." He slobbered of his weight onto me, like an iron ball chain, squeezed my waist with his hands, and held my throat under his chin. Heavy breathing: *his lungs, beating heart.*

A hug or pro-wrestler lock? I couldn't move.

Rex was stammering, swallowing words, like *Rainman*: "Oh it doesn't matter. What does it—I invited you to Europe. You should have come."

My silent psychostab: *Gosh, guy really wrapped in the failure of his cock.*

"Hateful. Deceptive. Manipulative. All I wanted was to love you—" Rex, hysterical.

He's a bit of a drama queen. Can I get that suitcase now? Like water trapped in rock pulses—silent, I was.

Praying for booze; barely a nibble my Popeye spinach…

"—And then you brought Mitch. Mitch. Juggernaut. Fucking weasel." Rex was mad at the mouth.

Like the popping green head on an infectious blister; paisley gold walls; Crème de Fleur; peach Botticelli sculpted lady in painting; face-engraved chair; copper-paned window—all turned a lavish blast of pulsing electric hyperspace-glassy-green car-wash blindness, everything: surrounded me.

While Rex's sputter echoed: "Black. Sam Black. Black."

Because, you see—Black is precisely Sam's last name.

Umm

"I've watched you lie from the start…"

Now, I may not have finished a semester at any major university—and Rex ripe to trashed me solid on, "your false NYU schtick," but I did collect my oh-fiddle-sticks scorched dry as desert gonad bones awhile later in this whole sprung-upon yee-haw-puddle-wrestle-smother scene, and found it most amenable to whine, "I was embarrassed! Rex, please understand I just wanted you to like me. I do attend school full-time. I do! Simply, none so elegant, as your past, so proper."

This wasn't untrue. Perhaps I wasn't a big liar or con, I was just insecure and wanted the privileged man to like me.

However, I did know a thing or two on background checks. We were almost nine months into the year 2000. I was aware, hearing his tirade, "Private Equity, Satins Touch, Lily's Secret," Rex went hobnobbing locations, the last four clubs I had danced, in NY. I moved a lot so I didn't have to fill out w-2s. If I ever made it big, I didn't want smudge on my track.

I was white, listening to him listing my own birth date; my real father's full Italian surname—*Rex only needed one fact to begin digging. Where did he fish?* My brain backpedaling—*never brought an I.D. near Rex. How does he know?*

Sam's DOB; Me and Sam's wedding date, Little White Chapel, Vegas…

Ouch, Did I ever let him close enough to tail cab? I don't think! I never once used the old Nokia for a call or text besides Rex. Looking swivel up-down-all circles and answers. Rex, no less, was still laying flat on top of me; I could barely eek-voice. Kicking me: *Stupid girl, too shy to sing public without Sam; should never have brought him to Lucky's.*

—wham. I turned like rabid rat in cage. Suddenly wanted to scream: *I've done nothing wrong. Whatever I have or have not shared with you is up to me to decide if and when. Stoop to snoop? Grow up! Walk, or ask. You made a choice to game me; don't berate me with your tantrum. Low-class coon.*

What did Sam always say? 'Harness rage it's a lot more powerful…' Hail Mary back to calm, I placed bets on an old winner's rule: *When in the hole, ya cop to some things, which make you look flush. Never must you come completely clean.*

Cooed, "Oh darling, you must be exhausted! Riddled ashamed, all that silly hum-goblin stuck between your beautiful ears," me, airily. "Please, Rex, that is your name is it not? Never even occurred to me to have you trailed or ask for I.D.! I simply trust you based on my instinct! Please, call me Cindy. *I prefer* it! My mother gave me an ugly old thing. Of course, I plan to sign your kissy promissory as I suggested, with the notary and my passport! So, what's this fuss? Sweetheart. You need a drink, you have jet lag."

"Mitch is your husband," Rex bellowed.

I don't see any photo proof. I do have a real brother. I'll say he has a nickname if Rex throws his name…

Another rule: In every truth, there's a good lie that explains it, which well could be true under another circumstance.

Sand, "Mitch wanted to make sure you are good for me. He was concerned you were stringing me along!" My mind was still searching: *Who gave me up?*

"In case you question my genuine nature. You are a liar," Rex flatly.

Mental ping came through just then: *Shit, I did finally get stupid sweet and signed some forms at Darlings.* I had rightly forgotten.

My favorite old Darling's manager Barry, round little gnome looking man with the grey beard, glasses, had nabbed me one night, after a shift. "Fucking Giuliani clamping down on the dancers, waiters, too, drivers, all taxed." The club was getting trouble to report. Wouldn't put me on schedule without filling out the old W-2.

Thinking back, I remembered that sweet moment when he pointed out the surname on my I.D., grinning, "My wife's a pizza bagel, too!"

First time she'd walked in that place, he'd insisted, "You have the soul of a Jewish girl." My long, dark eyes.

"Think Mom's side was half," I'd answered him one day.

"That makes you full-blood one of us," the grey goat gloated and became the first person to inform me about the womb—making-the-Jews thing. No one had made note of my heritage before, other than simply Caucasian—and told by modeling and acting agents that I was 'exotic or ethnic' because I had full lips, a wide chin, and dark eyes. In this case, with the Darling's manager, I had it found cute to be extra liked by someone I hardly knew for having done nothing but exist with the right lineage in his mind. It didn't change my life, anyway.

Fucker maybe sold my info out to Rex for cash? I couldn't see it really, but—*hey.* I did walk out, disappeared, and took up outside with a cash spending client of theirs. I hadn't thought about it that way before that moment.

But that's not this.

Yeah, thing is here—you can seek vitals on a pigeon, practically. Funny, I hadn't realized or thought about it any differently, during that whole time Rexing. Looking back after the malarkey blew over, and I was off traveling European film festivals with an acclaimed horror film director, a few years into the millennial decade one, I even said to myself, "I must have been so stupid. Rex seeking my identity: That musta been fuckin' cake."

Revan eventually clambered off me, in that Penthouse Penn. I was left smooshed like a hot marshmallow on the bed, staring down the, what I considered to be beautiful, landscape of my sort of paralyzed panty-donned centerfold curves.

Meanwhile, Mr. Eeyore Bagpipe pasted-thick some drippy-love-goo Neil Diamond; howling aloud like he was the most romantic fuck alive.

"Oh but, Star, that's what makes *us* so special! I knew all your dour lies from the start, and yet I still loved you. I believed in you!"

That: a hard nut to swallow. I was prepping for playing out a drawn-out meme-who-dunnit. Pointing my ring-clad finger back each time Rex popped new accusations. I was looking forward to a win.

No: instead. I went half-deaf in some weird way. I stopped hearing words. I didn't have to. Ping-pong of Rex's words, there forward, that day, just washed over my body, mind, brain, like shell encasings. Frame by frame. It was like I had already run the script for this scene. There I was. Frozen in time. Sucked into a black hole, and yet watching every crisp image. Like I was just popping corn to the back of my throat, nestled in some dark theatre, and viewing myself on some late-night movie. Some move I had seen a million times, and knew every line, and every outcome. So there I was a voyeur in my own world, suddenly. On a day I had been waiting for, for almost two years. There I was— some part of me—floating above myself, above Rex, almost bone dry sober, against my will, and watching, thinking…*Oh! Now here's that day…*

I knew exactly how the play started, and how the play ended. No, I didn't *want* to watch it. Yet, I couldn't turn it off…My body just stood there. My own brown, root beer as I liked to call them, shiners welled up; yet I was still. I made no shake. No stammer. I didn't even blink.

Maybe my lip quivered.

Creebies

I don't claim, or care to be able to, scientifically—I mean, who can really prove anything. We live in a world of constantly changing vibrations; instinctively moving toward, pushing away, expounding off of, forming pattern, falling apart. Energy never dies; it only transforms. There is no real proof or way to cement a finite moment and call it 'real.' Perception is variable and is constantly changing, forward desire, backward glance, present realm.

I don't know much, or claim to. I know what I've seen, what I feel. I'd buy options on betting: In our deepest unconscious hour—our soul decorates.

I mean, I have heard it said, somewhere, "Our souls set up everything that happens in our lives before we arrive at that moment. We actually intuitively know or feel in the resonance of vibration and movement, what is going to happen five minutes before we consciously experience it. Supposedly, too, our soul is moving energetically toward conception, birth, the other DNA vibrations in our family, our physical death or transition, beyond." To me, that's a hard beef, when it's applied to some of the heavy hits we see going on in this world. I don't believe the future is etched in stone.

I *do* think that we, our soul, our vibration pulse in the universe, thing that is moving through our visceral bodies, minds, with the intention of living, continuing to live, is always seeking to burn through whatever blocks are holding us back from energetic expansion and transformation. Just like the sun is constantly exploding so that it can expound and shed more light. We are chemical equations, and we are unconsciously self-organizing the experiences we have, a lot more than we want to know or admit.

Imagine: one breezy, outdoor lunching afternoon. Delicately crisp, cool linen is laid precisely under some pristine silver cutlery, not a centimeter off. It is arranged exactly so the slight angle of light, sun-glare, hits the sliver moment right, and catches someone's eye, and for a moment they are blinded. Person may not remember that particular table, may not know the reason or even care. To them, it's a passing moment, like a fly in the eye. Yet, somewhere, in the deep unknown of limitless expansion, the person who was arranging that table unconsciously was aligned, each move's outcome would affect the next, and—the person whose eye went blind for that one moment, had a shift in sight. This shift inevitably affects a thought, creates an idea, a move, a change. Who knows how—yet it is possible: We humans do know it *all.* In the unconscious pool, the space that all of life resonates: Life's vibration carries a vast knowledge, and we each are being guided on some levels by soul intuition.

That's the kinda creebies I felt, on that early evening in the Penn suite with Rex Raven. Numbness on the skin of my feet, touching the marble floor. Little grits of dust, caked between my toes. They were like the kernels of awareness, knowledge that I know I hold on to, and believe we all do. Often we ignore or find it annoying, and want to carry on, but we know, and we can choose to listen—and even if we don't listen, we will be forced to move in certain directions, because our soul commands it, for our survival.

Revan knelt knee before me nude in his blue moon croon, throwing out things I had said; ways he'd perceived me, experienced me, "this feminine being," since the day we met.

He is reminiscing again the day we had started 'dating,' at Hudson. I thought, first. You know how I hated recounting a moment over and over.

Yet, Revan's words were compelling, pulling me toward him, into wanting something that I couldn't put my finger on. *Fuck-o sap suck it, go cold,* I kept trying to tell me; but I wasn't drunk at all. I couldn't so easily go cold. I was rocked in this thing call presence, feeling, vibration, "fucking rattling on raw, I need a shut me up," I may have called it then.

Yet, in those very finite, pristine and fragile moments, I felt prickling. I felt an invitation of the numinous through Revan's language, and it sent me looking down at my pink flesh. Like a gaping-holed sheet left hanging off a stick in the breeze, waiting for the wind to disintegrate it, to become dust, dirt: *I am naked? Am I here?* I was stricken, confused in the Raven presence and glory.

I was wavering on my feet, and I heard harmonics; my body was frigid cold, dumbstruck listening to his totally familiar, and completely unrecognizable story...

Rex was planting roses, "You said it, Dear Cindy. By a taxi stand in the rain, our first or second night out. You kissed my cheek. I felt tingles. You said, 'Darling, Rex, some people make decisions for the heart in their mind. I am a person who is led by her heart. Those people often end up happier.' I wrote it down when we parted Cindy. I realized then, that what you need a man, me, to provide for you is emotional. It's not the bells and whistles, or 401K. What you need is to be understood, and cared for, deeply. I found myself in love with you from that moment on!"

225

Who is she? If I could get to know that woman, the woman he says is me; the me I am to him or he sees me as, I might like her.

If you'd asked me to tell you precisely what my heart and mind ideals were, then—I'd have said, "No time for that kind of luxury of feeling or thought; just trying to get by."

Who knows, maybe I never even said any of it; Rex just wanted to mess with me, Primal print feeling: I felt I was standing, surrounded in sound vibration: A woman in feather-light slow, with some mother soothing my skin…My own fingers under my own goosebumps, soothing.

Rex's words reminded me of a woman I didn't know anything about, but whose every move I felt I had known the whole of existence, since conception.

Maybe life is one big funhouse mirror, glaring back at me my innermost spiderweb chaos, I thought.

In each of us there is another self we do not know. There is a formless form that wants to make itself form.

Rex's voice echoed like a squash court inside of my head, as he galloped on saying, "I have adored your class, stature, sensibility. I have tried to show that to you, by presenting opportunities to help you gain confidence."

I shook my body hard to try to get the cobwebs out. *Any other girl in her right mind would understand how to handle Rex,* I scolded me.

Rex went on saying, "I have seen how hard you work, how you are suffocated by life."

Resolute, Cindy stepped back into navy Chanel pumps. Cocked a pose. Leaned my straight arm, over the gold-carved chair. Shifted my hip, lightly caressed my inner thigh, trying to peek Rex's interest.

I began to hum. Hummed up a hymn; A siren's song. Like a mystical melody from a mountaintop, breathes and intertwines the senses.

Rex wouldn't quit: "…truly believed when you learned to let someone be kind to you, understood what it feels like to be loved, you'd take all that I offered; come to me. All I wanted to do was love you."

Really, I wanted rip Rex's head—those three words, *'I love you.' I don't even know what I feel or what it's supposed to feel like.* Boys have been telling me that my whole life, then get pissed off at me if I didn't say it back. *Shut up! Hum more…*

"All I ever wanted. To love you. Be that one man. You spit on my hand."

My melody lingered from cool stream within to dead pool.

"I love you," was all I heard dangling the air, Rex.

I stood—stared cold.

Rex: "I want you to see me as a man, want you to be able to accept love…"

226

A voice in me began commanding: *Do what most people would tell you to do: Take what he offers. You will learn to love Rex; he's being good to you. Wrap your arms around him; claim love eternal, undying. You've worked so hard. Money sitting right there. Just a few more steps, a place in the sun will be yours—I mean with baggage of the old man, but...*

Rex, continued with his wants, "...all a man has to give, in your life..."

All of it right then, registered as *pressure*. All I could do, to keep myself from grabbing my clothes. *Walk.* The pounding in my head.

I did hear a man say recently, like in life today, "We create problems in our lives because we need to experience the solution for some healing."

Fuck knows, may be unconsciously I did, would have, set a thing like that up, to start to learn a thing about—well, life, addiction, abuse, self-love, inner peace, serenity, you fill in the blank. I have come to learn that whatever you project onto the meaning of what I am saying, has more to do with you learning from you, rather than whatever I am telling you in words to think, see, perceive.

"Hell no!" I would have said, then. "Bet low, win high—this is all I want to learn."

"Stay..." I eeked to Rex aloud.

Silence.

I didn't want Rex to stay. I also didn't want to be left alone with *her,* the inner whip.

Fuck, I hate when people confuse business with emotion. Really is a drag— I strutted to the curtain in my string tartan, my overripe jugs bouncing nude. *If I'm playing funhouse mirror, may as well do it with some pizzazz.* I leaned on the window and checked out the sunset hues, views of Manhattan.

I recovered and began: "Mr. Rex, you have promised me money and I've taken it. I'm not any better off than I was before. You got the best of me." Staring in the huge glass pane, reflecting back the room; I saw me and the man.

Rex's drone continued. I heard his voice like through a filter, half sound, half boom echo.

"You ought to be ashamed of yourself, putting yourself in this position, dear," Rex said. Laughing, "I knew it. You, every woman claims to be led by love. They say they don't have a price. In the end, you all have a price. I, me, I have been searching for the one single delicate female who is simply pure, true. I believed it could be you, but—Hell, songbird! You can't even sing!" Rex stooped to.

I turned, watched him. *I shoulda known better than to mess anything with a fucking putz-guy softee. Entitled pompous, dangling rich-fluff—got to hang with me, some kinda younger starlet thing from a red den, that's what he got. Now he's crying like he lost something.—What?*

227

Dick went on, "For the record, I paid those blokes to get you on stage—a tawdry singer you are!"

I felt as if someone had slapped my kid or something. Over to wicked voice, *Sounds about right, I suck—I'd be the first to tell you.*

Rex was dressed by then. In the wall mirror reflection, I saw him—stark across the suite on the other side of the bed—I watched him.

Rex opened the green Samsonite, flashed a view my way: stacks of hundreds.

I turned and faced him.

"Eat it up, my lady. If you contact me again, I will have you arrested on some grounds that will cost a liter of those crappy chair dances you peddle, to pay a lawyer to get you off." Rex snapped it locked, full.

Pounce him now, knock him out. I believed I could take that chance—*run, change it all, and probably win.* But no—I stood, stone sculpture. It wasn't even about the money. Money was about something else.

Rex Revan nicked the air, like chin of a baseball MVP. "Don't worry about me dear," he piped. "My lawyer was right. I lost weight. Got over my marriage. Even begun regular therapy, due to my sheer poor choice of dating *you*. These are things my wife had been trying to get me to do for years!"

I swallowed. *I could follow him. Call downstairs. Claim he stole the case from me.* I watched Rex slip that orange Hermès package I had gifted him, under his pudging forearm; *like a spoiled boy off to school with his books,* I thought.

"Who's pulling whose tail now, Cindy?"

That was almost the last time I ever saw Revan's glinty-tooth smile again. Stalemate.

I guess he liked the tie at least, I thought.

I just lay there. Drank the minibar.

Labor Day

Dolphins. When one is ill, or wounded, the others in their pack surround it in a circle and hum together, sonar, to heal it.

That kind of grouping idea wasn't for me.

I thought, *maybe some other girl may have gotten a regular job, roommates cheap.*

No one to fall back on; nothing to fall forward on. I kept standing, throwing punches at whatever, whoever came my way. I couldn't tell you why.

Some people feel they are nothing without holiday plans.

Sam was off boating in upstate New York, with the Sleepy's commercial guy, Jess doppelganger from the Flatiron Martini bar.

I was parked at the railroad, blood running down the insides of my thighs. It wasn't by accident.

The doctor had given me a shot in the vein. That's what they do when a girl rather not lie flat, legs spread, with a vacuum sucking her girl-life parts out. Modern new-fangled way, I chose to get injected. Then insert a thing up inside me at home, a few days later, after injection. Done.

It seemed common sense: *Kill a baby.* One of the only choices I was actually aware I had back then, and knew how to set in motion.

Lying on the floor, bleeding. Huge raging hot, like in *Carrie* the film— Violent red from silver bucket. Fetus size a quarter, turned out. Now a bloody pool on my bathroom floor. I was lying on the floor, cool tremble, in doubled-over cramps. Wailing like a little, traumatized child.

I had been calling Sam on the phone, over and over—no answer.

He knew why I was calling. I knew why he wouldn't answer.

I had told him I had a doctor's appointment. I might have told him as he left for his boating. I didn't remember him packing.

He wanted me to come along, "Boating. We need a vacation," he said. "Let's deal with this all later."

Sam said he wanted me to have it.

Twenty-four hours later. I had no idea it would hurt that much. Cold vodka felt right about then.

Labor Day weekend, no joke. I got myself cleaned up.
I packed. Bolted. Never returned to Sam. Didn't even leave a note.
Maybe left one voice message, "Good-bye."
Where did I go?—does it matter?
I have always loved the sound of heels clicking on pavement.

***

It was seven years after that day I left Sam, that I finally dropped sauce—five years since now. Time. Shit Sherlock, I could pick up a bottle any day; now, here forward. Nothing is etched in stone. It is a daily reprieve. A consistent process of coming back to intimacy with self, and source, when the loss or disconnect from the other is actualized in the midst of seeming intimacy. Here, I reclaim my sense of self, and wish to live, again.

"A flower comes from a stem. A consciousness comes from the Earth. This gives new pitch, new focus to mystery." ~ Carl Gustav Jung.

~ Finis ~

Epilogue

If you're one of those people, gotta know it all—what, when, how who. Some kinda closure thing, shit all wrapped up, grips on the hell happened next. I say, fuck, young Jedi Fucker Warrior. Sit in the unknown.

Cool, you care though, so—I stayed with Director O, if you must know. On the couch. That was his deal. "You must give me nothing," insisted he. I didn't tell him what had happened, none. Just I'd left Sam, "Need a place to sleep, a week." Think I'd have remembered, most men don't let a chick sleep on the couch. I got there with my bag. O happily gifted me a copy of *Divorce Italian Style*, 1961 Academy flick, Pietro Gerni directed, Marcello Mastroianni.

Night rolled around "But you must sleep in my bed," he went on, "you must let me give you sensual massages—I will not ask for sex." Or he wouldn't let me stay. He kept his words. I went on, blanking my body.

Within a week, I'd hawked the Rex ring—7 grand, got me. Actually, I sold it all, entire Chanel spring collection. Rich Upper East Side Lady's consignment shop. Except the suit, Borsalino. They've hung around. Got my own pad. Flew to Germany. Dir. O gotten Betty Paige flick I starred, was airing *Bravo* TV—into Oldenburg Film Festival 9/5-9/9. Well, only showed once— was Director O's flick, one I met him doing extra work, Ben Gazzarra, Rita Moreno, got raves the fest.

Guess 9/11 made me feel something. Towers went down while I was there, in Frankfurt airport. Watched it on TV waiting for my flight back to Gotham— British horror film director I'd just met zipped me directly up Maharati style to London selling a full hand-drawn map of Bin Laden carved fire roads in Afghanistan, to UK American Embassy. Champagne by night his bathtub singing Irving Berlin, "Cheek to Cheek."

Last time I saw or spoke Rex—when I got back stateside, close to October. Phoned him. Met for a drink. I came clean—even showed proper I.D. Rex didn't care. He said he didn't. I don't know what I wanted. Don't know why he showed up. I didn't think twice about him after that. Or anyone—but Sam.

I bumped into Sam's 1-800 Mattress guy. *Random.* Drinking afternoon reds some Middle Eastern belly dance and cocktail spot, near my then-new apartment, by Queensboro Bridge. "Boating," he told me details, I don't know why, guess I asked, guess I was digging clues. Said he and Sam been upstate kayaking that weekend I left, up in some motel high as hell on eightballs. "Sam's idea," he said. They'd called a prostitute, tag-teamed her—ya know a two-fer, both together. Didn't say much else.

Never went back to Sam. I did start a band, few years later. Sam did stand in the audience and watch. We didn't speak that night. Or see each other since. I never went back to Darling's. Oh, then the hawkshaw thing—

When I did quit sauce, I started getting quiet, intimate with my heartbeat, truth. *Your soul beauty is a gift, a responsibility, to calm and inspire; mirror other peoples' beauty, help them feel at rest, not at odds. Not to sell products. Not to manipulate suckers for money.* So, I tried devote my life to teachings of the spirit. Though I still like shoes.

Father

I saw my dad the other night for dinner. In life like today. We were sitting in a cafe in Grand Central Station. Hadn't spoken at all in ten years. Started having dinners together once every three, four months, the past five years. Meet at Grand Central every time, celebrate one of the holidays on the Roman Calendar—. I hadn't seen him in six months.

Dad's birthday, it was. Yep. He requested checkered shirts as a gift. This time, I bought them at Brooks Brothers. Dad said he wanted to talk, before dinner and his gifts. Guess Dad been cc'ed on some emails between Aidan, I. See, Aidan had gotten in touch with me, wanted to get together. I told him, "No. For now, our relationship works best for me quiet," that I love him, wish him all best. Dad asked me why.

I told my dad. We started talking about me and Aidan as kids with mom. I told him what happened—some of the things went down in the house when I was a kid. I'd never told him. Never told anybody else in my family before. Still haven't. It was kind of big and all at once. I didn't plan it, though it had been suggested at some point I try talking to my parents about it. I was stuttering and hot uncomfortable, trying to tell dad, how Mom's boyfriend would push me on the bed, didn't get too graphic. I don't know what I was trying to accomplish. Guess a closeness; an understanding. Dad didn't say much. He started talk trash on mom. Told me I was his favorite child, that I shouldn't tell either of my siblings, but I'm the one he brags to his friends about. *Guffaw.*

I told him how much it hurt, him not speaking me for ten years.

"I basically figured you'd turned out just like your mother, an underachiever baby maker," he said.

"It's a strange thing to abandon your kids and then criticize them on the progress they make in life," I actually said. *Guess he doesn't know how Mom used to beg me in high school, "don't tell anyone what goes on at home, they might haul me in for neglect." I never said.*

Dad told how much he respects Bridget for being a strong woman. *I'm not sure where the strength lies in shutting people out; I suppose he means something in the department of good boundaries, hard professional work.* Still afraid to talk to him—afraid *he'll leave again.* He went on, "Was it that long we were out of touch? Work really consumed me," he said. "How did we get back in touch?"

I got all choked. *He doesn't remember how*—that's another story, another day. I could eek, all that time I thought deep down, *well if my dad doesn't care if I'm alive or dead and I don't then who does.*

"I don't want to see you upset," dad's blue eyes smiled. Flipped topic. "Let's go have a nice celebratory Birthday dinner!" He jollied. We left the cafe and entered the restaurant. Politics. Travel. Work. —was nice.

I walked him down to his train. We said good-bye. He walked away and got on it. This time I told me; *it wasn't my fault he left. He wanted to. He isn't coming back the way you want it. And that's what the universe intends for your soul awakening.* Then I feel some bad for the guy; *must really have a negative opinion of himself if he thinks his offspring would be so valueless.* Underneath that, I feel a deeply broken heart—

He did get in touch. A week later. Brief "Thank you," email. A text the following holiday, Christmas—telling me he was on an island with his wife and her sons and grandkids.

***

Hey, each time I do see my dad, we talk a little more. Spend a little time getting into the big stuff—I want that relationship in my life, so I accept what is and try to work with it. I figure, you share DNA with your parents, and it's like a huge mirror. These days, I say I'd rather get to know me through it, rather than negate. I figure, if we both hang in, don't ditch the other, getting closer will happen; life never looks how I think it's supposed to.

An elder man, friend, confidant, spiritual guide with six kids in fact, sent me this recently. I don't know who said it, or where from: "Father. He can cast a giant shadow over his children, keeping them in thrall long after he is gone by tying them to the past, squashing their youthful spirit, and forcing them down the same tired path he followed himself. His tricks are many. At every crossroads you must slay the father and step out of his shadow."

I don't mean like be a rebel. That's same as going with the grain just the opposite. I figure it means, you must sit down, get with you, yourself, from your source—not live the predecessors' projection, what they: parents, society, institutions, think you are, want from you; or trapped in shadow of your own past glories, fuck-ups.

I say, strap on young Fucker Jedi Warrior. Create, re-create, see new, refresh, push through, awaken—and take a ride to the unknown, fucker man. Go blind. Just go. And ride the wave of your art. Like water. Just like water.

CPSIA information can be obtained
at www.ICGtesting.com
Printed in the USA
LVHW052049291121
704746LV00004B/211